Devolution, Asymmetry and Europe

Multi-Level Governance in the United Kingdom

P.I.E. Peter Lang

Bruxelles · Bern · Berlin · Frankfurt am Main · New York · Oxford · Wien

7 Day

University of Plymouth Library

Subject to status this item may be renewed
via your Voyager account
http://voyager.plymouth.ac.uk
Tel: (01752) 232323

Rosanne PALMER

Devolution, Asymmetry and Europe

Multi-Level Governance in the United Kingdom

"Regionalism & Federalism"
No. 14

Second round of interviews (2003), part-funded by Leverhulme-Trust programme "Nations and Regions: The Dynamics of Devolution" under Project IGBN "Multi-Level Governance in the EU".

© P.I.E. PETER LANG S.A.
   Éditions scientifiques internationales
   Brussels, 2008
   1 avenue Maurice, B-1050 Brussels, Belgium
   info@peterlang.com; www.peterlang.com

ISSN 1379-4507
ISBN 978-90-5201-390-9
D/2008/5678/24
Printed in Germany

Bibliographic information published by "Die Deutsche Bibliothek"

"Die Deutsche Bibliothek" lists this publication in the "Deutsche Nationalbibliografie"; detailed bibliographic data is available in the Internet at <http://dnb.ddb.de>.

CIP available from the British Library, GB
and the Library of Congress, USA.

Contents

8

List of Abbreviations

ACs   Autonomous Communities (Spain)
AM   Assembly Member (Wales)
CLRAE   Congress of Local and Regional Authorities of Europe
CO   Cabinet Office
COES   Cabinet Office European Secretariat
CoR   Committee of the Regions
COSLA   Convention of Scottish Local Authorities
CSG   Consultative Steering Group (Scotland)
DEFRA   Department of the Environment,
          Food and Rural Affairs (formerly MAFF)
DETR   Department of the Environment,
          Transport and the Regions (subsequently DTLR)
DfEE   Department for Education and Employment
          (subsequently DfES)
DfES   Department for Education and Skills
DGN   Devolution Guidance Note
DTI   Department of Trade and Industry
DTLR   Department of Transport, London and the Regions
EC   European Community
EEAD   European and External Affairs Division (Wales)
ESG   European Strategy Group (Wales)
EU   European Union
FCO   Foreign and Commonwealth Office
GM   Genetically Modified
IGC   Inter-Governmental Conference
JMC   Joint Ministerial Committee
JMC(E)   Joint Ministerial Committee (Europe)
MAFF   Ministry of Agriculture, Fisheries and Food
Minecor   Ministerial Group for European Co-ordination
MoU   Memorandum of Understanding
MSP   Member of the Scottish Parliament

NAAG	National Assembly Advisory Group
NAW	National Assembly for Wales
REGLEG	Conference of European Regions with Legislative Power
SE	Scottish Executive
SEA	Single European Act
SEERAD	Scottish Executive Environment and Rural Affairs Division
SNP	Scottish National Party
SP	Scottish Parliament
SSA	Sub-state Authority
TEU	Treaty on European Union
UK	United Kingdom
UKRep	United Kingdom Permanent Representation to the European Union
WAG	Welsh Assembly Government
WEC	Wales European Centre

Preface

The present book examines the implications of devolution in the United Kingdom for that country's domestic EU policy formulation process. Although the period of data collection, mainly in the form of interviews with civil servants and party officials, ran from 2000 to 2003, a number of the conclusions drawn continued to apply until 2007 as the Labour Party effectively continued to dominate the three executives examined here. However, the devolved elections of May 2007 dramatically altered this party political balance. The implications of such "governmental incongruence", considered by many to be the key challenge to intra-UK relations post-devolution, are considered in the Postscript.

A number of people deserve to be thanked for their assistance during the course of the researching and writing of this book, not least the civil servants and party officials at the devolved, Whitehall and Brussels levels, who gave up their time to discuss their work and share the experiences of managing EU policy processes post-devolution. Interviews took place in 2000/01 and again in 2003. The second round of interviews took place under the auspices of the project "Multi-level governance in the EU" (Project IGBN), part of the Leverhulme Trust-funded programme "Nations and Regions: The Dynamics of Devolution", headed by the Constitution Unit at University College London.

Particular thanks are due to Professor Charlie Jeffery, Professor William E. Paterson, Professor James Mitchell and my anonymous reviewer for their comments and feedback, as well as other colleagues at the European Research Institute, University of Birmingham, and at Cardiff University's School of European Studies for their support and encouragement. Any errors contained in the text are the author's alone.

It remains only to thank my parents for their unending support and to dedicate this book to my Nan, for whose strength, love and belief in me I will always be grateful.

RP
October 2007

Multi-Level Governance in the United Kingdom

Devolution in the United Kingdom (UK) formed a central element of the constitutional reform programme of the Labour Government elected in May 1997. This process of devolution recognised the territorial differentiation evident in the United Kingdom and substantively altered structures of territorial governance. Literature on devolution in the UK, both from the 1990s and from the earlier 1970s debate, suggests an agreement that devolution involves the transfer of powers from a superior decision-making body to an inferior one (Bogdanor, 1999: 2; Bradbury & Mawson, 1997: 11). In the case of the UK, these subordinate bodies are directly elected and relate to specific geographical areas – Scotland, Wales and Northern Ireland. In the following discussion, devolution is thus interpreted as signifying "the transfer to a subordinate elected body, on a geographical basis, of functions…exercised by ministers and Parliament." (Bogdanor, 1999: 2)

As this devolution process unfolded, it necessarily led to a re-adjustment in government structures within the UK. It also contributed to a recalibration of relations between the UK and the European Union (EU) by reshaping the system of interaction between the multiple levels of government and governance within the UK. The introduction of devolution thus created the opportunity to examine a newly evolving model of multi-level governance in an EU Member State – the EU-related activities of the devolved Scottish and Welsh institutions and the attitudes and reactions of the central government towards these changed circumstances. The unpredictable nature of politics in Northern Ireland, the intermittent suspension of the Northern Ireland Assembly and then its long-term suspension in autumn 2002, only lifted in 2007, resulted in the exclusion of the Northern Ireland Assembly from the scope of this study.

The overall aim of the analysis that follows is to provide a grounded theoretical understanding of the role of the devolved authorities in domestic EU policy formulation within the UK. In addition, it will raise the question of the extent to which our understanding of developments in the UK can be informed by the experiences of sub-state institutions in other EU Member States. The term "sub-state" is preferred here to the term "regional". Although Scotland and Wales are referred to as "regions" for EU administrative purposes, they are generally considered to be nations or countries that form constituent parts of the UK.

A comparative approach of this kind will allow us to understand whether developments in intra-UK relations derive largely from system-specific factors or reflect broader trends in sub-state mobilisation in the EU. As part of this comparative approach, existing academic literature dealing with the phenomenon of sub-state mobilisation in the EU will be considered in Chapter 1, with a particular focus upon the approaches adopted for the purpose of explaining this development, as well as the experiences of inter-governmental relations within other federal or devolved EU Member States. In particular, the concepts of paradiplomacy and of "European Domestic Policy", the latter developed by the German *Länder* during the 1980s, will be explored as potential complements to enhance the explanatory potential of the concept of multi-level governance for understanding the dynamics of sub-state mobilisation in the EU in general, but in the UK in particular.

The study is not restricted to a particular policy area where EU and devolved competences overlap, but rather looks at experiences across a range of policy areas to investigate the potential for differing levels of engagement on the part of the devolved administrations and different attitudes towards devolution on the part of central government departments. It thus moves beyond the earlier focus upon sub-state authorities in the field of EU regional policy in studies of the operation of multi-level governance in the EU.

Chapter 2 will then consider the pre-devolution EU policy formulation process in the UK, focusing in particular upon the representation of territorial concerns and interests in that process. This focus is considered more important to understanding developments in the post-devolution UK than an examination of the pre-devolution system of multi-level governance covering the engagement, or lack thereof, of UK local authorities with EU-related issues. Examining the representation of Scottish and Welsh interests in central government pre-devolution will allow changes in the post-devolution process to be discerned, as well as identifying potential areas of friction in the relationship between central and devolved levels of government.

The next chapter will examine the provisions made for the involvement of the devolved administrations in the UK's domestic EU policy formulation process. The framework within which the relationships take place is central to understanding the management of intra-state relations. The chapter will trace the development of this framework from the proposals contained in the 1997 White Papers, through the Acts of

Parliament to the Memorandum of Understanding (MoU) and the Concordats that create the non-binding framework for the relationship. It will also enable the key principles intended to underpin these relationships to be identified.

The subsequent three chapters provide the empirical basis of the analysis presented here. These chapters are substantially based upon interviews carried out with a range of officials (including party and legislature-based) at devolved, UK and EU levels, as well as primary source documentation, including government press releases and the official reports of the devolved institutions. The period of data collection covers the first term of the Scottish and Welsh institutions from the transfer of powers in July 1999 to the second-ever devolved elections in May 2003.

Chapter 4 will examine the experiences of the Scottish Executive and Scottish Parliament during this time period, whilst Chapter 5 focuses upon the Welsh Assembly Government and the National Assembly for Wales. The penultimate chapter considers the central government's experience of managing the EU policy formulation process post-devolution and the perception of the involvement of the devolved institutions by actors at the centre. Chapter 7 then seeks to gather these strands together and review them in light of the hypotheses posited in Chapter 1.

CHAPTER 1

Multi-Level Governance
in the European Union

Introduction

This study explores the involvement of the United Kingdom's devolved institutions in domestic EU policy formulation. In order to
enhance our understanding of this involvement, the aim here is to examine their experiences during the first four years of devolution in the
context of those of other decentralised or federal EU Member States. To
this end, this chapter will focus upon the key interpretations of sub-state
mobilisation that have been developed since the late 1980s. Given that
most integration theory focuses upon the balance between state and
supranational levels, "grand" theories of integration generally fail to
acknowledge the (potential) engagement of sub-state actors with EU
policy-making. As a consequence, this chapter will concentrate upon
those interpretations that seek specifically to explain sub-state mobilisation, rather than discussing broader integration theory.

We begin with an overview of the channels developed for facilitating
sub-state engagement, before moving on to consider early explanations
of sub-state mobilisation, namely the concepts of a "Europe of the
Regions" and a "Third Level". Attention will then turn to "multi-level
governance", widely accepted as the central model for understanding
sub-state mobilisation in the EU. However, this study adopts the approach that no one of these interpretations of sub-state mobilisation is in
itself wholly convincing and examines two potential complements for
enhancing the explanatory potential of multi-level governance: paradiplomacy and "European Domestic Policy". From this basis, and drawing
upon the experience of sub-state authorities (SSAs) in other Member
States, a series of hypotheses relating to acceptance, tension, asymmetry
and resources will be developed for testing in the UK case.

A "Europe with the Regions"

The issue of the mobilisation of SSAs in the EU forms part of a larger debate surrounding the consequences of European integration for the

Member States and their respective "regions". The source of this debate can be located in the two apparently contradictory trends that were discernible from the 1970s onwards – the accelerated pace of European integration at the supranational level and, domestically, the legislative and/or executive decentralisation that took place in a number of Member States including France, Italy and Spain. This reallocation of decision-making authority placed dual pressures upon the states with policy competences being transferred both upwards to the supranational (European) level and downwards to the sub-state tier. It is within this context that sub-state mobilisation in EU policy-making has taken place.

This mobilisation has manifested itself in a number of different ways in both the domestic and EU arenas. Hooghe (1995) distinguished between institutionalised channels in the EU, institutionalised channels in the domestic arena and non-institutionalised channels. Amongst the institutionalised channels in the EU were Article 146 (TEU) allowing a Member State to be represented by a sub-state minister in the Council of Ministers (now known as the Council of the European Union) if an issue of sub-state competence was under discussion; the Committee of the Regions (CoR), also established by the Treaty on European Union (TEU); and the principle of "partnership" introduced by the 1988 Structural Funds reforms.

In the domestic arena, she identified several opportunities for sub-state engagement, although acknowledging that these vary greatly from Member State to Member State. These included the ratification of European treaties (Belgium, Germany), sub-state observers attached to Member State representations in Brussels (Germany, Spain), the opportunity to send delegates to Council and Commission working groups (Austria, Belgium, Germany), and, crucially, the opportunity to influence or develop Member State negotiating positions in areas of domestic sub-state responsibility (Austria, Belgium, Germany). Non-institutionalised channels include sub-state offices in Brussels, umbrella lobbying organisations such as the Assembly of European Regions (AER), inter-regional associations and independent collaborative projects between two or more SSAs.

It can thus be seen that sub-state mobilisation has taken a wide range of different forms, varying from Member State to Member State with some SSAs, such as those in Belgium, in a much stronger position to engage with EU policy formulation than others, such as the Spanish Autonomous Communities. These forms of mobilisation seemingly result from the interaction between those two apparently contradictory processes of decentralisation and European integration which have combined to create an overlap between the competences of the different territorial levels of governance. It is in the context of this overlap that the mobilisation highlighted here takes place. To date, a number of possible explanations for such mobilisation have thus far been identified:

– That a "Europe of the Regions" is developing with a potential corresponding decline in the role of states as a federal Europe develops (Knemeyer, 1990; Hrbek & Weyand, 1994: 13);

– That SSAs have been deliberately mobilised by the Commission as potential allies in an attempt to weaken central governments by "squeezing" them from above and below (Tömmel, 1998);

– That mobilisation is an attempt to create the "Third Level" of a balanced three-tier federal EU structure (Bullmann & Eißel, 1993);

– That mobilisation has taken place in response to the advent of new funding opportunities and participation in the formulation of regional policy at the European level as a result of the reform of the Structural Funds in 1988 (Marks, 1992; 1993);

– That mobilisation is a reaction to the ever expanding scope of the EU's policy competences which have been perceived as a threat to SSAs' own legislative or executive responsibilities. Such expansion has been interpreted as a "Europeanisation" of domestic politics as the EU agenda increasingly cuts across the domestic division of competences (Jeffery, 1996; 1997).

Let us begin by looking at the earlier interpretations of sub-state mobilisation, generated at a time when such sub-state activities were a new development in the EU system. The remainder of this section will focus firstly upon the concept of a "Europe of the Regions", and whether such a development was precipitated by the European Commission, and secondly on the potential emergence of a Third Level.

A "Europe of the Regions" was a concept that was widely used as a slogan by SSAs mobilising in the EU, but which suffers from a number of problems of definition, not least the issue of how to define a "region" (Hrbek & Weyand, 1994: 13-19). As such, it has been interpreted in a number of different ways by different groups according to their own interests. For example, the Catalan nationalists of "Convergence and Union" (CíU) promoted the concept as a way of gaining recognition for Catalonia, whereas Flanders has been interested in promoting it as a means of gaining protection for cultural identity and minority languages, a "Europe of the Cultures", and the German *Länder* seized upon the concept of a "Europe of the Regions" as a means of protecting their own institutional rights and competences (Keating, 1998: 164).

The concept has been identified as "originally meaning a federal Europe with a reduced role for nation states" (Keating & Loughlin, 1997: 1), representing the concept in its most idealistic form with the argument being that as European integration progressed, the state would increasingly find itself squeezed between the sub-state and supranational levels. One argument contends that many of the reasons behind SSA mobilisation are economic in nature (Keating, 1998) and this coincides with the idea of the rise of "region-states" (Ohmae, 1993) in response to economic globalisation. Ohmae argued that region-states are natural economic zones and the state is no longer the best-equipped geographic entity for responding to the challenges raised by globalisation and economic interdependence (*Ibid.*: 78). In this scenario, sub-state mobilisation would be viewed as a stage in the demise of the state more generally, not just in the EU arena.

This early conception of regions ousting the states as key players has been variously dismissed as "idealistic", "utopian" and "simplistic" (Keating, 1998: 161; Keating & Jones, 1995: 10; Anderson, 1990: 445). One very important reason for this dismissal is the fact that the concept ignores the strength and depth of the resources of the Member States as well as the resilience of the political elites at state level and the important interests invested in the state as an entity (Keating & Jones, 1995: 10). In addition, the negotiation of future treaties on integration essentially depends on interaction between Member State governments.

A second interpretation of the concept considers the European Commission to be the driving force behind sub-state mobilisation, seeking to build up SSAs as allies in attempts to gain control over ever larger areas of policy competency and to weaken the states as centres of authority (Stewart, 1997: 140; Tömmel, 1998: 53-4). From this perspective, the Commission employs the "Europe of the Regions" concept in order to place a squeeze on central governments from above and below and by-pass central governments by dealing directly with SSAs when requiring information or assistance in policy implementation.

Three particular factors suggest weaknesses in this interpretation of sub-state mobilisation. Firstly, it has been argued that the Commission's interest in sub-state authorities stem from technocratic concerns regarding the effect of regional disparities upon the construction of the Single Market, rather than an attempt to utilise SSAs as a means of weakening Member State governments (Keating & Jones, 1995: 290). Secondly, the Commission was initially unenthusiastic with regard to the activities of the CoR (Jeffery, 1995). The Commission's attitude towards the CoR can be interpreted as a signal that mobilising SSAs was not an overriding concern of the Commission. Thirdly, although SSA mobilisation may provide the Commission with allies against Member State dominance of the policy process, active SSAs also introduce new interests and concerns into that process. Increasing numbers of actors may act as a constraint upon the Commission's ability to create an impact upon policy outcomes, rather than facilitating the exercise of its influence.

Interpretations which represent the Commission as the driving force behind SSA mobilisation moreover ignore a further factor. The Commission, as with the Member States, does not constitute a monolithic actor. Rather, it is a set of sometimes loosely connected, or even competing, directorates consisting of officials from all the Member States. Such interpretations also presuppose a Commission activism that has scarcely been evident since Jacques Delors finished his last term as Commission President.

There is no firm evidence for the establishment of such a Europe of the Regions, whether driven by federalisation, economics or the European Commission. Although it can be argued that the role of states is undergoing a re-assessment, there are no clear signs that states are in decline or that their place in policy-making processes is being taken over by the supranational and sub-state levels. The depth of resources and the strength of vested interests supporting them ensures that they remain central in EU policy-making, even though they may not be the only actors able to have an independent impact upon policy outcomes.

So, from early enthusiasm about the emergence of SSAs as important actors alongside the supranational level in a challenge to the supremacy of states' decision-making authority (Borkenhagen *et al.*, 1992; Scott *et al.*, 1994), more pragmatic perceptions about the role of the regions began to emerge (Hooghe, 1996; Keating & Jones, 1995). Alongside these more pragmatic perceptions about this future role as European integration continues, alternative interpretations of what a Europe of the Regions actually signifies also emerged, with the slogan being taken to mean an enhanced role of the regions in EU policy-making (Keating & Loughlin, 1997: 1), rather than the squeezing out of the state by decision-making at the supranational and sub-state levels. A perceptible shift from the notion of a "Europe of the Regions" to one of a "Europe with the Regions" (Leonardy, 1992: 57-8; Le Galès & Lequesne, 1998: 267; Hooghe, 1995: 179) has taken place.

Less idealistic than the concept of the demise of the state, but highly ambitious nevertheless, was the conception of sub-state mobilisation in the European Union as the emergence of a Third Level in the EU's nascent political system leading to the establishment of a balanced three-tier federal system (Jeffery, 1997a: 65). With the Third Level concept, the three-tier system would incorporate the SSAs into the policy-making process and include state governments, resulting in a more balanced structure than that suggested by the concept. The development of the Third Level would see the institutionalisation of the role of SSAs in the

EU, giving them a distinct role in EU decision-making with the creation of a "regional" chamber to participate in the EU's legislative processes.

The concept of the Third Level in the EU system is most frequently associated with the German *Länder* and draws from their experience of the federal system there. After the conclusion of the Single European Act (SEA), the *Länder* challenged the Federal Government for involvement in European policy-making processes both domestically and at the European level. The Third Level concept was one of two principal strategies which the *Länder* employed in their efforts to secure participatory rights. It represented a horizontal strategy for developing transnational alliances with other European regions in a bid to establish a Third Level targeted at boosting the role of SSAs in the European integration process (Jeffery, 1996: 261). The second strategy, applying the concept of "European Domestic Policy", was aimed primarily at securing constitutional changes within the Federal Republic to ensure *Länder* participation in European policy formulation in the domestic arena and will be examined later in this chapter.

These conceptions and strategies stimulated intensive debate both in the *Länder* and in SSAs in other EU Member States and can also be linked with the highly contentious debate surrounding the application of the principle of subsidiarity in EU policy-making. Subsidiarity was seized upon by the SSAs in their quest to entrench their role in EU policy-making. However, a fundamental dispute about the definition of subsidiarity rapidly became apparent during the negotiations surrounding the Maastricht Treaty.

For the stronger SSAs, amongst others, subsidiarity as a principle signified that decisions should be taken at the lowest appropriate level, (thereby securing a sub-state role in the EU policy-making process and protecting "their" competences from further European encroachment). It was also argued that decision-making at the lowest possible level would help to reduce the impression that European integration was distancing decision-making from the citizens of the Member States and would thereby help to enhance legitimacy by reducing the so-called democratic deficit (Scott *et al.*, 1994).

However, the state governments of some of the more centralised Member States (notably the Conservative government in the UK) viewed subsidiarity as a device for keeping the then EC's institutions in check and preserving as great a decision-making authority as possible at the state level (*Ibid.*: 49-52). The centralised states of the EC thus created a major stumbling block for the campaign by "strong" SSAs for the creation of a Third Level as a consequence of this resistance to the idea of devolving power away from central government. These state executives were also opposed to a clear division of competences between the three levels of government, as this would effectively require the drafting of a European constitution.

Two phases can be discerned in the debate over the concept of a Third Level. The first is a promotional phase, with debate centring upon how this level could be created and what level of institutionalisation it would require. The second phase came with the observation that the German *Länder* in particular, one of the main driving forces behind the concept, had begun to distance themselves from the strategy of creating a Third Level.

During the first phase, the concept of the Third Level was used to promote a third, sub-state, level beneath the supranational and state levels in the future development of the EU political system (Hrbek & Weyand, 1994: 155). An example of such demands followed a meeting of *Länder* premiers in Munich in 1990 when a statement was released detailing the need for the future construction of the then Community to have a three-tier structure and a clear division of powers between the three levels (Borkenhagen *et al.*, 1992: 236). Some contributions to the literature on the Third Level were also marked by a comparative approach as authors considered the respective strengths and weaknesses of the SSA level in different Member States (Engel, 1993).

This process of comparison, however, also served to contribute to the growing realisation that the differences between SSAs in the Member States meant that the prospects for the early emergence of a coherent sub-state level across the EU were remote. As it became increasingly clear that a uniform layer of sub-state government was not about to be created across the Member States, the stronger SSAs began to distance themselves from the promotion of this cause in favour of entrenching their own positions in the decision-making process.

A good illustration of the reasons for this disillusionment with the Third Level concept can be seen in the weaknesses apparent in the operation of the Committee of the Regions, a body created by Article 198 of the Treaty on European Union. The establishment of a body of sub-state representation had been one of the key objectives which the *Länder* had inserted into the Federal Republic's Maastricht agenda. However, the Treaty provision established a purely consultative body and only required that policy documents in a very limited number of areas be automatically passed to the CoR for its opinions. In its operational form, the CoR has faced a number of difficulties stemming from the disparities which exist in the sub-state government structures of the Member States. States which have no "regional" tier nominate local authority representatives, whose interests and concerns differ markedly from those of representatives of "regional" authorities, making it difficult to agree common positions for the CoR to present.

The problems engendered by operating across this regional-local divide led to a growing disillusionment with the CoR as a way of influencing policy in the EU political system on the part of the stronger SSAs who have been unable to shape the work of the Committee in accordance with their own wishes and concerns. With the Committee incapable of operating in the way the stronger SSAs desired, the *Länder* in particular began to argue for its division into local and regional chambers (Jeffery, 1997a: 70).

The operation of the new "regional" institution in the EU and a process of comparing SSAs in different Member States meant that the limitations of the Third Level's potential, at least in the short- to medium-term, became increasingly apparent. The distancing of some of its key supporters from the promotion of the concept further weakened its potential, and represented a clear move away from the enthusiasm surrounding the possible creation of a Europe of the Regions or of a Third Level in the early 1990s.

The Third Level approach envisaged interaction between the processes of decentralisation and European integration as creating a uniform sub-state level in a balanced three-tier federal European polity. However, there are no signs of such a homogenous sub-state level developing across the EU. The decentralisation processes of Member States have varied widely and some states remain centralised, particularly those, like Luxembourg, that are smaller than some of the large SSAs. It has therefore become apparent that this heterogeneity at the sub-state level will not noticeably diminish in the short- to medium-term.

This has been further emphasised by the increasingly pragmatic approach of those "strong" SSAs who have concentrated on protecting their competences and employing intra-state channels to represent their interests and concerns (Jeffery, 1997a). Horizontal links between SSAs have increasingly refocused upon functional arrangements aimed at achieving concrete policy outcomes in areas like transport, rather than more abstract attempts to strengthen the role of the sub-state level in the EU system, although the "Conference of European Regions with Legislative Power" (RegLeg) has remained active in its attempts to engage with debates about the future direction of European integration.

These early interpretations, often built upon the enthusiasm of sub-state actors rather than evidence of concrete developments, thus have little to offer in understanding changes in the UK's EU policy formulation process post-devolution. In the academic sphere, however, one concept came to dominate approaches to understanding sub-state mobilisation, and it is to this concept of multi-level governance that we now turn.

Developing Multi-Level Governance

Originally developed by Gary Marks, seeking to explain the increase in activity of the sub-state level of government in the EU arena, the concept of multi-level governance has developed into one broader dimension of the debate on governance in the EU. Since its initial development, it has become increasingly common in academic analysis of EU decision-making processes. Unlike the previous interpretations addressed here, multi-level governance does not see sub-state mobilisation as a threat to the continued existence of the state. Rather, it recognises that states cannot be viewed as monolithic actors and therefore questions theoretical approaches to European integration and EU policy-making which only encompass supranational and central government levels, arguing that there is a need to conceptualise the EU policy process as "a system of continuous negotiation among nested governments at several territorial tiers" (Marks, 1993: 392). It also uses the term "governance" rather than "government" to denote interaction between "public and private actors, social groups and institutions in order to attain clear aims, which are debated and defined collectively, in uncertain and fragmented environments" (Le Galès & Lequesne, 1998: 243). So the multi-level governance approach does not view the state as a single cohesive actor but looks beyond to the internal decision-making and communication procedures existing within the states.

In contrast to other, more radical, interpretations of SSA mobilisation, however, multi-level governance does not predict the emergence of a uniform sub-state level of government across the Member States of the EU. Rather it accepts a likelihood that the territorial structures of governance in the Member States will remain highly differentiated and that levels of access to the decision-making process will vary from SSA to SSA according to their own legislative, administrative and financial resources, and the structure of the Member State within which they are located (Hooghe, 1995: 178-179). In addition, it is expected that levels of participation will vary considerably between policy sectors.

In the multi-level governance literature that has subsequently developed (for example, Hooghe & Marks, 2001; Bache & Flinders, 2004), four core characteristics of the concept can be recognised. Firstly, multi-level governance involves the sharing or dispersal of authority across multiple territorial levels, leading to the relative empowerment of actors other than the state. Secondly, it is genuinely multi-level, most notably in the EU, and involves actors from a number of distinct territorial levels in policy processes (Peters & Pierre, 2004). Thirdly, despite continuing contestation of definitions of the term, it is "governance" in that it extends beyond traditional state actors. Finally, it expects policy sector variation, anticipating fluidity in the constellation of actors involved in negotiating different policy issues.

Marks originally suggested that potential and actual sub-state mobilisation was an unintended consequence of the major reform of the Structural Funds in 1988 which was initiated by Member States and the Commission (Marks, 1992: 192, 206). He thus adopted a traditional two-tier perspective when considering the actual negotiation of the reforms, with no place for sub-state representation in the initial bargaining process. The new procedures which resulted from this reform, however, included sub-state actors in both the planning and implementation phases, thus presenting them with an opportunity to mobilise and, in some instances, have direct contact with Commission officials. Sub-state developments in response to these reforms thus indicated a potential for mobilisation at that level.

The argument followed that the reforms created new arenas, involving new participants, in which EU decision-making would take place, thus emphasising the lack of a clear distinction between EU and domestic politics – at least in EU Regional Policy and the Structural Funds. Nevertheless, in this complex multi-tier system, state executives remained central in the policy-making process, though not as completely dominant as state-based approaches would contend. Subsequent multi-level governance approaches to EU policy-making continued the initial focus upon Structural Funds policy (Hooghe & Keating, 1994: Hooghe, 1996; Smyrl, 1997), until supplemented by more recent work drawing upon research into governance in other policy sectors (Knodt, 2004; Schout & Jordan, 2005).

As the debate over multi-level governance has progressed, three notable trends have developed that divide and shape the existing literature. Firstly, there has been a continued focus upon the differences between state-centric approaches and multi-level governance (Hooghe & Marks, 2001a; Jordan, 2001; Knodt & Große-Hüttmann, 2004). Secondly, there has been a division between research focusing upon the "multi-level" aspect and that concentrating upon "governance" (for the former, see Bomberg & Peterson, 1998; Jeffery, 2000; for the latter Kohler-Koch, 1999; Schout & Jordan, 2005). Finally, Hooghe and Marks have argued that two different types of multi-level governance can actually be discerned, one territory-based form and one task-specific form (2001b). The concept can thus be seen to have developed in a number of different directions since its initial conception. Whilst such strands are interesting and relevant to the broader topic under discussion here, the key focus of this study remains upon the motivations for sub-state mobilisation.

Inevitably, the concept of multi-level governance has also been the subject of much criticism, both from proponents of state-centric approaches to European integration and also from those seeking to enhance understanding of the concept and its practical operation. Perhaps the central criticism is that although multi-level governance offers an accurate description of the EU policy-making process (Rhodes, Bache & George, 1996: 372-373), there are several problems with its interpretation of causation, particularly when domestically "strong" SSAs such as those in Belgium, Germany and elsewhere are taken into consideration, and it is this issue that the following study seeks principally to address.

Firstly, the concept of multi-level governance was, as highlighted above, largely derived from, and applied to, analysis of a single policy sector and reforms associated with that policy. By viewing the emergence of multi-level governance as a spin-off from interaction between Commission and Member States, multi-level governance approaches failed to draw upon the experiences of SSAs in other policy sectors where they have domestic responsibilities. The German *Länder*, for example, were not solely interested in engaging with Structural Funds policy issues, as many of the western *Länder* benefited little from the Funds. The concept of multi-level governance in its original form cannot therefore account for the mobilisation of those SSAs that were determined to prevent the erosion of their exclusive or joint policy competences in areas other than regional economic development, or of those SSAs who receive little or no Structural Fund aid.

Secondly, it is a "top-down" approach (Jeffery, 2000), that is SSA mobilisation is viewed as being a by-product of the interaction between state executives and the Commission, implying a state-centric focus on these two levels. It also implies that SSAs were essentially passive until offered the opportunity to engage in the policy process by the state and supranational levels. Yet this does not account for the pro-active positions adopted by SSAs like the German *Länder* and Belgian regions and communities, both through inter-regional associations such as the AER, and within their respective Member States, as they sought to enhance their opportunities to access European policy-making.

The limitations of the explanatory factors provided by the original conception of multi-level governance can be further highlighted by considering the mobilisation of SSAs in the international arena by regions outside the European Union. Such mobilisation has been termed "paradiplomacy" by some (Aldecoa & Keating, 1999), whilst others have differentiated between paradiplomacy, which is seen as supplementary to the foreign policy conducted by the central government, and "proto-diplomacy", which can be understood as the representation of an SSA's interests in a separatist manner (Mitchell & Leicester, 1999). The concept of paradiplomacy will be returned to shortly.

The multi-level governance approach thus argued that Structural Fund reform generated SSA mobilisation, but this fails to account for deliberate actions by SSAs aimed at enhancing their participatory rights in the EU policy process, with evidence for this pro-active stance demonstrated by a series of conferences entitled "A Europe of the Regions" by the German *Länder* in 1990 and the declarations of RegLeg with regard to the 2001 European Council at Laeken and the 2004 Inter-Governmental Conference.

Such intentional actions clearly demonstrate a "bottom-up" impulse with SSAs pro-actively seeking to engage with the formulation, in both the domestic and EU arenas, of EU policy positions that will impact upon their own policy competences. The original approach also ignores the fact that such actions were not just aimed at achieving participation in the formulation of Structural Funds policy, but in every policy field in which the SSAs were involved in domestic decision-making. Problems are also raised for this approach by studies which establish the occurrence of sub-state mobilisation in non-EU states including the US and Canada. Taken together, these factors indicate a clear need to complement the model of multi-level governance in order to better explain the motivations of the more powerful sub-state authorities with domestic legislative and executive competences for mobilising in the EU arena.

The multi-level governance approach can thus be said to accurately describe developments in the EU policy process, and it recognises that new networks are being created that involve both sub-state and private actors in the policy process. It also accepts that the pattern of sub-state mobilisation will be uneven and those SSAs that are deeply entrenched in their domestic political systems are more likely to participate in EU policy-making than others. Crucially, it also recognises that the EU policy process is no longer separate from the domestic political system. However, the problems with its interpretation of the motivation for such mobilisation need to be addressed by complementing the multi-level governance approach to provide an enhanced understanding of why SSAs mobilise.

Complementing Multi-Level Governance

This section will now consider two potential complements for enhancing our understanding of sub-state mobilisation. The first is the concept of paradiplomacy, highlighted above. The second is the strategic concept of European Domestic Policy, developed by the German *Länder* in response to the continuing European integration process. The paradiplomacy approach offers a further range of motivations that may prompt sub-state mobilisation, concentrating as it does upon understanding the enhanced profiles of SSAs internationally, not just within the EU. Although many of the explanatory factors employed are economic in nature, interpreting this international mobilisation as a response to the new circumstances created by the changing global economy, the approach also recognises that political and/or cultural elements can also have a role in explaining the mobilisation of certain SSAs.

Considering SSA mobilisation from this wider perspective, studies of para- or proto-diplomacy explore motivations that are more complex than simply being a response to new funding opportunities. SSAs outside the EU could not have mobilised in response to Structural Fund reform. Nevertheless, many of the motivations identified for this kind of mobilisation are economic in nature. Instead of being concerned with receiving funding from a supranational organisation, they are concerned with the challenge of attracting inward investment (Keating, 1998: 139) or seeking to expand the external market for products made in the region. It has been argued that these new economic imperatives for regions (beyond the sub-state authority) have been generated by important changes to the global economy.

A significant element of the changed context for regionalism is the globalisation of the economy (Keating & Loughlin, 1997: 25). The changing nature of the global economy, characterised by the interdependence of states, the rise of multi-national corporations and a growing emphasis upon free trade and a free market by the governments of western liberal democracies, has created a new environment in which SSAs and their territories must operate. Their responses to this challenge have been shaped by the retrenchment of some central governments from centrally-led "regional" development policies and, in a number of states, a trend of decentralising power away from central government down to the SSA level. Such shifts in central government policy have encouraged the creation of endogenous regional development strategies by sub-state authorities (Keating, 1998: 138-160).

The second category of motivations for seeking an international presence can be broadly defined as cultural. Objectives of mobilisation stemming from cultural motivations may be to protect a minority culture of language through external appeals, particularly if it is the majority culture in another state, as is the case with Quebec in Canada and France, or to promote a distinctive minority culture or language, as is the case with Catalonia (Keating, 1999: 4-5).

Finally, territories may have political reasons for their international activity. For example, nationalists in areas such as Quebec may seek recognition of the legitimacy of their aspirations for a special, or even independent, status (Balthazar, 1999: 153). It is this kind of activity that may be termed as proto-diplomacy, being perceived as detrimental to the interests of the state to which the territory belongs.

In common with studies of SSA mobilisation within the EU, studies of paradiplomacy indicate that two sets of factors combine to shape both the nature and intensity of an SSA's international mobilisation. The first is the resources at the disposal of the authority itself, for example its financial resources, or its bureaucratic expertise in specific policy sectors (Hocking, 1999: 28; Hooghe, 1995: 178-179). The second set of factors can be defined as the opportunity structure within which the SSA is located. This would include elements such as formal and informal communication channels with the central government, the immediate international environment within which the state, and hence also its SSAs, operates, and potential points of access for SSAs to this broader environment (Keating, 1999: 6-10).

This approach can, to a certain extent, be adopted to explain particular dimensions of the mobilisation of SSAs belonging to EU Member States. For example, the role of the Welsh Development Agency in enhancing Wales' international profile focused heavily upon changing economic circumstances and endeavoured to promote Wales as a trading partner and a location for inward investment. However, such economic factors fail specifically to account for demands to engage with the EU policy process where it overlaps with domestic policy competences. The fact that the paradiplomacy approach can also be applied to the mobilisation of SSAs outside the EU signifies that Structural Funds reform is not the sole reason for SSA mobilisation, but also suggests that the factors identified by paradiplomacy cannot be employed to fully explain the challenge of SSAs for engagement with the EU policy process.

Nevertheless, the paradiplomacy approach contains a key element of use to the study of sub-state mobilisation in the EU which relates to the level and quality of SSA engagement with the policy-making processes, namely the extent of an SSA's resources. The importance of resources was also proposed by Jeffery (2000) who argued that an SSA's resources, including its administrative and financial capacity, affect the extent to which an SSA is able to engage with the formulation of EU policy, both domestically and at the EU level. This suggestion echoes that of the multi-level governance approach which argues that the depth of an SSA's domestic entrenchment affects its ability to engage in EU policy-making. Linked to the constitutional position of SSAs, it can therefore be argued that resources create the opportunity structure through which the SSA is able to engage with EU policy processes, helping to determine the level and quality of this SSA engagement.

Paradiplomacy, then, provides, at best, a partial explanation of the specific motivations behind sub-state mobilisation in the EU. One potential complement to the multi-level governance approach therefore remains – that the expansion of the EU's policy competences has led to an overlap between EU and domestic politics, leading SSAs to perceive a potential threat to the exercise of their domestic responsibilities. This concept of an overlap between EU and domestic policy was incorporated in the *Länder* concept of "European Domestic Policy" which they constructed to substantiate their claim to be involved in the formulation of Germany's European policy positions.

Marks (1993) argued that there was little reason to believe that the patterns of multi-level governance apparent in Structural Funds policy would be replicated in other policy areas. However, it is clear that SSAs have sought to mobilise in other policy areas where they have domestic responsibilities. The concept of European Domestic Policy offers a potential explanation for why SSAs mobilise in specific policy areas. This concept was formulated by the German *Länder* during their challenge to the Federal Government for access to EC policy-making which followed the ratification of the Single European Act. They effectively argued that the (then) European Community could no longer be considered as an international organisation in the conventional sense and thus did not form part of the Federal Government's exclusive foreign policy competence. Instead, they claimed the Community was increasingly assuming state-like qualities and, as such, they claimed rights in EU policy-making equivalent to those that they would have if the policy issue was being dealt with domestically (*Bundesrat*, 1997: 143-168).

The concept assumes that states are not monolithic actors and furthermore implicitly suggests that European integration has an inevitable impact upon decentralised state structures. By following this argument through, the *Länder* also demonstrated the deliberateness of their actions, contradicting the argument that their mobilisation occurred as a spin-off of interaction between the Commission and Member States governments.

It is also clear from this argument that the *Länder* no longer perceived the existence of a clear distinction between domestic and EU policy arenas in the same way that they perceived a demarcation between domestic politics and the wider international arena, with their claim that the Community could no longer be considered an international organisation like any other. From their perspective, the Community had increasingly come to be seen as an additional tier on top of the domestic policy-making system, rather than a separate international organisation. This notion of the EU level as an additional tier helps to demonstrate the accuracy of the multi-level governance model as a description of the EU system, with its acceptance of a number of actors at several different levels engaging in EU policy-making.

This approach therefore sees the mobilisation of sub-state authorities in the EU policy process as being an outcome of the interaction between the domestic decentralisation of decision-making authority and the transfer of policy competences to the EU level, the two apparently contradictory processes highlighted earlier. The combination of these two processes leads to an overlap between EU and sub-state responsibilities which prompts SSAs to seek to engage with the EU policy process. By combining this concept with the multi-level governance model, understanding of the engagement of SSAs in the EU policy process could be enhanced.

Writing in 2000, Jeffery argues that the changes occasioned by sub-state mobilisation have in fact occurred largely in the intra-state arena and the changes brought about have been wrought within the framework and logic of each Member State where the SSAs are concerned with maintaining the integrity and purpose of the internal distribution of competences. The lack of uniformity found in the multi-level governance model will thus also be apparent with European Domestic Policy. He went on to argue that the concept of European Domestic Policy may also assist in understanding with which policy areas SSAs will seek to engage. If the argument of European Domestic Policy holds, SSAs will seek to engage in EU policy in those areas where they hold domestic responsibilities. The variation in the competences of SSAs in different Member States may also help to explain differences in SSA mobilisation from policy sector to policy sector.

The concept also allows for a "bottom-up" approach, that is SSAs actively seeking to mobilise in areas where they have domestic responsibilities. The concept therefore addresses a number of the deficiencies of the multi-level governance approach by offering the possibility of an underlying trend to account for the mobilisation, actual or attempted, of sub-state authorities in EU policy-making. This leads to the formulation of the main hypothesis tested in the case of the UK:

> The concept of European Domestic Policy, as developed by the German Länder governments in response to the continuing process of European integration, will apply in the post-devolution UK. This will see the increasing overlap of European and sub-state politics reflected in the involvement of the devolved Scottish and Welsh authorities in EU policy formulation, both within the UK and in the EU arena.

If the concept of European Domestic Policy applies in the UK case, then the Scottish Executive (SE) and the Welsh Assembly Government (WAG), will be active in EU policy formulation in areas of competence other than the Structural Funds. The policy areas in which they are active in EU policy formulation will correspond to those in which they have domestic responsibilities. Acceptance of this participation by the

UK central government could indicate a growing acceptance of the idea of Europeanised domestic policy-making.

In Germany, the different interpretation of the nature of EU policy – the question of whether or not EU policy was foreign policy – created a challenge of cycle and resistance between the two levels of government. Reluctant acceptance of the concept was eventually forced upon the Federal Government by the threat of non-ratification of the Treaty on European Union, as the *Bundesrat*, the federal level-organ of *Länder* government representation, must ratify European treaties alongside the *Bundestag*, the German parliament. The acceptance of this concept acknowledged the overlap that existed between EU and domestic policy arenas. If the idea that EU policy is not an element of foreign policy, but rather an extension of domestic policy, is accepted in the UK, this will be recognised by the involvement of the devolved administrations in the process of EU policy formulation. The extent of this involvement will demonstrate either UK central government acceptance of, or resistance to, the concept of this overlap.

A Potential for Tension

Despite the evidence of dynamics of challenge and resistance within the system, the EU policy formulation process in Germany has largely been characterised by a consensual approach since the constitutional entrenchment of the participatory rights of the *Länder*. Neither the Federal nor the *Land* levels have tested the limits of the existing settlement. However, the generally smooth operation of the German system has not concealed the existence of a number of dynamics and tensions, a situation that has also been the case in Belgium and Spain. It therefore appears inevitable that tensions will emerge as a consequence of the impact of European integration upon devolved policy-making structures and processes, leading to the construction of a supplementary hypothesis:

> The overlap between European and devolved domestic competences is likely to create (or exacerbate) sources of tension in the relationship between the devolved executives and UK central government over the degree and nature of the involvement of the devolved authorities in EU policy formulation.

From studying the experiences of SSAs elsewhere, seven potential points of friction can be identified. The first two point to the dynamics of challenge and resistance previously identified in relations between domestic levels of government. Subsequent points highlight more specific tensions which have emerged between central and sub-state levels:

– The exclusion of SSAs from European policy formulation

This tension has been evident in both the German and Spanish cases in particular, as can be demonstrated by the *Länder* push for participation in EU policy formulation detailed above. The Spanish government's stance was also, for a long time, marked by resistance to the involvement of the Autonomous Communities (ACs), with the Constitution explicitly reserving international affairs as a competency of the central government (García, 1995: 124). In the Spanish case, Catalonia and the Basque Country have most pro-actively sought engagement with EU policy-making, but there were no constitutional provisions regulating sub-state engagement in EU affairs. The framework for sub-state engagement, the Agreement of 30 November 1994, was not legally binding (Jones, 1997: 50).

– The loss of competences from the sub-state to the EU level with no redress for the SSAs to engage in decision-making in these policy areas.

The second area of tension has also emerged in both cases, and in Germany at a particularly early stage of the European integration process, with the transfer, under Article 24 of the Basic Law, of sub-state competences to the EU level without any requirement for *Länder* consent. This issue of the loss of competences was highly controversial for the *Länder* from as early as 1951, as they perceived it as the creeping centralisation of power at the federal level (*Bundesrat*, 1997). With the insertion of a new Article 23 post-unification, this was reduced as an area of tension in the German case.

The Belgian regions and communities are in a strong position in this regard and this issue has been less salient since the federal reform of 1994. Responsibility for signing international treaties is divided according to the domestic allocation of competences (Kerremans, 1997), reducing the loss of competences as a potential source of tension in the Belgian system. Having joined the EU at a later date, Austria acceded to an organisation that already held extensive policy competences and few transfers of sub-state competences have taken place subsequently, while the Spanish Autonomous Communities hold no veto over the transfer of competences to the EU level. The devolved authorities of the UK find themselves in a weaker position in this respect, one that more closely resembles that of the Spanish ACs, but this may be reduced as a potential source of friction given that most of the policy competences devolved in the UK have a pre-existing EU dimension as a result of transfers of competences that pre-date devolution.

– The question of sub-state representatives participating in Council of the EU meetings where sub-state competences are under discussion.

This particular tension relates to the question of access to the Council of the European Union (formerly known as the Council of Ministers) when issues of sub-state responsibility are under discussion. The right of sub-state ministers to participate in Council meetings was gained by the Belgian regions and is enshrined in Article 146 TEU. The German Federal Government had refused to place this *Länder* demand on its negotiating agenda for the TEU, but accepted the possibility of a *Land* minister representing the Federal Republic on occasions when an exclusive *Land* competence was under discussion following the Belgian move. The Spanish central government, on the other hand, chose not to allow sub-state ministers to represent Spain under this clause. The question of Council participation has potential to cause tensions in the UK, particularly if exploited in a party political manner by the opposition parties.

– The information flow.

The flow of relevant information from federal to *Land* level was another key point of friction in Germany. Access to information is crucial to ensuring that relevant positions can be adopted quickly to enable their input into the policy formulation process. The issue of a lack of a reliable and sufficiently extensive information flow was a serious area of contention between federal and *Land* levels, but the German *Länder* now have a constitutional right to information as do their Austrian counterparts.

The complexity of the Belgian federal system and EU co-ordination system has meant information is delivered directly to the regions and communities from the Permanent Representation through the mechanism of weekly co-ordination meetings (Kerremans, 1997). The right of the Spanish Autonomous Communities to information is not constitutionally entrenched and complaints have been made about the late receipt of information making it impossible to influence policy lines already adopted. The necessity for a regular flow of appropriate information to enable participation will also exist in the UK's devolved system.

– The legal/constitutional entrenchment of the participatory rights of SSAs.

The question of legal, then constitutional, entrenchment of the rights of participation has been a vexed question for SSAs in Member States across the EU, and an obvious point of tension in relations with the centre. In Germany, constitutional entrenchment was finally achieved some forty years after the first demands heard at the time of the founding of the European Coal and Steel Community (*Bundesrat*, 1997). However, this is less likely to be an area of dispute in the UK where a very different perception dominates attitudes towards the necessity for constitutionalisation, given the UK's lack of a formal written constitution. Despite this, it may still be the case that the devolved administrations seek legal clarification of their rights in legislation passed by the Westminster Parliament and thus the question of legal clarification could become an area of tension between the two levels.

– The need to establish collective positions – the tensions of a multi-lateral system for negotiating policy positions.

The multilateral process for managing intra-state relations in other Member States has the potential to generate friction in those systems where there is a need to establish majority positions on behalf of the SSAs, notably Germany and Spain. The Belgian system is, again, somewhat unusual in this respect, but should the regions or communities fail to agree a policy position on an issue where they are domestically competent, the Belgian delegation effectively abstains from voting at the EU level.

This aspect of tension is unlikely to be recreated within the UK system, as the relationship is likely to be managed predominantly on an informal bilateral basis, rather than through formal multilateral fora. This informal system is based upon the tradition for managing relations within the British civil service which appears to be preferred by UK ministers and officials. However, its informal nature may create frictions if there is no document that the devolved administrations can call upon to guarantee their involvement.

– The dominance of the policy formulation process by executives at the expense of sub-state parliaments, compounded by the difficulty of establishing a role for parliamentary committees in EU policy.

With regard to the final area of tension identified here, it is clear that the executive dominance of sub-state involvement can be anticipated and the constraints upon the *Landtage* and other sub-state parliaments may be replicated in the Scottish Parliament (SP) and the National Assembly for Wales (NAW) with regard to matters such as the scrutiny of executive activity. Difficulties in determining the best role of the EU committees of these devolved institutions can also be expected. Challenges to perceived exclusion may well emanate from the political parties represented in the devolved institutions, with party political tensions more likely to be apparent in the UK than in some of the other, more consensus-oriented, EU states such as Germany and Austria.

The list of sources of friction given here is far from exhaustive, and points to generic tensions across different models of multi-level governance. It is also possible that system-specific tensions occur in the different Member States of the EU, a possibility that will be considered further in Chapter 2.

The Issue of Asymmetry

Yet more dynamics may also be created in the UK case. If European Domestic Policy applies in the United Kingdom post-devolution, the new sub-state authorities will adopt pro-active stances to seek engagement with the EU policy process. The asymmetrical nature of devolution combined with pro-active positions may lead to the unleashing of another set of dynamics within the policy process. Neither of the processes under discussion here, devolution and EU integration, are static and they therefore inevitably create dynamics between the different actors involved. However, the fact that devolution in the UK has created asymmetry between the competences of the Scottish and Welsh institutions could create an additional set of dynamics within the system, specifically a campaign by the National Assembly to be granted further competences to equal those allocated to the Scottish Parliament.

Under the UK's devolution process, the Scottish Parliament was granted primary legislative responsibilities in a large number of policy areas. The National Assembly for Wales, under the Government of Wales Act 1998, was initially only granted secondary legislative competences. This arrangement meant that the Assembly was only able to take primary legislation adopted by the Westminster Parliament and pass the secondary legislation required to adapt it to meet specific Welsh concerns and requirements. The National Assembly was therefore heavily dependent upon the legislative programme of the Westminster Parliament and also upon the amount of detail contained in the initial UK primary legislation. The more detailed the UK legislation, the less opportunity for secondary Welsh legislation. Although the Government of Wales Act 2006 subsequently altered the situation, asymmetry continued to exist. Such asymmetry contained the potential to create pressure for further devolution to the National Assembly, pressure which could translate into a challenge for enhanced competences which may be further encouraged if the Assembly is already adopting a pro-active stance on the issue of seeking engagement in EU policy formulation.

This challenge for further competences is well illustrated by the process of decentralisation or "rolling devolution" (Hazell, 1999: 24) that has unfolded in Spain since democratisation, with the creation of sub-state authorities with differing levels of responsibility. This asymmetry has resulted in a situation where Spanish Autonomous Communities with fewer competences seek to gain further responsibilities to bring themselves up to the same level as the Basque Country and Catalonia with their greater range of devolved competences. The latter then seek extra powers to emphasise the difference that they perceive to exist between their strong historic and national identities and the weaker regional identities of the other Autonomous Communities. It is clear, therefore, that asymmetrical devolution in Spain has not resulted in a stable equilibrium.

The nature of the processes involved, supported by the evidence apparent in the Spanish case, suggests that the National Assembly will actively seek to gain further devolved competences to allow it the same range of responsibility and room for action granted to the Scottish Parliament. Unlike the Spanish case, however, this is less likely to result in the spiral of rolling devolution where every new grant of authority to the weaker Autonomous Communities creates fresh demands from the so-called historic nations. The UK's historical experience suggests less motivation for the Scottish Parliament to specifically demand a greater range of competences than the Welsh, although the Scottish Parliament may also seek further decision-making authority in certain areas.

The combination of asymmetrical devolution and the pro-active search for mobilisation resulting from the acceptance of the concept of European Domestic Policy therefore gives rise to a further supplementary hypothesis:

> The UK devolution process does not create a stable equilibrium. Its asymmetry is likely to result in Welsh attempts to attain the same level of devolved competences as Scotland.

Evidence for this hypothesis will be evident in the existence of demands from the National Assembly, the political parties or other relevant organisations for a greater range of competences to be devolved to the National Assembly.

A Question of Resources

This asymmetry of devolution is also likely to affect the level and nature of the engagement of the devolved administrations in the UK with the EU policy formulation process. Scotland's primary legislative competences suggest that the Scottish Executive is likely to be more deeply engaged with the EU policy-making process across a wider range of policy areas than their Welsh counterparts. There are also indications from the German experience that better resourced (and often larger, western) *Länder* have been in a stronger position to engage with the EU policy formulation process.

Jeffery (2000) identified four resource variables that may affect an SSA's ability to impact upon EU policy formulation: constitutional position, intergovernmental relations, entrepreneurship and "legitimacy", in the sense of the cohesiveness of the SSA's "regional" identity and civic support for the "region" as an entity. The identification of these resources would suggest that Scotland, with its primary legislative powers, is likely to be more deeply engaged than Wales. In particular, the constitutional position of an SSA is a core resource as this provides the key opportunity structure for engagement, as identified in studies of paradiplomacy.

The asymmetry in the UK gives the Scottish and Welsh devolved institutions differing levels of competence and capacity, although interestingly the Memorandum of Understanding and Concordat dealing with the management of EU affairs provide exactly the same opportunities to both (see Chapter 3). Thus their "constitutional" positions differ, but the opportunity structure is the same. This situation may, therefore, lead to the National Assembly adopting different strategies for pursuing its engagement such as horizontal relationships with other sub-state authorities. The final supplementary hypothesis can therefore be formulated as:

> In addition, the asymmetry and the different level of resources available to the devolved authorities will affect both the level and nature of their engagement in EU affairs.

Subsequent chapters will now draw upon empirical evidence of the evolving relationships between the devolved institutions and UK central government in the first four years of devolution to test these hypotheses. First, however, the following chapter will focus upon the pre-devolution system for EU policy formulation in the UK to enable a better understanding of the management of the EU policy process post-devolution. It will identify the key institutional actors and any role played by the Scottish and Welsh territorial offices in EU policy preparation. It will also seek to determine whether any further potential sources of friction may exist that are specific to the UK's political system and traditions, rather than being more generally connected to the interaction between the EU, state and sub-state tiers of governance.

CHAPTER 2

EU Policy-Making
in the Pre-Devolution UK

Introduction

To fully understand the impact of devolution upon the UK's domestic processes for formulating EU negotiating positions, it is evident that the pre-devolution policy-making processes must be examined. This chapter will therefore provide the domestic context for understanding the implications of devolution for the UK's EU policy process by determining the key components and characteristics of that policy process pre-devolution. In particular, the role played by the Scottish and Welsh territorial offices in this process will be considered with particular consideration of the opportunities for, and limitations upon, the representation of territorial interests and concerns.

The Position of the Territorial Offices within Central Government

Before devolution, the UK was regularly characterised as a "centralised" or "unitary" state, particularly in comparison with other EU Member States (Wright, 1996: 158; Armstrong & Bulmer, 1996: 334). Yet within this apparently centralised system, there existed long traditions of administrative decentralisation, most notably through the territorial departments, with the Scottish Office being established in 1885, the Welsh Office in 1964 and the Northern Ireland Office in 1972. These arrangements, notably with regard to the role of the Scottish Office, have been depicted as those of a "union" state (Mitchell & Leicester, 1999), rather than a unitary state, because they allowed for territorial distinctiveness to be taken into account. The policy competences of the territorial offices, modest at the outset, subsequently expanded in scope, with their functions cutting across those of individual functional departments in Whitehall, covering policy areas such as education, environment, agriculture and transport.

The territorial offices were headed by Secretaries of State who held seats in the Cabinet. They were considered to have the dual role of representing territorial interests in central government and of representing central government's interests in Scotland and Wales. Although the Secretaries of State were both members of the Cabinet, they were generally considered to be of lesser status than some other Cabinet posts and were therefore not always automatically included on the most important Cabinet committees. In addition, the wide range of functions allocated to the territorial offices made it impossible for the Secretaries of State to develop the same degree of policy specialism as their ministerial colleagues, or to attend all committee meetings with a (potential) territorial interest (Kellas, 1989: 27, 46-7).

With the exception of the territorial offices, all central government departments operate along functional lines. The existence of the territorial offices thereby created a situation where more than one government minister had responsibility for most policies under discussion (Mitchell, 1997: 414). The territorial offices were thus almost inevitably affected by decisions taken within other departments, leaving their officials and ministers to negotiate with counterparts from functional departments for recognition of particular Scottish or Welsh interests and concerns, thereby creating a need for co-ordination with other government departments (Kellas, 1989: 45-46).

In certain circumstances, officials from the territorial offices appear to have enjoyed a certain degree of autonomy in policy implementation. This discretion with regard to implementation was particularly apparent in the work of the Scottish Office (Keating & Jones, 1995: 101; Armstrong & Bulmer, 1996: 271-272). Scottish Office officials were also engaged in drafting Scotland-only legislation for passage through the Westminster Parliament, necessitated by the fact that following the 1707 Treaty of Union, Scotland maintained quite separate and distinct legal and education systems. Welsh administrative structures, on the other hand, were not distinct from those of England and greater constraints existed upon the exercise of discretion by the Welsh Office and its ability to diverge from UK policy.

A further factor that played a role in the extent of the territorial offices' discretion over policy implementation was the degree of political saliency of a policy issue (*Ibid.*). In general terms, the less politically salient an issue, the greater the discretion of the territorial offices in implementing policy. Increased discretion meant that territorial interests and concerns could be better taken into account when a policy was implemented.

A Highly Centralised System?

Despite this evidence of administrative decentralisation, the British system was still characterised as a highly centralised unitary state, especially with regard to the presentation of the UK's EU policy positions, described as "coherent", "consistent" and "highly effective" (Wright, 1996: 161; Spence, 1993: 68). The ability to present a coherent policy position in the EU negotiating arena has been considered both a characteristic and a strength of the UK's EU policy formulation process. This capacity was widely considered to derive from the UK's mechanisms for providing strong central co-ordination, thereby ensuring that policy positions presented within the EU aligned with the UK Government's over-arching policy objectives (Bender, 1991: 17).

Research into the UK's domestic procedures for formulating EU policy positions identifies a small number of key components as the most important elements: the Cabinet and relevant Cabinet committees, the Cabinet Office and in particular the European Secretariat, the Foreign and Commonwealth Office (FCO) and the United Kingdom Permanent Representation to the European Union (UKRep) and "lead" government departments (Spence, 1993: 52; Bulmer & Burch, 1998: 612, 615-616). The importance allocated to these key components within the policy-making process varies, but is frequently considered to depend upon the nature of the policy issue under discussion. Observers have identified two main types of issue which are dealt with quite differently.

Lead Departments

The two types of policy issue are, firstly, those which are highly technical in nature and, secondly, those that require inter-departmental co-ordination or have, or may develop, a politically salient dimension. This distinction is crucial in determining the way in which policy is co-ordinated. The first type of issue, a large proportion of the workload emanating from the EU, is routinely dealt with by departmental specialists as a consequence of its technical nature (Armstrong & Bulmer, 1996: 261-262). Virtually all functional departments in Whitehall now have a European dimension in at least some, if not all, of the policy areas they cover.

As the scope of the EU's competences has increased, this has drawn a growing number of departmental officials into the process of EU policy-making. A number of departments, for example the former Ministry of Agriculture, Fisheries and Food (MAFF), now part of DEFRA, the Department of the Environment, Food and Rural Affairs, established their own European divisions partly as a central conduit for information and also because all new policy initiatives need to be checked to ensure that they do not contravene existing European legislation (Dowding, 1995: 130). The role of the departments can also be observed in the growing numbers of departmental officials travelling to and from Brussels, either providing support to their Minister in the Council of the European Union or attending official-level working groups (*Ibid.*: 136). Direct links between sectoral ministries and the European Commission also developed over time (Spence, 1993: 62; Wright, 1996: 155).

Thus functional departments have a clear role in the formulation of EU policy positions where the issue is of low political salience or requires minimal inter-departmental co-ordination. Issues with a strong political dimension, or those requiring considerable inter-departmental co-ordination are likely to trigger the involvement of the Cabinet Office in the policy formulation process.

The Role of the Cabinet Office

A European Unit was first established in the Cabinet Office (CO) under the Wilson Government which attempted to negotiate British accession to the European Economic Community in 1966-7. This Unit took over the general task of co-ordinating negotiating issues across Whitehall. During accession negotiations, it shared its co-ordinating role with the FCO, but has since, as the European Secretariat (COES), developed its role as the principal co-ordination mechanism within Whitehall (Bulmer & Burch, 1998).

From the beginning, the Cabinet Office was considered to be in a better position to fulfil this role than the FCO. Firstly, the Cabinet Office was historically the administrative co-ordination centre of the British Government. Secondly, it was an administrative department rather than a policy-making department and thus considered to be more neutral than the FCO and better placed to act as an independent arbitrator between departments in instances of conflict over policy direction (Armstrong & Bulmer, 1996: 269).

Spence (1993: 55-57) identifies five key functions of the COES:

– It is responsible for preparing and placing EU business on the agenda of the Cabinet and ministerial committees;

– It is responsible for co-ordination between departments on cross-cutting issues;

– It provides authoritative guidance on issues of concern for overall UK policy;

– It monitors the process of parliamentary scrutiny of European business; and

– It monitors the implementation of Community legislation.

Thus COES provides the overarching framework within which the formulation of EU policy positions takes place. The second and third points mentioned above clearly identify its role in dealing with cross-cutting or political issues. It also has a key role in ensuring the flow of necessary information through the system and has generally been re-garded as being inclined to be pro-active in engaging the policy-making departments in the overall co-ordination of policy (Bender, 1991: 16; Burch & Holliday, 1996: 88). It also takes responsibility for organising weekly meetings, traditionally held on Fridays, with UKRep to further ensure the presentation of a single UK line in forthcoming EU negotia-tions (Buller & Smith, 1998: 171). The UK was generally considered a good performer in terms of its implementation record, aided by the culture and centralised nature of its administration (Armstrong & Bulmer, 1996: 263) and a procedure which, out of long practice, auto-matically took into account the different Scottish legal system.

A key element of its responsibility for inter-departmental co-ordination is the anticipation of both potential problems and opportuni-ties and alerting the relevant department(s) to their existence. COES calls and chairs most co-ordination meetings, bringing together officials from the departments concerned. With the expansion of the scope of EU policy competences over recent years, there has increasingly been a tendency to forego formal co-ordination meetings in favour of *ad hoc* informal meetings to deal with specific issues (Bulmer & Burch, 1998: 616).

Thus the Cabinet Office plays a central role in the co-ordination of cross-cutting or politically salient policy issues. With two routes for policy issues to take, this suggests two potentially contradictory trends in EU policy formulation – one of fragmentation, with policy depart-ments taking the lead on specific sets of issues, and one of centralisation with the Cabinet Office at the centre of policy co-ordination. The route taken by a policy proposal through the process therefore depends on its political saliency, the degree of technical specialisation required and the number of departments involved.

Cabinet and Ministerial Committees

Another key role of the Cabinet Office is to support the work of the Cabinet and associated ministerial committees. Theoretically, the Cabi-net is regarded as the central co-ordinating mechanism for policy-making in the UK. Although its exact composition varies from government to government, being decided by the Prime Minister, it generally consists of between 20 and 24 members, most of whom are ministers heading important Whitehall departments. It does not contain all government ministers (Budge *et al.*, 1998: 206-207). Cabinet discussions are confidential, making it difficult for observers to comment upon the exact nature of proceedings and the levels of influence enjoyed by different Cabinet ministers.

The size of the Cabinet is widely considered to be too large for the discussion of detailed policy issues and its workload is such that it is known that most Cabinet business is conducted through ministerial committees, composed of those ministers with an interest in the issues under discussion. Such committees can either be standing, dealing regularly with recurrent important issues, or *ad hoc*, set up by the Prime Minister to handle a specific issue. The key ministerial committee for the discussion of European questions is the Ministerial Sub-Committee on European issues, a sub-committee of the main Defence and Overseas Policy committee, chaired by the Foreign Secretary. It is supported by two official committees, one composed of senior officials with co-ordinating and oversight functions and the other dealing with detailed co-ordination at official level (Bulmer *et al.*, 2001: 43).

The main role of the committees is to deal with policy co-ordination across departments and to resolve conflicts. Policy issues that fall within the responsibility of a single department are expected to be handled in-house and are thus unlikely to be drawn into the Cabinet system. Issues requiring co-ordination, or where there is an obvious conflict of departmental interests, will be drawn into the committee system much earlier, as will important new policies, or issues where new spending commitments or parliamentary legislation are required (Burch & Holliday, 1996: 68-70). These reflect the triggers that bring COES in to co-ordinate issues through the official-level policy network, with a growing tendency evident to deal with issues on a more *ad hoc* and less formal basis.

There is routinely a European item on the weekly Cabinet agenda, although this serves predominantly to provide ministers with information, rather than as a substantive issue for discussion (Spence, 1993: 58). The main role of managing EU policy is therefore focused on the ministerial sub-committee and the two shadow official committees, with administrative support provided by COES as the permanent centre for co-ordinating activity. A large amount of EU business passes through the official, rather than the ministerial, committees.

The senior official committee, the formal shadow of the ministerial sub-committee, includes representatives of the key departments involved in formulating EU policy, for example the FCO, the Treasury,

DEFRA, the Department of Trade and Industry (DTI) and the Treasury Solicitor's Department. Officials from other government departments attend as necessary. The Treasury can also have an important role to play in both domestic and EU policy formulation. Its involvement across all policy areas derives from its control of government expenditure (Smith, 1999: 146-161), allowing it an impact upon policy co-ordination, although it does not represent a central co-ordinating mechanism for EU policy formulation.

The official committee, the "workhorse" of the EU policy co-ordinating network, meets formally once or twice a week, although there are also frequent informal co-ordination meetings. Most departments would only send officials to meetings of direct concern to their policy responsibilities (Spence, 1993: 55). This committee is at the centre of an extensive Whitehall network, though as the volume of EU-related business continues to expand, subsidiary networks have been constructed to deal with recurrent issues.

Minutes from the official committee are circulated to network contacts throughout Whitehall. The committee has two principal responsibilities: the first is one of "line-clearing", that is ensuring that departments are aware of any requirements upon them entailed in EU legislation and sorting out any points of contention that may arise; second, to provide guidance, either procedural, tactical or strategic, for officials engaged in drawing up EU policy positions (*Ibid.*, 1993: 59).

This system of committees and networks of officials is the co-ordinating mechanism operating as a counterbalance to the autonomy of lead departments in the formulation of EU negotiating positions. It is also this system of official contacts, and membership of the relevant ministerial and official committees, that enabled the territorial offices to participate in the formulation of EU policy within central government.

The FCO and UKRep

Alongside COES, the FCO has always been a key component of the process for co-ordinating EU policy in the UK. The FCO provides an institutional framework within which the practicalities of day-to-day co-ordination can take place. However, its role as a conduit for material emanating from the European Commission is increasingly by-passed as functional ministries receive these materials direct from the source. The role of the FCO becomes more important in the build-up to European Councils, for which it prepares briefing materials, and the UK Presidency, dealing with over-arching political matters rather than policy issues. It also has prime responsibility for preparing for General Affairs and External Relations Councils (meetings of EU Foreign Ministers) and is the lead department for Common Foreign and Security Policy.

Its role in the co-ordination process has led it to receive criticism for encroaching into domestic policy issues (Dowding, 1995: 137-138). Such criticism indicates the extent to which EU policy is overlapping with domestic policy. However, the FCO's focus upon over-arching political matters suggests that a distinction is made between policy areas that relate purely to foreign policy and issues that relate to domestic policy.

Internally, the FCO has a European Unit department divided along three principal lines – Internal, External and Bilateral (HMSO, 2001). Most commentators agree, however, that the key branch of the FCO in co-ordinating EU policy is UKRep, the UK's Permanent Representation to the EU. The permanent representations of the Member States in Brussels usually consist of between 30 and 50 officials. In the case of UKRep, half of these are usually members of the diplomatic corps, whilst the other half are seconded from other Whitehall departments. During the 1990s this generally included at least one official on secondment from the Scottish Office (Mitchell, 1997: 415). UKRep fulfils several key roles in the policy co-ordination process.

Firstly, UKRep acts as a monitor of developments in the EU's institutions, relating important information back to Whitehall. It also maintains links with the other permanent representations in Brussels, enabling it to alert Whitehall to potential shifts in negotiating positions by other Member States. Secondly, it provides a base in Brussels for Whitehall ministers and officials attending negotiations, as well as being a source of advice to those officials, particularly on the question of negotiating tactics. As well as providing assistance and advice to these officials, UKRep is frequently represented alongside them in negotiations. This leads to its third function as prime negotiator in most Council meetings as well as servicing the UK delegation in Council meetings at all levels (Spence, 1993: 63-64; Dowding, 1995: 143-145).

UKRep thus works closely with both Commission and home officials, as well as being at the centre of the lobbying network in Brussels for British interest groups affected by Commission proposals (Spence, 1993: 48-49). It is widely regarded as being an efficient and tightly knit unit which liaises closely with Whitehall, although this can also be perceived as a constraint as well as an advantage (Wright, 1996: p. 161). UKRep is well trusted as a source of information and advice by policy makers in Whitehall (Wallace, 1996: 65) and participates regularly in the domestic European policy-making process, as well as representing the agreed policy lines in the EU arena, being a member of the weekly Friday meetings to discuss the overall direction of policy.

Thus it can be seen that the FCO is generally involved with the external relations of the EU and over-arching political objectives, rather than the development of technical policy positions. UKRep has a key role as a centre for co-ordination and as an important resource that can be employed by government departments. UKRep is also the external face of the domestic EU policy formulation process, with this face generally being one of unity, any disagreements within Whitehall being suppressed in the EU arena.

Having thus considered the domestic EU policy formulation process in the UK pre-devolution, attention turns to the position of the territorial offices in this system. Of particular importance are the points of access available to the Scottish and Welsh Offices under this system, the extent to which they could influence policy decisions taken and whether particular types of issue can be identified that it was easier for the territorial offices to influence.

The Participation of the Scottish and Welsh Offices in UK European Policy Formulation

Pre-devolution, the Secretaries of State for Scotland and Wales were, as previously mentioned, members of the Cabinet. Nevertheless, they and the territorial offices were widely regarded as "junior partners" in central government, with no automatic right to membership of key Cabinet committees, though they did hold places on the Sub-Committee on European issues, giving them access to the ministerial forum where EU policy was discussed. However, given the secrecy surrounding the proceedings of the Cabinet and its committees, it has been impossible to assess their role in proceedings and the degree of influence they were able to exert on decisions taken (Kellas, 1989: 44-45). The number of fora in which EU decision-making takes place also meant it was possible that territorial concerns and interests were not represented in all relevant fora.

Another problem for the territorial ministers, more so than their officials, was that the wide range of functions allocated to the territorial offices pre-devolution meant that they were less specialised in any policy area than their Whitehall counterparts (*Ibid.*: 47). Nevertheless, it was still possible for them to have an impact upon policy areas where they had specialist knowledge, for example on fisheries, where the Scottish Office sometimes led, or on hill farming (Keating & Jones, 1995: 100). Territorial office ministers were included in negotiating teams for the Council of Ministers where they had specific knowledge or, occasionally, specific concerns, to contribute. However, such appearances were few. According to figures presented by the SNP during the parliamentary passage of the Scotland Act in 1998 (Hansard Vol. 304, Cols 63-64, 12 January 1998), the Scottish Office was represented at 8 Councils out of 125 in 1992; 8 Councils out of 125 in 1993; 6 Councils out of 125 in 1994, 7 Councils out of 83 in 1995 and 15 Councils out of 84 in 1996 (this increase was attributed to the increase in discussions on fisheries policy and the mounting political and economic crisis surrounding BSE).

Even out of those limited appearances, many were in a junior capacity and most related to fisheries policy. This was despite a deliberate attempt by the Scottish Office to increase its level of engagement in EU policy formulation as a consequence of the increasing impact that EC/EU business was having upon their work (Bulmer & Burch, 1998: 616). Comparable figures are not available for Wales, but indications suggest that Welsh attendance was even more rare than Scottish, with Wales having fewer distinctive policy concerns than the Scots, demonstrating that levels of territorial engagement were not equal prior to devolution.

The Scottish record of attendance also demonstrates quite clearly that the UK functional department almost invariably took the lead on EU policy issues, despite the fact that the co-existence of territorial and functional departments meant that more than one minister held responsibility for the issue under discussion. For the lead departments, it was a question of balancing specific concerns and interests as represented by the territorial offices against broader UK interests. The territorial offices appeared largely dependent upon Whitehall for policy leadership (Keating & Jones, 1995: 113), although this did not preclude the possibility of them pursuing policies that differed from those of UK departments (Armstrong & Bulmer, 1996: 271-272).

In spite of the fact that the Scottish and Welsh Offices appear to have had the same opportunities for involvement in EU policy formulation, it is here that their approaches and actions differ. In domestic issues generally, as well as in EU matters, there was a discernible tendency for the Welsh Office to adopt UK policy lines without significantly adapting them to particular Welsh circumstances, whilst the Scottish Office took a more independent line (McAteer & Mitchell, 1996: 10). However, both Offices took the approach of behind-the-scenes lobbying rather than attempting high profile tactics to represent their interests (Bulmer & Burch, 1998: 616). It is also clear that they were more able to influence issues of low political saliency, where officials were dealing directly with functional counterparts. On highly politicised issues, there was a tendency towards UK-wide uniformity (Keating & Jones, 1995: 101) which was imposed by central government if considered necessary.

As the impact of EU business upon their work increased, both Offices also established European Affairs divisions which had two key roles. The first was to co-ordinate the management of EU business within their respective Office and then between the territorial office and Whitehall, in instances where this was not being handled directly by divisional specialists. The second was the administration of the Structural Funds within the territories (Jones, 1997: 397).

The main difficulty in studying the involvement of the territorial offices in the UK's EU policy formulation process pre-devolution is determining at what point and to what degree ministers and officials were able to exercise influence over the policy decisions taken. This is partly a consequence of the tradition of confidentiality that surrounds UK central government. Equally, access to the relevant decision-making fora, not always guaranteed in itself, does not guarantee influence over the decisions made. This was the case for the territorial offices on both domestic and EU policy issues though influence over issues of low political saliency or on highly specialised issues was more likely. Taken together with the important role of lead departments on specialised or low-key EU policy issues, it is likely that opportunities for the territorial offices to exert influence were highest when officials were co-ordinating directly with their counterparts in functional Whitehall departments. As is the case for all departments, territorial or functional, it was much harder for them to exercise influence over joint decisions taken in multilateral fora, a situation exacerbated for the territorial offices by the assumption that their position was as "junior partners" within central government's policy-making processes.

In total, four factors have been identified as affecting the degree of influence that it was possible for the territorial offices to exercise (Mitchell, 1997: 409, quoting Moore & Booth, 1989: 39): the issue; its political saliency; the strength of the argument deployed; and the character/influence of the Secretary of State. It has also been argued that the influence of the territorial offices declined under the Conservative governments of the 1980s in particular, when the lack of electoral support for the Conservatives in Scotland and Wales and the personalities of the Secretaries of State tended to ensure that uniform UK-wide policies were followed (Keating & Jones, 1995: 101).

Even when the territorial offices were able to influence policy, they most often had to be content with minor modifications to policy in the domestic arena (*Ibid.*) and thus consequently in the EU arena. They were also confronted with the possibility that even if they succeeded in incorporating their own distinct interests into the UK's negotiating line that these may be traded away in the creation of a "package deal" during the negotiations.

It therefore appears that opportunities for the territorial offices to influence UK EU policy, while they existed, were limited by a number of factors. The relevant literature also indicates a difference in the level of engagement of the Scottish and Welsh Offices, with the Scottish Office being more pro-active than its Welsh counterpart. This involved active engagement in the Whitehall policy process, but also the development of a policy of seconding Scottish Office officials to UKRep or to the European Commission to build up a cadre of officials with specialist knowledge of the *modus operandi* of the decision-making process at the EU level (Mazey & Mitchell, 1993: 110).

The Wider Political Context

In contrast to the more consensual, coalition-based systems of government in other EU Member States, the British system is based upon single party majority rule and has a long tradition of adversarial party politics. Issues relating to both British membership of the EU and the future path of development of the European Union have been highly contested. Attitudes towards European integration not only divide the British political parties, but also create divisions within them (Baker & Seawright, 1998), being particularly problematic for both the Labour Party (in the 1970s and 1980s) and the Conservatives (from the 1980s on). Over-arching issues of European integration, particularly issues relating to state sovereignty, are highly contested in the parliamentary arena, and European debates in the House of Commons are often of a symbolic nature (Armstrong & Bulmer, 1996; Bulmer & Burch, 1998).

The capacity for parliamentary supervision of the government's activities in the EU arena is rather weak, a consequence of the executive-centric nature of EU decision-making processes. In the case of the UK, the House of Lords has the more effective procedures for scrutinising technical EU legislation (Armstrong & Bulmer, 1996). A perceived lack of involvement of legislatures in the European policy process is not unique to the UK, but rather is widely regarded as a problematic issue for Member States across the EU. Both factors highlighted can be identified in the areas of friction already suggested in the multi-level relationships developed post-devolution.

Domestic European Policy Formulation in the Pre-Devolution UK

So far, the principal components and characteristics of the UK's EU policy formulation prior to devolution have been identified, together with the role that the Scottish and Welsh Offices were able to play within this system. This section will examine further those details that seem likely to impact upon the opportunities for participation of the Scottish and Welsh authorities after 1999. It will also consider possible areas of tension between the different levels of government with regard to the formulation of EU policy positions – that is the tensions created by the overlap of responsibilities contained within a multi-level policy process.

Firstly, it is clear that there are two distinct, and potentially contradictory, trends in the UK's European policy-making process. The first is one of fragmentation, whereby Whitehall departments take the led on specialist policy issues. The second is one of centralisation, with the engagement of the Cabinet Office in co-ordinating the development of policy positions in order to present a coherent UK line during negotiations at the EU level. The co-existence of two different sets of procedures for policy formulation will thus inevitably affect the degree of participation of the devolved administrations.

Another feature of the pre-devolution policy-making process with implications for the role of the devolved authorities was the position of the territorial offices as the "junior partners" in central government. With responsibility for policy areas divided between functional Whitehall ministries and their territorial counterparts, more than one minister was responsible for certain policy areas. This situation is perpetuated post-devolution, but with a substantial increase in the number of Scottish and Welsh ministers involved, allowing for their greater specialisation in policy fields. Unlike the territorial office ministers, however, the Scottish Executive and Welsh Assembly Government ministers will not have access to the Cabinet process, suggesting that influencing the policy line of the UK department will be of crucial importance to representing Scottish and Welsh interests.

Also noticeable from the role of the territorial offices in the policy-making process was the extent to which the representation of Scottish and Welsh concerns and interests took place by means of behind-the-scenes activity, rather than through open confrontation or high profile lobbying. This suggests that the most effective means whereby the devolved administrations can seek to influence policy positions is through bilateral communications, particularly at the level of officials. High-profile lobbying is more likely to create friction between the central government and devolved levels, particularly if the principle of confidentiality is not respected.

The post-devolution relationships between the new administrations and UK central government on EU issues were intended, to a large extent, to be based upon existing policy practice, as will be demonstrated in Chapter 3. Relationships are therefore likely to be bilateral, with contacts predominantly taking place between officials where possible and behind closed doors in respect of the principle of confidentiality.

The territorial offices were, and are, part of central government. The devolved administrations are not. However, central government was never likely to exclude the devolved authorities from European policy-making, given the accepted participation of the Scottish and Welsh Offices in that process prior to devolution. Nonetheless, the possibility existed that the devolved administrations might be less involved than the territorial offices, creating a potential area of friction in the UK's multi-level system.

Another area of potential conflict was widely identified by observers in the build-up to the transfer of devolved powers taking place (Sloat, 2001: 11) and it continues to be considered the principal test of the mechanisms and procedures established to manage intra-UK relations post-devolution. This is governmental incongruence, that is having different political parties in government at different levels within the political system. Difficulties created in this situation would derive, to a large extent, from the adversarial tradition of party politics in the UK and an apparent inability of the main parties (with the partial exception of Labour and the Liberal Democrats), including the two nationalist parties, to co-operate or reach consensus. This is further exacerbated by the fact that differences in policy positions will be exploited for party political advantage. Despite the early rhetoric of "new politics" and "inclusivity" at the time the devolved institutions were established, the adversarial traditions of British politics continued to exercise a powerful influence over post-devolution party behaviour.

Another broad area where tensions may emerge relates to the secrecy in which central government discussions take place and the confidentiality of the relevant materials when circulated. Given this tradition of confrontational opposition between political parties, and the likely exclusion of the Scottish Parliament and the National Assembly for Wales from the policy formulation process, parties in opposition may seek to exploit this lack of transparency and the inability to trace the influence of the Scottish Executive and Welsh Assembly Government upon decisions taken.

The principle of confidentiality as it is employed in the UK means that the role of the civil service is crucial in the multi-level system established by devolution, in particular with regard to the incorporation of the Scottish Executive and the Welsh Assembly Government in the domestic EU policy formulation process (Mitchell & Leicester, 1999). If tensions were to emerge between officials at the centre and officials in Edinburgh and Cardiff, this would be highly detrimental to the representation of Scottish and Welsh interests in the drafting of EU negotiating positions and may ultimately result in public conflict between politicians in the centre and their counterparts in the devolved administrations. A key element to maintaining good working relationships between the different parts of the civil service will be the maintenance of the information flow. Based upon the experience of SSAs elsewhere, any exclusion from the information "loop" is likely to provoke challenges from the devolved administrations for access to the policy formulation process.

The potential areas of friction identified suggest that in addition to tensions that are related more generally to the situation created across the EU by the existence of multi-level governance, as identified in Chapter 1, there may also be tensions in the relationship between the devolved administrations and central government that are UK-specific. Thus the particular nature of devolution in the UK, in particular the asymmetry, combined with the party political context, will impact upon the development and operation of the multi-level system post-devolution.

The key potential areas of friction identified from experiences elsewhere and from the pre-devolution processes of EU policy formulation in the UK are summarised here:

Table 2.1: Potential Sources of Tension in Intra-State Inter-governmental Relations

EU experiences	Pre-devolution UK
Exclusion	Exclusion
Information flow	Information flow/ importance of the civil service
Loss of competences	–
Exclusion of parliaments/ executive dominance	–
–	Confidentiality/lack of transparency
–	Party politics

This study of the pre-devolution process for formulating EU policy in the UK has enabled the identification of key elements of the co-ordination and policy-making processes, further developing the hypotheses constructed in Chapter 1 in the process. It has also allowed the opportunity structure for access and input of territorial interests and concerns into these processes to be determined. The following chapters will present empirical evidence about the development of the UK's EU policy formulation process post-devolution, based upon documentation and a range of interviews conducted between 2000 and 2003. The next chapter focuses upon the documents that accompanied devolution, allowing for an examination of the attitude(s) of central government towards the participation of the devolved authorities in EU policy formulation, testing the level of central government acceptance of the participation of these administrations in EU affairs.

CHAPTER 3

White Papers, Acts and Concordats

A Framework for Managing Relations?

Introduction

The process of devolution through Acts of the Westminster Parliament was also accompanied by a number of White Papers and Concordats (inter-executive agreements) which contained *inter alia* the provisions for the involvement of the devolved institutions in the UK's domestic EU policy formulation process. The relevant provisions of these documents, their drafting, and the associated debate, will be considered here in chronological order to allow the development of the debate to be assessed.

Of particular interest in this process is any evidence of Government retrenchment or nervousness concerning the role of the devolved administrations in EU policy-making as plans for devolution became more concrete. This would reflect any UK Government resistance to the engagement of the devolved tier with EU policy. In addition, any evidence of a challenge for greater participation from Scotland and/or Wales will be examined. As well as indicating a challenge to the UK central government, such demands indicate a pro-active pursuit of engagement with the EU level. In addition to the potential sources of tension identified previously, additional sources of tension contained within the framework created by the documents will be explored.

The development of the devolution process will be traced chronologically from the arrival in power of the Labour Government elected in May 1997 to the publication of the first tranche of Concordats on 1 October 1999. This approach will enable changes in position on the part of those involved in the process to be discerned, and in particular any change in attitude on the Government's part.

The Devolution "Settlement"

When the new Labour Government came to power in May 1997, it was committed to the devolution of power to Scotland, Wales and, eventually, as part of a peace settlement, to Northern Ireland. By the end of 2000, the Scottish Parliament, the National Assembly for Wales and the Northern Ireland Assembly had been established (although devolution to Northern Ireland was suspended in 2002 as a consequence of the peace process faltering). London had a directly elected mayor and the 25-member Greater London Authority whilst Regional Development Agencies had been set up in the eight English regions. Debate in England centred initially upon plans to extend the number of directly elected city mayors and/or create regional assemblies. However, a disinterested public often failed to vote on plans for city mayors leading to the rejection of such plans in a number of places. This situation led to the debate focusing upon the potential for regional assemblies. Subsequently, moves towards the establishment of the first regional assembly were scuppered by a negative vote in an all-postal ballot, held in November 2004, in the North East in what was viewed as a test case for the strength of regional interest in devolution in England (Rallings and Thrasher, 2005).

The first move of the new Government was, however, towards devolution for Scotland and Wales. Figure 4.1 outlines the key events of the devolution process for Scotland and Wales between the general election in May 1997 and the transfer of powers to the SP and NAW in July 1999.

The White Papers, published in July 1997, formed the basis of the referendum debate. In Scotland, the White Paper's proposals, both for devolution and to give the SP a tax-raising power, were clearly approved: 74.3% voted "Yes" to the devolution proposal and 63.5% voted in favour of the SP having its own limited tax-raising powers (McFadden & Lazarowicz, 1999: 4). In Wales, the outcome was much less clear-cut, as the White Paper's proposals just scraped through with an extremely slender majority given by a 50.3% "Yes" vote (Balsom, 2000: 151-160).

The Scottish White Paper proposed a Parliament with primary legislative competences in a wide range of policy areas, including health, education, environment, rural affairs and culture. It thus proposed a clear division of competences between the Scottish and British institutions, with each responsible for legislation in their respective policy areas. In addition, it proposed that the SP should be able to vary the UK rate of income tax by +/- 3 pence in the British pound.

Table 4.1: Key Dates in the Scottish and Welsh Devolution Processes

Date	Event
2 May 1997	Labour Government takes office
May 1997	Referendum Bill introduced to Westminster Parliament
July 1997	White Papers – "Scotland's Parliament" (Cm 3658) and "A Voice for Wales" (Cm 3718) published
July 1997	Referendums (Scotland and Wales) Act receives Royal Assent
11 September 1997	Referendum in Scotland approves White Paper proposals
18 September 1997	Referendum in Wales approves White Paper proposals
26 November 1997	Government of Wales Bill introduced into Parliament
17 December 1997	Scotland Bill introduced into Parliament
31 July 1998	Government of Wales Act 1998 receives Royal Assent
19 November 1998	Scotland Act 1998 receives Royal Assent
6 May 1999	First elections to the Scottish Parliament and the National Assembly for Wales held
26 May 1999	National Assembly for Wales opened by the Queen
1 July 1999	Scottish Parliament opened by the Queen. Official transfer of powers to the new institutions in Scotland and Wales takes place.

Source: Summarised from Hazell, 2000: 2, 6.

The proposals for the National Assembly were very different in nature and have been described as offering a "unique scheme of executive devolution" (Patchett, 2000: 229). Unlike "Scotland's Parliament", the Welsh White Paper, "A Voice for Wales" did not propose devolving primary legislative competences to the Assembly. It only proposed the power for the National Assembly to make subordinate, or secondary, legislation within the framework of primary legislation passed by the Westminster Parliament. As with the proposals for a Scottish Parliament, a wide range of policy areas were nominated in which the NAW could carry out its executive competences.

The Acts passed by the Westminster Parliament substantially followed the pattern suggested by the White Papers, with Scotland gaining a strong legislature with extensive policy competences. In the Scotland Act 1998, the powers reserved by Westminster are listed with the Scottish Parliament taking responsibility for all other policy areas. In the Government of Wales Act 1998, the areas of executive competence transferred to the National Assembly are listed. The exercise of its competences was thus dependent upon the discretion to act allowed it by the legislation issued from Westminster – the more prescriptive the primary legislation, the less discretion for the National Assembly to enact subordinate legislation adapted to the needs and interests of Wales.

The Acts thus created a highly asymmetrical form of devolution, with the Scottish legislature being far more powerful than the National Assembly. This asymmetry was further highlighted by the lack of devolution to the remaining (and largest) constituent territory of the UK, England. It is this asymmetry that could be expected to generate Welsh demands for more extensive policy competences to place it on an equal footing with the SP.

Following the parliamentary passage of the Acts in 1998, the first elections to the new institutions were scheduled for 6 May 1999. These took place under a new form of electoral system for the UK, the Additional Member System, which gave constituents two votes: one for a constituency representative and one for a regional list. 129 seats were contested in Scotland, 73 constituency and 56 regionals. In Wales, there are 60 Assembly Members, 40 constituency and 20 regional. In the first devolved elections, the Labour Party won most seats in both, but failed to gain an overall majority in either, a situation that was subsequently repeated in 2003.

In Scotland, this led to the formation of a Labour-Liberal Democrat coalition, originally headed by the late Donald Dewar as First Minister. In Wales, a short-lived minority administration was formed under First Minister Alun Michael. As will be discussed subsequently, this minority administration later collapsed and was eventually replaced by a Labour-Liberal Democrat coalition. However, following the 2003 election, Labour formed an administration with a majority of one.

Process and Content

Publicly, the Labour Government continually maintained a positive outlook on the involvement of the devolved administrations in EU policy affairs. In a pre-devolution lecture delivered by the Rt Hon Donald Dewar MP to Scotland Europa in Brussels, whilst still Secretary of State for Scotland, he spoke of the role of EU Member States being complemented by that of their strong regions within the EU and mentioned the German *Länder* congratulating the UK Government on its "wisdom" in allowing Scottish Ministers to speak for the UK if appropriate (Scottish Office News Release 1900/97, 1 December 1997).

The Labour Government was thus publicly committed to sub-state involvement in the EU and spoke of learning from best practice elsewhere to make the UK's new tier of government a source of strength for the UK in Europe. However, any arrangements with regard to devolved engagement with the EU must respect one underlying factor – it is the Member States alone who are signatory to the EU treaties. As such, they are expected to speak with one voice on the EU stage, irrespective of their domestic political structures, a fact which the government did not ignore in drafting the EU provisions of the key documents of devolution.

White Papers – the Drafting Process

The drafting of the White Papers began immediately after Labour's general election victory. The Government was intent on preparing its proposals carefully in order to avoid any repeat of the 1979 referenda when devolution proposals were accepted by the Scots, but by an insufficiently large majority, and were rejected outright in Wales. The subject of devolution had long been a difficult issue for the Labour Party, causing deep division within it between pro- and anti-devolutionists, and the situation was little different in May 1997 (for further detail, see Hazell, 1999).

Commentators on British politics, such as Brian Taylor of BBC Scotland noted a lack enthusiasm for devolution on the part of some members of the Cabinet, several of whom argued in favour of limiting the powers of the proposed devolved authorities, particularly the Scottish Parliament (Taylor, 1999: 92, 96, 99, 104). Divisions were particularly evident on issues relating to the distribution of competences, with ministers reluctant to let go any of their department's responsibilities, and on the thorny issue of finance, giving the Treasury a key role. These two factors, so-called "turf wars" and finance can be identified as two of the most likely sources of tension in a decentralised policy system. Some of this reluctance was overcome by the commitment to devolution of the Rt Hon Donald Dewar MP as Secretary of State for Scotland, whose position was strengthened by his good relations with Prime Minister Blair and with Whitehall officials (*Ibid.*: 96, 104-105).

Taylor (*Ibid.*: 99) identifies the biggest dispute over the allocation of competences as being the responsibility for EU affairs. There was scepticism about the workability of arrangements for the involvement of the devolved administrations in some parts of central government. However, Scottish Labour in particular needed to be able to counter the Scottish National Party (SNP) position on Europe, and particularly the SNP's slogan of "Independence in Europe" by being able to point to the proposals for the Scottish Executive's involvement in EU affairs. This only emphasised official concern about the workability of proposals that were drawn up at least partly out of party political motivations.

In the end, both White Papers contained substantial sections on the management of EU-related affairs, conceding a role to the devolved administrations but representing a balance between different interests. This demonstrates the existence of dividing lines between those advancing the interests of the new administrations, like Mr Dewar and his officials at the Scottish Office, and central government interests wishing to retain as great a range of responsibilities and scope for manoeuvre as possible at the centre. However, bringing about a compromise of these interests was not a debate that was carried out in the public arena.

Content

This careful compromise of interests (Interview, 2000) is in evidence in both White Papers. It is made explicitly clear that foreign policy, including EU affairs, is a reserved competence, as this example from the White Paper "A Voice for Wales" illustrates:

> Foreign policy, including issues arising from the membership of the European Union (EU), will remain the responsibility of the UK Government which must continue to ensure the UK meets its obligations and exercises its rights. (Welsh Office, 1997: 21)

It is clear, given the potential level of engagement contained in the White Papers' provisions, that the UK will continue to speak with one voice in the EU (Scottish Office, 1997: 16-17). Nevertheless, the White Papers also conceded that the devolved administrations should be involved in EU affairs:

> But European issues also impact on wide areas of domestic policy which will be within the remit of the Assembly. This means that the Assembly will need to be involved as closely as possible in developing UK policy on European matters. (Welsh Office, 1997: 21-22)

As well as representing a balance of different political interests, this also represents a pragmatic approach to the issue – the overlap of competences between the devolved and EU tiers is explicitly recognised, as are the experiences of other decentralised EU Member States (Scottish Office, 1997: 16).

The two White Papers identify six principal areas where European and devolved responsibilities overlap and potential consequences deriving from this situation:

– The responsibility of the devolved authorities for ensuring the implementation of EU regulations in areas of devolved competence;

– Their role in scrutinising EU policy proposals in areas of devolved responsibility (Scotland only);

– Management of the devolved administrations' involvement in the formulation of the UK's policy positions in areas where policy competences are devolved;

– A potential role for Scottish Executive members in the UK's negotiating team in relevant Council of the European Union meetings. "A Voice for Wales" originally provided for the Secretary of State for Wales to participate in relevant Council meetings (Welsh Office, 1997: p. 22) but with the publication of the Concordat on the Co-ordination of European Union Policy Issues, this had changed to members of the Assembly Cabinet (Welsh Assembly Government) and their officials;

– The relationship of the devolved administrations with UKRep; and

– The possibility of the devolved administrations establishing their own representative offices in Brussels.

This is effective recognition that the nature of the two trends of European integration and domestic decentralisation is such that the exclusion of devolved administrations with their own decision-making powers was no longer feasible, or even, according to some Scottish Office news releases, desirable (Scottish Office News Release 1900/97, 1 December 1997). This represents effective acceptance of the overlap of EU and domestic responsibilities and thus the concept of European Domestic Policy.

However, it must be borne in mind that the White Papers had two audiences: the Scottish and Welsh publics, who would vote on the proposals, and the Westminster Parliament which would debate any subsequent parliamentary legislation. As a consequence of this, it is made explicitly clear in the White Papers that ultimately the UK Government decides. For example, the UK lead Minister is responsible for deciding the composition of delegations to EU negotiations and is thus responsible for extending invitations to attend to members of the devolved executives where s/he considers it appropriate (Scottish Office, 1997: 16-17). Members of the devolved executives may request to attend specific meetings, but participation is by invitation, not by right. The Conservative Party argued that any involvement of the devolved authorities would weaken British influence in the EU, particular if different parties were in power at sub-state and central government levels (*The Economist*, 6 September 1997: 29).

Neither White Paper rejected the idea of direct representation for the devolved executives in Brussels by way of a "regional office". In "Scotland's Parliament" this is regarded as a potential complement to the work of UKRep and a useful means of supporting direct contact with sub-state governments elsewhere in the EU (Scottish Office, 1997: 18). Reference is also made to this possibility in "A Voice for Wales", but in a less forceful manner than in the Scottish White Paper (Welsh Office, 1997: 22). Implicit in the opening of information offices in Brussels is the notion that the Scottish and Welsh executives would build up new, or enhance existing, links with other EU SSAs. The White Papers were silent, however, on what purpose such relationships would serve.

Heavy emphasis was placed throughout upon the principle of confidentiality. This was considered crucial to the smooth running of relations between the UK's different levels of government (Scottish Office, 1997: 15). This was particularly significant with regard to relations between central government and the National Assembly. NAW's proposed status as a "corporate body" had raised concerns about policy information being leaked into the public arena before negotiations had taken place at the EU level (Interview, 2000). As a corporate body, the National Assembly was initially intended to be viewed as a single legal personality, with no formal distinction between the Cabinet, later known as the Welsh Assembly Government, and the plenary Assembly.

As well as confidentiality, emphasis was also placed upon "collaboration and trust" (*Ibid.*: 18). Thus the provisions for devolved engagement contained in the White Papers appeared heavily reliant on the existence of good will and good relations between the devolved and central levels of government. Nevertheless, given the evidence of scepticism at the central government level pre-devolution, the White Papers outlined a remarkable scope for the involvement of the devolved authorities.

"Warm Words are No Substitute for Hard Laws"

(Mr Jim Wallace in *The Herald*, 31 March 1998).

The Scotland Bill and the Government of Wales Bill both substantially followed the same lines as the respective Scottish and Welsh White Papers (Patchett, 2000: 230). In the case of the Scotland Bill, parliamentary passage was eased by the strong support for the devolution proposals demonstrated in the referendum result. This made it more difficult for anti-devolutionists, notably in the Conservative Party, to oppose the Bill. The two Bills differ in form and content, a reflection of the asymmetry of devolution. However, explicit in both is the position of all foreign policy, including EU matters, as a reserved power of the UK Government.

Neither Bill contained any form of the White Papers' pledges to involve the devolved authorities. In fact there was little reference to the EU at all, apart from emphasising the devolved administrations' responsibility for the implementation of EU legislation (Clause 106 in the Government of Wales Act; Clause 53 in the Scotland Act). This is of key importance to the UK Government as it is the Member State which would be taken in front of the European Court of Justice in cases of infringement, not the devolved administrations. Thus it required a means for ensuring that the devolved administrations would be held account-able for any infractions. The actual mechanisms for this are contained in the Concordats.

The absence of any provisions for the involvement of the devolved administrations was a reflection of the fact that the UK Government did not want to establish any statutory participatory rights for the devolved executives which would be binding upon future UK Governments. However, this position was strongly challenged by both the SNP, in the case of the Scotland Bill, and Plaid Cymru (The Party of Wales) in the case of the Government of Wales Bill. The Liberal Democrats also tabled amendments in an attempt to guarantee participation of the devolved authorities in EU affairs.

The issue of representation in Council of Ministers (Council of the EU) meetings was particularly controversial during the passages of both Bills through Parliament. Schedule 5 (6) (1) of the Scotland Bill set out reserved matters, but also allowed for the Scottish Executive to provide assistance to UK Government ministers in international fora (House of Commons research paper 98/1), including the EU. This highlights the point made in the White Paper that participation would be by invitation, not by right. This concept of "participation by invitation" quickly emerged as a potential flashpoint of devolution during the Westminster debates and remained so during the parliamentary passage of the two Bills.

Plaid Cymru demanded an automatic right to representation as ex-pressed by Dafydd Wigley during the Second Reading of the Govern-ment of Wales Bill:

> We want the Ministers, or Secretaries as they will be known, of our national assembly included as of right in the UK delegation to the Council of Minis-ters when issues within the assembly's competence ...appear on the agenda. (Hansard, Vol. 302, Col 707, 8 December 1997)

The Conservatives, on the other hand, remained opposed to any form of representation.

The subsequent passage of the Scotland Bill demonstrated the same tensions, with the SNP demanding a statutory right for Scottish Minis-ters to attend Councils of Ministers. Jim Wallace, then leader of the Scottish Liberal Democrats, claimed that the opposition parties were united in condemning the Scotland Bill as "ambiguous and inadequate" with regard to Scottish representation in Europe (*The Herald*, 31 March 1998). One thing that became clear from the parliamentary debate was that all the opposition parties wanted either a clarification or a formali-sation of the role of the new authorities with regard to the EU (Inter-view, 2000). However, all amendments tabled to insert such provisions into the two Bills were rejected by the Government, which, at the time, controlled a substantial majority in the House of Commons.

The potential for the question of EU participation by the devolved administrations to cause dynamics of challenge and resistance between the two tiers of government is made quite clear by such exchanges. The issue of representation in Council meetings had already become a point of tension between the political parties given its highly symbolic nature. In particular, it presented an opportunity for the SNP to contrast what the UK Government was offering – no statutory right of participation – with its demand for Scotland to be an independent Member State, with its own seat at the EU negotiating table.

The Government remained firmly opposed to all amendments aimed at formalising any rights of participation in EU policy formulation (although examination of the Acts demonstrates that this is also the case for the formulation of reserved issues domestically). With its overwhelming majority, the Government was able to steer the Bills through with the only significant amendments, particularly to the Government of Wales Bill, being initiated by the Government itself. Jim Wallace condemned the lack of statutory rights of EU participation by arguing that "warm words are no substitute for hard laws". Nevertheless, the lack of explicit provisions in the new Acts of the White Papers' pledges on EU affairs demonstrated that the management of the involvement of the devolved administrations in EU affairs would be reliant on good will and pre-devolution practices (Interview, 2000), as was re-emphasised by the Concordats.

Drafting the Concordats

The Concordats represent informal agreements between the UK Government and the devolved executives. Four over-arching Concordats between the devolved and central executives are attached to the Memorandum of Understanding (MoU), officially entitled the "Memorandum of Understanding and Supplementary Agreements between the United Kingdom Government, Scottish Ministers and the Cabinet of the National Assembly for Wales" (Scottish Executive, 1999). The MoU sets out the four principles expected to underlie relations between the executives – communication and consultation, co-operation, exchange of information and confidentiality – as well as other matters relating to the management of relations, such as correspondence. The first supplementary agreement relates to the operation of the Joint Ministerial Committee (JMC), which was intended to operate as a principal forum for the discussion of reserved matters with implications for devolved responsibilities and other matters of mutual interest, as well as serving as a forum for dispute resolution. The next supplementary agreement – the first of the Concordats – is the "Concordat on Co-ordination of European Union Policy Issues". The three subsequent Concordats deal with Financial Assistance to Industry, International Relations and Statistics.

Bilateral Concordats were also drawn up between UK Government departments and their devolved counterparts as a framework for the management of relations between the two. These allowed guidelines to be drawn up for specific technical issues, for example Competition Casework in the DTI (Concordat between the Scottish Executive and the Department of Trade and Industry, Annex C, 25 November 1999), which are only of relevance to a limited number of divisions.

The MoU and overarching Concordats were published on 1 October 1999, three months after the official transfer of powers to the devolved institutions. The first tranche of bilateral Concordats was published on 11 November 1999. The timetable for publication changed on several occasions. Originally, the over-arching Concordats were intended to be produced before the May 1999 elections. This was then changed to after the elections had taken place and they eventually appeared in October 1999. The official reason given was that the documents had to be agreed by the devolved executives and this could not happen until the new executives were actually in place.

The Concordats were drafted by an informal network of officials, with the Cabinet Office, at its centre, carrying out most of the actual drafting. The drafting process went smoothly with the Cabinet Office demonstrating its aptitude for compromise and drafting mutually acceptable formulations. From the perspective of now devolved officials, they also proved easier to negotiate than the White Papers or the Parliamentary Bills (Interview, 2000).

As with the Acts of Parliament, there was no intention of creating legal obligations on either side. Rather the Concordats were expected to formalise existing arrangements (Mitchell & Leicester, 1999). Joyce Quin, then Minister for Europe at the FCO, in a speech given to the Northern Ireland Assembly, said:

> The Concordats will provide a framework for practical co-operation.

The UK Government's emphasis was therefore clearly based on a pragmatic approach. The second clause of the MoU states:

> This memorandum is a statement of political intent, and should not be interpreted as a binding document. (Scottish Executive, 1999)

Officials drafting the Concordats tried to avoid giving the impression that the documents were overly prescriptive. The documents had to be agreed by the new devolved executives, but any appearance of a "directive" from central government would be an invitation for the opposition parties, particularly the SNP and Plaid, to go on the offensive. Such an attack on the Concordats had already taken place at an early stage. During the Second Reading of the Scotland Bill in the House of Commons, Alex Salmond MP, leader of the SNP, spoke of the importance of defining the new Parliament's European role, citing a document apparently leaked from Ministry of Agriculture, Fisheries and Food (MAFF) as evidence of central government/Whitehall reluctance to involve the devolved authorities and describing the Concordats as potential "diktats" (Hansard Vol 304, Col 60-1, 12 January 1998). The SNP had also spoken out over its concerns that the Concordats were being drawn up "behind closed doors in Whitehall" (*The Scotsman*, 9 March 1999).

Further concerns arose among the opposition parties with regard to the lack of parliamentary input into the process. In the Scottish Parliament, the over-arching Concordats were debated and a vote was taken, but no committee stage scrutinised the details of the documents. In Wales, the National Assembly was only asked to "take note" of the document. Emphasis was clearly being placed upon the documents' position as informal agreements between the executives.

Asking NAW only to "take note" of the Concordats was a deliberate decision (Interview, 2000), representing an attempt to establish a firmer separation of the powers between Cabinet and plenary. It was also a reflection of the fact that central government departments would not be prepared to reveal policy positions to the plenary Assembly prior to EU negotiations taking place for fear of information leaking into the public arena, emphasising once again the importance attached to the principle of confidentiality.

The flow of information to sub-state tiers of government is crucial to their effective engagement with the EU policy process. In this instance, the flow of information to the Welsh Assembly Government was not in question, but the availability of information to the plenary Assembly was, potentially contributing to the exclusion of the plenary Assembly from the policy process.

As with the parliamentary passage of the Bills, a principal cause for concern for the opposition parties was the lack of legal standing given to arrangements for participation in EU policy formulation. However, the exclusion of the SP and NAW from the process must be noted, with the emphasis being placed on confidentiality rather than transparency. From a central government perspective, this is a necessary requirement for effective policy presentation in Brussels and the agreement of a single UK line. For the devolved plenaries, however, it can be interpreted as exclusion or a lack of transparency in the arrangements, perceptions that can be employed in the party political war of words.

The Concordat on the Co-ordination of European Policy Issues

The non-binding nature of the Concordats allows greater flexibility in the management of the UK's intra-state relations. Essentially, the EU Concordat adopts a pragmatic approach to the involvement of the devolved executives in EU affairs. As was indicated by the tone adopted in the White Papers and in the discussion surrounding the parliamentary passage of the Bills, strong emphasis is placed upon the principle of confidentiality in return for involving the devolved administrations in domestic EU policy formulation. Rather than representing absolute guarantees of participation, the Concordat represents a statement of intent.

The Concordat itself covers the following issues:

- Provision of information;
- Formulation of UK policy;
- Attendance at Council of Ministers and related meetings;
- Implementation of EU obligations;
- Infraction procedures (Scottish Executive, 1999).

The EU Concordat goes considerably further than the proposals set out in the devolution White Papers which had glossed over how relationships between the tiers of government would actually be handled when devolved affairs cropped up as issues in EU negotiations. Instead they concentrated upon the responsibilities involved for the devolved authorities and on potential points of access to the EU policy process. The common annex to the Concordat, which contains most of the relevant detailed information and applies equally to all three devolved authorities, acknowledges the importance of exchanges of information in the EU policy formulation process and commits the Government and the devolved administrations to pass on comprehensive information as soon as they are able. The second part of the annex deals with the participation of the devolved administrations in the formulation of UK policy positions. It anticipates that most issues will be dealt with bilaterally between lead UK and devolved departments, with overall policy co-ordination being provided by the Joint Ministerial Committee (JMC).

The third key section handles the issue of Scottish and Welsh ministerial attendance at Council and other EU meetings. It recognises that there should be a role for devolved ministers and officials at relevant Council meetings, with decisions on the composition of negotiating teams being taken on a case by case basis by the lead UK Minister. If the lead Minister considers it appropriate, it is possible for the devolved representative to speak, representing a previously agreed UK line. It is important to note that this is a previously agreed UK position, not an opportunity for a devolved Minister to put forward a separate devolved position. They represent the UK as a whole and present policy lines already negotiated domestically.

The remaining sections deal with the implementation of EU obligations and mechanisms for dealing with infraction proceedings. Again, emphasis is placed on the role of the lead UK Departments and UKRep. The status and function of UKRep remains unchanged post-devolution. The devolved authorities are permitted to establish their own Brussels offices for contacts with the EU institutions and with SSAs from other EU Member States, but these offices are expected to work closely with UKRep. This reflects the pledge of the White Paper and implicitly allows for the construction of horizontal relationships with sub-state governments in other Member States, although, as in the White Paper, the intended purpose of these relationships is not clarified.

The clauses relating to infraction proceedings are quite clear. Where proceedings are instituted against the UK by the European Commission through the European Court of Justice, the Cabinet Office will co-ordinate the response which will be delivered through UKRep. If the infraction in question has only occurred in Scotland or Wales, the draft reply will be formulated by the devolved administration, agreed with the relevant Whitehall department and delivered through UKRep. Responsibility for meeting the cost of any penalties imposed for infractions in the devolved territories will be met by the devolved authorities. This is the UK Government's attempt to ensure that the devolved administrations take full responsibility for ensuring the implementation of EU legislation in areas of devolved competency. It is quite clear from the Concordat that it is the UK as a whole that is responsible for any submissions to the European Commission and the ECJ with regard to infractions, irrespective of whether the infraction has occurred at the devolved or UK level.

The content of the Concordat in fact allows for fairly extensive participation by the devolved authorities in EU policy issues with implications for devolved responsibilities. There is an option for annual review contained within the MoU and the Concordats to allow for their progressive revision. However, their status as an informal document means that they do not contain the same legal guarantees as settlements achieved by SSAs elsewhere in the EU, for example the German and Austrian *Länder*.

Summary

The arrangements for the participation of the devolved administrations in EU policy are not the most extensive in an EU Member State. The provisions put in place in the UK do not constitute legal rights or guarantees of involvement. Nevertheless, the Scottish and Welsh administrations had, at the outset, opportunities for involvement which sub-state governments elsewhere had to challenge their respective central governments in order to achieve. The possibility for engagement established in the framework indicates that the overlap between EU and devolved competences had been accepted by the UK central government.

The existence of this implicit acceptance is further demonstrated by a key characteristic of the debate on devolved EU involvement between 1997 and 1999, namely the acceptance on the part of UK central government as a whole of the unfeasibility of excluding the new devolved executives from EU policy formulation in areas of devolved responsibility, indicating a recognition that EU policy can no longer be demarcated from domestic, including devolved, politics. This acquiescence to the involvement of the devolved administrations in EU policy arose partly from practical considerations and partly from party political motivations.

On a pragmatic level, the territorial offices had a history of involvement in EU policy formulation. The process of devolution acknowledged that Scotland and Wales have distinctive policy concerns and interests and it would thus have been difficult for the UK Government to explain why Scottish and Welsh involvement in EU policy formulation ceased when the devolved institutions assumed most of the responsibilities of the territorial offices.

There were also party political considerations for the Labour Party, particularly in Scotland with the SNP's "Independence in Europe" slogan. The EU is an increasingly important centre of decision-making and exclusion from this arena would have presented the SNP with an opportunity to promote their view that Scotland would be better represented in the EU as an independent state. With an election campaign for the devolved institutions approaching, the Labour Party did not want to present the nationalist parties with electoral ammunition.

Despite the broad acceptance of devolved involvement, there were still some signs of nervousness at the central government level. This was demonstrated during the process of drafting the White Papers and is also evident in the texts, for example the emphasis placed upon the principle of confidentiality. These concerns were also reflected in concerns about the status of the National Assembly as a corporate body. Nevertheless, there was little sign of actual retrenchment by the Government between the proposals of the White Papers and the frameworks established by the Concordats.

The central government managed to create a framework for close liaison on EU affairs without granting statutory rights of participation. The non-binding arrangements could therefore be revised by future central governments given the possibility of annual revision contained in the MoU and the Concordats, although attempts to restrict participation in any new agreement would still have to be agreed by the devolved executives. This is a situation that could be particularly difficult if opposing political parties formed the different administrations.

The model of participation requires close co-operation on the part of the different executives, a type of involvement most likely to operate effectively if the same party is in government at both levels. In her speech to the Northern Ireland Assembly, Joyce Quin announced:

A key principle is that there should be *no surprises*. (emphasis added)

This comment refers to the need for good open channels of communication between central government and the devolved authorities on EU issues. It is also a telling comment, however, on the position adopted by the UK central government. With the channelling of Scottish and Welsh activity through central government channels, it could be argued that the UK Government is attempting to prevent itself being "surprised" by Scottish or Welsh "paradiplomacy". Experiences in other EU Member States, such as Germany and Spain have shown the difficulty of preventing strong sub-state governments from developing autonomous activities in EU affairs if they are determined enough. The UK Government chose to deal with this by directing participation through specific channels rather than attempting to prevent it.

With regard to the issue of tensions being created by the overlap between EU and domestic competences, it is clear that the UK Government pre-empted the initial source of challenge and resistance by allowing for devolved engagement in the EU policy process. Nevertheless, other potential sources of friction are present within the framework established, primarily concerned with the nature and level of devolved engagement.

The first specific issue is the non-statutory nature of arrangements – without guaranteed legal rights, there is still a possibility of the devolved administrations being excluded from the EU policy process. This issue may provide a focus for the challenge of the devolved executives to achieve guaranteed legal rights of participation rather than the existing informal arrangements which rely on continued goodwill between the two levels of government. This friction could emerge as an increasingly serious issue with different parties in power at different levels of government.

As highlighted in Chapter 1, another area of friction can be identified in numerous other multi-level systems – the information flow. Information was recognised as crucial by the European Strategy Group, established by the Secretary of State for Wales in 1998 to discuss the most effective means of representing Welsh interests in the European arena. The ESG emphasised the importance of information for effective interest representation (ESG, 1998: 14-15). Therefore, exclusion from the information loop also represents a potential source of tension as it would hamper the effective involvement of devolved officials and ministers.

There is also the potential for differing levels of engagement created by the non-statutory nature of the arrangements. This point does not link directly to any of the areas of friction already identified. The framework established allows decisions on participation in Council meetings and working groups to be taken on a case-by-case basis by the respective UK lead department. A possibility therefore exists that some central government departments may co-operate more extensively with their devolved counterparts than others, creating tensions from devolved divisions who feel excluded by comparison.

Challenge could therefore emanate from devolved ministers and departments who feel excluded from the Council decision-making process. Challenges could also be triggered by the lack of consistency in attendance by devolved ministers at Councils. The Councils represent a highly visible form of demonstrating presence in the EU decision-making process. It is easy to determine whether a minister from a devolved executive has been present or not. Any apparent lack of attendance can be seized upon by opposition parties as a sign of exclusion from this important locus of decision-making.

It may be easy to determine presence in the Council of Ministers, but concerns were voiced about the lack of transparency in the arrangements for devolved engagement with UK EU policy-making. It is not easy to establish the input and influence of devolved departments in the process of formulating the positions actually presented in Brussels. This issue of a lack of transparency is also open to challenge from opposition parties.

Thus the arrangements for devolved engagement with the UK Government's EU policy formulation process were shaped by a combination of party political and pragmatic concerns. Compared with the situation of SSAs in some other EU Member States, the framework appears relatively generous, but its non-statutory nature may prove a source of instability. In addition, there are other potential sources of friction evident in the arrangements made that may affect the management of intra-UK management of EU affairs. It is thus to the operation of the framework in practice that our attention now turns.

CHAPTER 4

A View from Edinburgh

Introduction

This chapter will examine the roles of the devolved Scottish institutions in the UK's EU policy formulation process. It will begin by considering the level and quality of the involvement of Scottish Executive Ministers and their officials in EU policy-making, before considering evidence of the involvement of both the plenary Scottish Parliament and its European and External Relations Committee with EU policy issues. The evidence presented will also consider the question of whether a party political dimension can be discerned in the debate over European engagement.

Executive and Officials

The term "Scottish Executive" refers to both Scottish Ministers and Deputy Ministers and to the civil servants who comprise the policy departments of the Executive. This section will begin by considering the activities of the Ministers and Deputy Ministers, before addressing the role of SE civil servants, looking at the work of the External Relations Division, the SE EU Office and the SE functional departments. This approach will allow for an examination of the levels of engagement of the Executive with EU issues, providing evidence as to the effectiveness of the framework for the management of intra-state relations discussed in the preceding chapter.

The Role of Scottish Ministers

The first Scottish Executive administration was formed in 1999 by a Labour-Liberal Democrat coalition agreement, a pattern that was repeated following the second devolved elections in 2003. Their key task is policy development and delivery in all devolved policy areas (Burrows, 1999: 60), making them primarily responsible for initiating policy legislation in the Scottish Parliament. As highlighted previously, EU affairs are a reserved policy area of UK central government and in the original SE line-up from July 1999, no Minister had direct responsibility for EU affairs. This changed in the re-shuffle of November 2000 when Jack McConnell had External Relations, including EU affairs, added to his portfolio as Education Minister. When Mr McConnell became First Minister in November 2001, responsibility for External Relations was transferred to the portfolio of the Deputy First Minister, a post held at the time by the leader of the Scottish Liberal Democrats, although Mr McConnell retained a marked interest in EU and external affairs.

Prior to Mr McConnell's portfolio being extended to cover External Relations, he had been the Minister with *de facto* responsibility for EU affairs in his role as Finance Minister, as the SE Finance Department's responsibilities included the management of the EU Structural Funds in Scotland. This position reflected the continued importance of the Structural Funds as an area of EU policy. However, the original decision not to appoint a Minister with explicit responsibility for European issues reflected both its nature as a reserved policy matter and the difficulty of establishing which ministerial portfolio has the greatest European dimension, given that almost all devolved policy areas have an EU dimension.

Despite the status of EU affairs as a reserved policy area, the UK central government had committed itself to engaging Scottish Ministers and officials in the development of UK policy lines. One element of this decision has been the invitation extended by lead UK Ministers for Scottish Ministers to attend both formal and informal European-level meetings. The first member of the Scottish Executive to attend a formal Council of Ministers meeting was John Home Robertson, then Deputy Minister for Rural Affairs with special responsibility for fisheries, who attended a European Fisheries Council in October 1999. He also spoke at the Council as a member of the UK delegation and attended subsequent European Fisheries Council meetings, as have his successors in the post.

Fisheries is undoubtedly an area of key importance for Scotland, with at least 60% of the UK's fishing fleet being based there. Previous attendance records for Scottish Office Ministers indicated fisheries as a policy area where Scottish involvement could be anticipated. However, other examples of ministerial involvement in Council meetings include attendance at Environment, Education and Agriculture Councils amongst others. This indicates Scottish interests are now being explicitly incorporated across a broader range of policy areas than pre-devolution where almost all Council appearances by Scottish Office Ministers were restricted to Fisheries Councils.

The political salience of this question of attendance at Council meetings was demonstrated by the tabling of questions about Scottish Executive presence in Councils by the SNP, the main opposition in the Scottish Parliament for its first two terms. According to answers to parliamentary written questions tabled by the SNP, SE Ministers attended 16 Councils out of more than 130 that took place between 1 July 1999 and 28 February 2001 (S1W-13367, 29 March 2001), as well as participating in two informal meetings (out of 33) taking place during the same period (S1W-13368, 28 February 2001). This response served to create some public embarrassment for the SE, however, when the SNP announced that their research showed that one Agriculture Council at which SE attendance had been claimed had actually been cancelled. In response to a written question submitted by the SNP MSP Richard Lochhead in March 2003, it was reported that Scottish Executive ministers had attended 12.9% of all Councils held between 1 July 1999 and the end of February 2003 (S1W-34840). The extent of the SNP's focus upon this question is demonstrated by the holding answer issued to Written Question S1W-31303 (submitted by Richard Lochhead, SNP) on 20 November 2002 when Jim Wallace referred to seven answers previously issued to questions submitted about ministerial and official attendance in Council meetings and working groups.

The fact that the SNP chose to table such questions demonstrates the considerable political salience of the issue as an area where the SNP felt able to attack the Labour-led Executive. Exclusion from Council meetings has previously been identified as a potential source of friction between the UK Government and the Scottish Executive. However, the Labour-Liberal Democrat SE showed no inclination to publicly challenge the UK Government over the question of its Council participation. Rather it portrayed itself as satisfied that it was able to attend on issues of particular Scottish interest and content that Scottish concerns are reflected in the UK line when no Scottish Minister is present. Council attendance remained, however, an issue of contention in the Scottish party political arena.

Attendance at Council meetings is not the only instance of Scottish ministerial contact with the EU level. There have been a number of bilateral contacts between the Scottish Executive and the European Commission, including meetings with Regional Policy and Justice Commissioners. There was also the high profile public launch of the new Scottish Executive EU Office in Brussels which took place between 11 and 15 October 1999, promoted as "Scotland Week", when a number of Executive Ministers visited Brussels and built up contacts with both the European Commission and also other sub-state governments with representative offices in Brussels. "Scotland Week", as a series of seminars and as an opportunity for SE Ministers to hold meetings in Brussels, has been repeated subsequently.

The holding of such meetings demonstrated that the SE pro-actively sought to engage with the EU level, committing itself to holding an annual event in Brussels to promote Scotland, both economically and as a tourist destination, and to engage in policy debates. The UK Government made no public objections either to Scotland Week or to the holding of meetings between Scottish Ministers and European Commissioners. This situation could change, however, if a Scottish Minister proposed to present a line contrary to the UK Government's proclaimed position on an issue. Nevertheless, such meetings and events suggested that the SE took advantage of opportunities to engage with EU issues that overlap its domestic responsibilities.

Back in the UK, relations between Scottish and UK Ministers have tended to take place on an informal bilateral basis. The Joint Ministerial Committee (Europe), originally intended as a key multilateral forum for discussing the general lines of EU policy, met only once during the first two years of devolution, a meeting that did not take place until 1 March 2001. However, following the replacement of Robin Cook as Foreign Secretary in the wake of the May 2001 general election, and the announcement of the Convention on the Future of Europe, JMC(E) began to meet on a more regular basis, with discussions focusing upon the work of the Convention (Carter *et al.*, 2005: 5), discussed further in Chapter 6.

Self-evidently, Scottish Ministers are not members of the UK Government's Cabinet, traditionally considered the locus of decision-making authority in the British political system. This means that they are excluded from the ministerial and official sub-committees dealing with EU policy co-ordination. To a large extent, this exclusion from Cabinet committees was circumvented by the existence of two alternative points of access to the central government European policy network – Minecor and official contacts – when discussions impact upon areas of devolved responsibility (Interviews, 2000).

Minecor (the Ministerial Group for European Co-ordination) was headed by the Minister for Europe at the FCO, until it was wound up in 2004, and provided a multilateral forum for the discussion of policy by the competent ministers from both central government and the devolved administrations (Carter *et al.*, 2005). Exclusion from Cabinet was also circumvented by informal work, particularly at the official level, to keep the devolved administrations informed and involved on issues impacting on devolved competences. Relevant information is circulated in written form either between officials or between Ministers.

The fact that Scottish Ministers do not belong to the UK Cabinet network raises the question of the information flow. It is clear that efforts have been made to defuse this as a potential source of friction by circulating information between the two tiers of government. Each UK ministry has handled this differently – some departments always write to their Scottish counterparts in parallel, whilst others may copy them into correspondence directly, generally making their decision on the basis of the material's content (Interviews, 2000; 2003).

It is clear from the above that the Labour-Liberal Democrat SE demonstrated a degree of pro-active engagement in the first eight years of devolution. SE Ministers were not shut out of the UK's EU policy process. Although areas of potential tension can be identified, they did not unleash the dynamics evident in other federal or devolved EU Member States. There were, however, clear suggestions of party political tension over EU affairs, which are explored further in the section on the Scottish Parliament.

The evidence examined so far suggests the possibility that a new system for EU policy formulation was not created post-devolution. Rather, existing EU policy networks were extended to cover the relevant members of the Scottish Executive, both ministerial and official, where EU policy discussions touch upon devolved responsibilities.

The External Relations Division

The External Relations division existed in the Scottish Office prior to devolution taking place. However, it was smaller than the post-devolution division and concentrated largely on Structural Funds issues (Interview, 2000). Post-devolution, the division was divided into two sections, one dealing with EU affairs and the other with non-EU issues, acknowledging the qualitatively different nature and greater intensity of intra-EU relations.

The main functions of the EU section were identified as:

– Providing advice to Ministers on, and handling, cross-cutting issues;

– Providing business or "corporate" services, for example organising ministerial visits abroad or arranging programmes for visiting dignitaries;

– Acting as a conduit for information from central government and EU levels;

– Maintaining a collective record on the implementation of EU legislation in devolved policy areas in Scotland;

– Exploring the potential for co-operation with sub-state governments elsewhere in the EU (*Ibid.*).

As stated previously, no one Minister was given specific responsibility for external relations in the early days of devolution. Although that changed subsequently, the External Relations Division continued to advise all Scottish Ministers on EU issues. Officials expected few changes as a consequence of external relations becoming part of a ministerial portfolio (Interview, 2000) and indeed little did change.

The EU division had little to do with the formulation of specific policy positions, unless an issue emerged which did not have an obvious lead policy department – such as the Convention on the Future of Europe. As is the case in the UK central government's EU policy networks, most policy formulation is carried out by departmental specialists. It is recognised within the division that there was, and could only be, a single UK line on a policy issue and that the important thing was to influence that line (Interviews, 2000; 2003). Officials were also aware that good and prompt information was a prerequisite for exercising influence over UK policy positions. In addition, direct contact with the European Commission that was not also referred to central government was effectively ruled out, with the suggestion made by officials in 2001 that, although the European and External Relations Committee of the Scottish Parliament had sent positions directly to the European Commission, the Scottish Executive would not do so without having informed central government in advance. This suggests a specific approach to relations with the Commission was adopted in order to facilitate the smooth running of relations with central government, one which would be unlikely to endure under governmental incongruence.

It was also recognised within the division that some central government departments were "more clued-up" than others about involving their devolved counterparts, particularly in the early stages of devolution (Interview, 2000). To a certain extent, this reflected the situation that existed pre-devolution – central government departments that had good relations with the territorial offices maintained good relations with the new devolved departments. Consequently, some SE policy departments were considered by officials at both levels to be more extensively engaged in EU policy formulation than others. For example MAFF/ DEFRA maintained good relations whereas other departments that were less aware of territorial circumstances, such as the Home Office, were starting from a less well-developed position. In many instances, this was viewed as a case of departments adjusting to, or even perhaps a certain ignorance of, the new circumstances created by devolution, rather than a deliberate exclusion of the devolved executives (Interviews, 2000; 2001; 2003).

The key contact for the External Relations division within Whitehall was the Cabinet Office, with the relationship between the two being described in positive terms (Interviews, 2000; 2003). The division also claimed good contacts with UKRep in Brussels and is, of course, closely connected to the Executive's EU Office. Maintaining regular contacts with officials based in Brussels allowed the Executive to be alerted to potential policy proposals, highlighting the importance of networks of officials and the passing of information in involving the Executive in the EU policy process.

The Scottish Executive EU Office

The Scottish Executive's EU Office was opened on July 1, 1999, the day of the official opening of the Scottish Parliament. A higher profile launch week took place in October 1999 with events being attended by a number of Scottish Ministers and also the then UK Foreign Secretary, Robin Cook. This was designated as "Scotland Week" and was repeated in October 2001. Scottish Ministers have continued attending Brussels "regularly" since then (Interviews, 2000; 2003).

It shares premises, known as "Scotland House", with Scotland Europa, a lobbying and information service with members from both the public and private sectors (including COSLA, the Convention of Scottish Local Authorities). It is located, quite literally, just around the corner from UKRep's offices. It originally comprised six full-time staff which later increased to nine, and was then subsequently adjusted to a policy team of seven with three support staff.

The principal functions of the EU Office were identified as being:

– To provide advice to Executive officials on EU matters, including practical advice such as potential contacts within the European Commission;

– To influence policy, either through speaking to Commission officials when legislation is at an early stage of drafting, or through UKRep's desk officers;

– Collection and distribution of relevant information;

– To provide "hotdesk" facilities for SE officials whilst they are in Brussels attending meetings;

– To promote Scotland's international profile (Interview, 2000).

Desk officers at the EU Office each cover a range of policy areas and it is recognised within SE policy departments that the desk officers can operate most effectively if they are given a very specific objective, rather than being expected, or asked, to cover large general subject areas. Contact with policy departments in Whitehall is left predominantly to Executive officials based in Scotland. The level of contact maintained by the Office with SE officials was largely issue-dependent (Interview, 2000). Contact between the Office and the Scottish Parliament itself was almost non-existent, with just occasional questions from researchers. Although these were dealt with where possible, there was a feeling that this was not the main role of the Executive's Office. In a later development, the Scottish Parliament established its own post of Parliamentary Adviser to act as a conduit in Brussels, a post which operates autonomously of the Executive Office and is housed in Scotland Europa.

Overall, officials felt that the early years of the Office's operation passed fairly smoothly. Once they had begun to "find their feet" (Interview, 2000), officials felt increasingly able to take decisions on where Scotland's key priorities lay, thereby enabling more effective management of the workload. The most crucial element of this "settling in" process was identified as the Office's relationship with UKRep.

The Executive's Office was set up by two Scottish Office officials actually based within UKRep for that specific purpose, before being formally established by the SE. This helped to strengthen links between UKRep and the new Office. The relationship between the two was perceived favourably from the Scottish side, particularly UKRep's readiness to share information with the Executive Office. Members of the EU Office also regularly attended UKRep's weekly briefing (Interviews, 2000).

This was met with reciprocity on the part of the Executive Office which kept UKRep informed about SE activities in Brussels, for example visits by Scottish Ministers or senior Executive officials. Members of UKRep are invited to attend receptions and other functions, invitations which are regularly accepted. They are also briefed in advance on the content of any Scottish ministerial speeches being given in Brussels. A high level of trust exists in their relationship and there were few instances of public conflict between the two.

Despite these positive evaluations at the time, the leaking of a confidential memorandum by the head of the Scottish Executive Office indicated that in fact a number of problems existed in relations between both Edinburgh and Whitehall and UK Rep and the SE EU Office. Without the original document, it is difficult to assess the accuracy of media reporting, particularly as the issue was made public at the beginning of an election year. The paper in question had been written in 2006 and references to it appeared in *The Herald* in January 2007. The memorandum allegedly referred to problems in the information flow and a feeling that the SE was held back from putting across key points. It was also reported to condemn the Scotland Office for failing to strenuously represent Scottish interests in the UK Cabinet.

Although the timing of this leaked document places it outside the period of data collection for this study, it is clearly of interest as it indicates that tensions, including some of those identified here, clearly exist in the relationship between the Scottish and UK levels. However, it is also clear that, unlike in other EU Member States, such frictions generally remain firmly behind closed doors, implying that there was, at the time, no political advantage to be gained for the then Scottish Executive by going public with the existence of such difficulties.

This level of openness and the high degree of reciprocity was undoubtedly a key factor in maintaining good relations. It also echoed the statement of Joyce Quin on the importance of "no surprises" in the relationship between central government and the devolved administrations. With central government kept fully informed about Scottish Executive activities in Brussels, any objections could be made quickly and privately, rather than risk a situation degenerating into a public row, as happened in Germany between the Federal Government and the *Länder* when they began to open their regional information offices in Brussels (Hahn, 1986). It also demonstrated the importance of all kinds of information to maintaining a smooth relationship between central and sub-state levels.

However, the question remained as to whether a Scottish Executive led by a different political party to the one forming central government would receive, or allow, such an open flow of information between "its" officials and those of central government, an issue explored further in Chapter 7. It also raises the question of whether the relationship was assisted by the fact that Scotland is the most prominent of the devolved territories and the fact that there are only three devolved territories in the UK. For example, with 16 German *Länder* or the 17 Spanish Autonomous Communities, it is likely it would be more difficult to sustain such open relationships and have such a high degree of information flow between central and sub-state levels, with the possibility that information on all such activities being carried out by all the *Länder* or ACs would be more overwhelming for German federal or Spanish government officials, than has been the case for UKRep.

From the perspective of officials based in Scotland, many of the SE policy divisions, such as Environment and Fisheries, maintained regular contact with the appropriate desk officers of the EU Office and copied them in on major policy submissions to ensure that they were kept up-to-date with the developing direction of policy (Interview, 2000). Officials in both Edinburgh and Scotland considered the Office to have become increasingly effective as both the policy departments and the Office became increasingly familiar with their roles and consequently better able to prioritise and present Scottish concerns and interests (Interviews, 2000).

SE Policy Divisions

The importance of the Scottish Executive's policy divisions to the involvement of the Executive in the UK's EU policy formulation process reflects the sectoral nature of much of the UK's EU policy-making as discussed in Chapter 2. SE officials engage in frequent discussions with their Whitehall counterparts about domestic and EU issues across a wide range of policy areas away from the public arena. Almost all of the policy areas for which the devolved authorities are responsible have an EU dimension. Executive officials are also engaged in discussions at the EU level on a regular basis, especially when issues with a distinctive Scottish dimension – such as the education system – are under discussion.

In addition to ministerial engagement in Council meetings, there is evidence that Scottish Executive officials have engaged in EU working groups across a range of policy areas. Unsurprisingly, Scottish officials are almost always involved in working groups on fisheries policy, but SE officials also regularly attend working groups on education and environment issues (Interviews, 2000; 2003). An answer to an SNP-tabled written question showed that Executive officials attended 99 European level working group meetings in the first 18 months of devolution, with attendance not only at meetings on the above policy issues, but also, for example, justice and home affairs and health policy. Involvement in working group meetings is highly important as this is where much of the actual policy-making and negotiation takes place. Ministerial Councils deal with the most difficult political decisions that need to be taken. It is therefore important to the representation of Scottish interests to be part of the delegation to the official-level working groups.

Executive officials also maintained contact with their Welsh and Northern Irish counterparts on a range of policy issues, although such links were rarely as intensive as contacts with Whitehall officials. The particular issue under discussion can also determine whether links with Wales or with Northern Ireland are more intensive. For example, there are more extensive links between Scotland and Northern Ireland on fishing policy because the Northern Irish fleet is more substantial than the Welsh fleet and bears a greater similarity to the Scottish fleet, fishing many of the same areas (Interview, 2000). This reinforces the impression that bilateral links with central government are more important to engagement in EU policy formulation than the multilateral fora. It also reflects the fact that, unlike in Germany, in the devolved UK there is no need to develop joint policy positions to present to central government. However, if the devolved administrations share a policy priority, presenting a common position may have greater impact on the policy positions adopted by the UK Government.

In general, there were few immediate dramatic changes to the role of many of the policy departments in EU policy affairs post-devolution from that played by Scottish Office divisions. The key change overall from the point of view of officials was the increased workload created by enhanced public and parliamentary scrutiny. The number of parliamentary questions to be answered increased greatly and there was also greater involvement in the drafting of legislation. Increasingly, as a result of this scrutiny, officials felt a need to be able to demonstrate their involvement in the EU policy process (Interviews, 2000; 2003).

There was no obvious exclusion of devolved policy divisions from the EU policy process, but involvement was not uniform. In sectors where there was traditionally a considerable degree of engagement, this continued post-devolution. This was the case, for example, in fisheries policy, where links between MAFF/DEFRA and Scottish Office officials were always extensive as a result of the importance of the Scottish fleet. Indeed, fisheries officials commented that there was not that much change from pre-devolution, with the working relationship being described as "business as usual" (Interview, 2003).

Some departments have found it more difficult to engage in the EU policy process, although officials argued that this did not necessarily reflect reluctance on the part of central government departments, but may also have been a consequence of a learning curve on the part of some SE policy groups, as well as the extent of their resources. An example of this was evident in the increased focusing on priorities as divisions realised that comments on one or two key priorities were more likely to be incorporated into the UK's final policy positions than extensive comments on every point (Interview, 2000). However, outside the Executive, notably amongst opposition parties, there were accusations of SE policy divisions being excluded from the formulation of EU policy positions.

Difficulties in relationships with central government divisions were generally considered by officials to stem from the need to adjust to the new circumstances created by devolution. An official from SEERAD commented that "MAFF colleagues understand that we are working in a different kind of environment" (Interview, 2000). The SE Education department also had good links with its Whitehall counterparts, although this reflected a situation that had developed incrementally over time, with work on improving relations also taking place for some time before devolution (Interview, 2000). Where understanding of the changed environment was absent, friction could be created with comments being made that with the exception of the FCO and the Cabinet Office, Whitehall had not always understood devolution particularly well. However, SE officials generally evaluated relations with central government departments during the first four years of devolution in positive terms, particularly those with the Cabinet Office, MAFF/DEFRA and UKRep.

One of the main reasons why relations between departments worked better in some instances than in others is the importance of inter-personal relations in the predominantly informal process of policy co-ordination. Maintaining good relations with central government officials was considered to be an important part of the job. Factors considered to be key to these relationships were identified as negotiation, compromise and trust (Interviews, 2000; 2003). Negotiation and compromise are an essential element of determining a single UK policy line. A growing level of trust, as SE officials continued to be reliable in maintaining confidentiality, helped to maintain information-sharing, a crucial element in enabling effective participation by SE officials. The importance of the information flow was widely recognised by officials, although information from central government could be, and was, disseminated to the SE in a format different to that in which it was circulated within central government.

SE officials were able to build upon the networks of relationships that existed between the Scottish Office and Whitehall departments prior to devolution. A number of policy divisions in both Scotland and Whitehall were spared extensive staff transfers at the time of devolution with many SE staff continuing in the same roles, in contact with the same Whitehall officials, for some time after devolution. The Scottish Office, of course, had a long history of experience of dealing and nego-tiating with central government departments.

However, the heavy reliance on inter-personal relationships inevita-bly meant that some officials got on much better with their contacts than others. Such a context can further aggravate the lack of uniformity in levels of engagement across different policy areas. Where good relation-ships between officials were maintained, behind-the-scenes Scottish involvement was generally managed smoothly, with disagreements over policy resolved privately.

Engagement in EU policy formulation was further facilitated by the existence of a small core group of officials who had developed EU policy expertise as a result of the Scottish Office's deliberate policy of seconding officials to placements either with UKRep or the European Commission. This led to the SE gaining a number of officials in differ-ent policy areas with first-hand experience of the EU's legislative processes and with networks of contacts within Brussels and other Member States (Interview, 2000). The Executive ran a first study trip to Brussels which provided officials with a basic introduction to the EU's institutions and legislative processes. Over-subscription of this initial trip led to at least one policy division organising their own equivalent, ensuring that they thus had at least one official in each of their units with a knowledge of EU institutions and the EU policy process.

During the first four years of devolution, there were no public rows between the Scottish Executive and central government about the level of Scottish involvement in EU policy formulation. No call was made upon the formal mechanisms for conflict resolution and the Concordats were viewed very much as a "safety net" (Interview, 2003), rather than as a recipe for conducting relations, and were only rarely consulted. The need for the Concordats was actually called into question by some officials on occasion. However, they were generally considered to be useful in spelling out previous practice and were available to be referred to should any difficulties arise in the relationship between the Executive and the central government (Interviews, 2003). The emphasis on informality appeared to suit both administrations, and reflected the way in which business was carried out between the Scottish Office and Whitehall policy departments. The informal nature of relations also enabled intra-UK discussions to keep pace with developments at the EU level, which would be more difficult if the more "cumbersome" official machinery was employed (Interview, 2000).

Nevertheless, potential for conflict and challenge remained present within the system. The first possibility – and the one most frequently mentioned by officials with regard to potential tensions – is the potential for conflict when administrations of different political persuasions hold power in Edinburgh and London. Labour dominance of the first two terms of devolution in Scotland made party political conflict between the two far less likely during the early years of devolution, but it was inevitably that the situation would arise, as it finally did after the 2007 devolved election results.

Secondly, there was the potential frustration created by the "participation by invitation" approach of Whitehall in deciding the composition of negotiating teams attending discussions in Brussels, particularly given the fact that some central government departments involved their devolved counterparts more than others. There were clearly frustrations with some of the larger Whitehall departments who appeared slower to adjust to the changed circumstances created by devolution. Nevertheless, there were no public challenges to central government for the Scottish Executive to establish a right to attend Councils. The SNP, as it did during the passage of the Scotland Bill through the Westminster Parliament, continued to press the issue.

There also did not appear to be a deliberate exclusion of departments where portfolios were held by Ministers from the Liberal Democrats, the "junior" coalition partner. The Liberal Democrat Ross Finnie, as Minister for Rural Affairs after May 1999, was one of the Scottish Ministers most heavily engaged in EU issues, attending a number of Agriculture Councils. Indeed, one official commented that Finnie and Elliot Morley (UK Minister with responsibility for fisheries) sought to present themselves as a team in Brussels. Nicol Stephen, then a Liberal Democrat Deputy Minister, actually led the UK delegation at an Education Council in 2000. However, the variation in levels of engagement across different policy areas raises questions about the actual quantity and quality of access to the EU policy formulation process, particularly if this lack of uniformity fails to decrease over time.

Thirdly, the extension of the existing policy process to incorporate the Scottish Executive demonstrated that the flow of information between UK and devolved levels was not cut off during this time. There was no evident dissatisfaction with the dissemination of information, nor was there any evidence of information being withheld for "power purposes" to gain the upper hand in discussions (Interview, 2000). Nevertheless, the possibility for information to be withheld remained, and could be provoked either out of party political motivations or as a result of breaches of confidentiality and the leaking of material into the public domain. Official documents issuing from the EU would still be available to the SE from other sources, but necessary information on central government's policy positions would not be. In order for the flow to be maintained, the climate of trust which existed in the first stages of devolution would need to continue. However, it was also noted that "cutting loose" the Scottish Executive, especially in fisheries policy, was "not a risk-free option" for MAFF/DEFRA, suggesting a further motivation for sustaining co-operation in order to present a single policy line (Interview, 2003).

These three points demonstrate that the lack of public tensions between the SE and UK central government between 1999 and 2003, and indeed up until April 2007, does not mean that the potential for friction was absent. In fact, it is inherent at several key points in the framework for managing post-devolution relations. The maintenance of a unified civil service has clearly helped to reduce tensions in many areas by allowing for a certain stability in relations between SE and central government officials. However, the reliance on informal methods of co-operation contains its own problems and is, in all likelihood, best suited to the type of bilateral contacts in evidence during the first eight years. In addition, the lack of highly salient dynamics of challenge and resistance between the two administrations does not mean that they are absent in the overall devolution framework. Evidence of such tensions will now be sought by examining the experiences of the Scottish Parliament and its European Committee since their establishment in 1999.

The Scottish Parliament

The Scottish Parliament at its establishment contained 129 MSPs. Unlike the original design for the National Assembly for Wales, the Scottish Parliament was intended to be completely separate from the SE, and, indeed, both perceive themselves as entirely separate institutions (Interview, 2000). The work of the Parliament is supported by its own staff, who do not constitute part of the home civil service. The SP is a unicameral legislature, and incorporates a strong committee system which is designed to counterbalance the lack of a second chamber.

The means by which the Parliament can scrutinise the work of the Executive are laid down in the Standing Orders and topics can be raised by MSPs either by asking oral questions, submitting written questions, or by giving notice of, or moving, a motion. As a consequence of its identity as a separate institution from the SE, the SP is not bound by the MoU or the Concordats which merely form an agreement between the governing executives. It was suggested that as its self-confidence increased and MSPs' familiarity with their roles and with policy likewise increased, that there would be a possibility of tension emerging between itself and the central government, particularly in the area of EU affairs. However, in order to have a sufficient degree of impact on policy to provoke such tensions, it would need to focus very carefully on the specific issues that it desired to influence (Interview, 2000).

Examining the operation of the full parliament between June 1999 and May 2003, it is quite clear that debates and questions across a wide range of policy issues often had an EU dimension. This reflects the extent to which EU and domestic policy issues now overlap, whilst also making it difficult for the SP to achieve the kind of focus on a policy area discussed above. Taking the example of written questions, those regarding policy issues with an EU dimension ranged across Structural Funds, rural affairs, the cashmere industry, bridge tolls, policing and planning applications. Unsurprisingly, most questions with a European dimension were concentrated on the key EU areas of agriculture, fisheries and the environment. With the exception of Structural Funds issues, far fewer written questions dealt explicitly with the EU itself, rather they acknowledged its influence over a traditionally domestic policy area. For example, only four questions related to the subject of IGC 2000 were tabled, all relating to Scottish Executive influence over the UK line and representation at negotiations.

Oral questions asked during Scottish Executive Question Time similarly covered a wide range of issues with an EU dimension. Again, these were mostly involved with fisheries, agriculture and the Structural Funds, but also included such diverse policy issues as GM crops, Skye Bridge tolls, and the display of the saltire on vehicle registration plates. Europe-related issues received far less exposure during First Minister's Question Time, although occasional questions relating to European Union issues did occur.

General plenary debates on the EU were rare, as were ministerial statements to the plenary on attendance at the Council of Ministers. However, despite the fact that there were only occasional general debates on "Europe" (for example, just two in the first 18 months of operation), Structural Funds debates and most agriculture and fisheries debates contained references to the EU, as did some on environmental, transport (specifically the tendering of contracts) and planning issues.

The lack of time devoted to specifically EU issues in plenary sessions emphasises the importance of subject committees, and particularly the European and External Affairs Committee, in scrutinising the Executive's EU activities. However, the debates which took place in plenary sessions clearly demonstrated a continuation of confrontational attitudes in party politics in Scotland, reflecting patterns in the UK as a whole (see, for example, Scottish Parliament Official Record of Proceedings, 10 November 1999, S1M-258, Cols 444-445).

The main party political tension in Scotland is between Labour and the SNP, and this is played out at both the local government and all-Scotland levels. As noted during Chapter 3, EU issues feature prominently with the SNP as part of their campaign slogan of "Independence in Europe". Particular reference is made to the anticipated benefits of membership of the EU as an independent Member State, such as a permanent seat at all Councils, the opportunity to hold the rotating presidency and so on.

Therefore, the SNP gave a high profile to the question of the Labour-led Scottish Executive's representation in EU-level negotiations, raising the issue of what they called the Scottish Executive's "absolutely atrocious" (*The Herald*, 14 February 2001) and "contemptible" (*The Scotsman*, 27 March 2001) record of attendance at Councils on a number of occasions. This record of attendance was the main point of attack on the SE's level of engagement in EU affairs during the first four years of devolution. After the appointment of Jack McConnell as Minister for Education, Europe and External Relations, the SNP particularly attempted to turn the spotlight on his apparent lack of attendance at Council meetings.

However, they also argued that they had been frustrated in their scrutiny of the Executive's performance by the lack of transparency in relations between the SE and central government, and by the lack of "independently verifiable information" released into the public domain (Interview, 2000). It was argued that this lack of transparency, particularly with regard to the engagement of officials in the EU policy formulation process, made it difficult to scrutinise how effectively the SE represented Scottish policy concerns and interests and the degree of influence that it was able to exercise over the final UK line.

Part of this frustration stemmed from the difficulty in accessing information about the SE's engagement with EU issues. Opposition parties are only able to table parliamentary questions, many of which receive singularly unenlightening answers designed to protect the confidentiality of negotiations with central government departments. An example of a typical answer follows:

> *Richard Lochhead* (North East Scotland) (SNP): To ask the Scottish Executive what discussions it has had with Her Majesty's Government about the impact of departmental expenditure limits on the allocation of European Union funding within the Executive's budget (S1W-34834).

> *Mr Andy Kerr*: The Scottish Executive is in regular contact with the UK Government on financial issues.

This demonstrates the clear division that exists between the work of the Scottish Parliament and the activities of the SE, with the Parliament being kept at a distance from the work of the Executive's officials. This lack of forthcoming information, however, does enable opposition parties, particularly the SNP, to draw their own conclusions about the Executive's level of engagement. This lack of transparency in the policy process led to accusations that certain central government departments were less than willing to involve the Scottish administration in EU policy discussions (Interview, 2000).

The SNP's suspicions regarding the engagement of the Executive increased further following the post-general election re-shuffle in June 2001 which saw Mr Jack Straw, former Home Secretary, move to the Foreign Office as Mr Straw was not considered a supporter of devolution (*The Herald*, 19 June 2001; Taylor, 1999).

Interviews with SE officials have demonstrated their involvement with the EU policy process. However, because this is not public or high profile, it left the Scottish Executive open to attack about their level of engagement as it is so difficult for external observers to determine and thus easy to exploit for party political purposes.

In addition to demanding an automatic place in the negotiating team for Scottish Ministers to attend Councils, the SNP also pushed Ministers to give pre-and post-Council statements either to the plenary session or to the relevant subject committee, a development that was eventually introduced in the work of European and External Relations Committee, as will be discussed subsequently. The SNP argued that Ministers should explain their position, or the outcome of the Council, or their reasons for non-attendance (Interview, 2000).

In response to this sustained focus on representation in Council, the Labour-Liberal Democrat SE countered that engaging with the EU's legislative process is more than just a matter of a "head count" at every Council meeting (Scottish Parliament Official Record, 10 November 1999, Col 439 – Mr Donald Dewar). The Deputy First Minister, Jim Wallace in the same debate, pointed out the importance of official engagement in preparing policy positions (*Ibid.*: Col 470) before UK delegations depart to attend negotiations. In addition, the Executive argued that it would be pointless to attend meetings that are not relevant to substantial Scottish interests and that Scottish interests are inevitably represented at all meetings that Scottish Ministers and officials do not attend, by the UK delegation as a whole (*Ibid.*: Col 470). These two arguments represented a continual theme throughout the period under consideration here.

Before the introduction of the new committee mechanism for receiving ministerial statements on Council participation, the SE refused to discuss policy positions before negotiations took place at EU level. Even following the new committee innovation, the heavy emphasis placed upon the principle of confidentiality in both the White Paper and the Concordats was maintained. This attitude on the part of the SE was designed to avoid breaches of confidentiality which could risk restricting the information flow seen as crucial to both ministerial and official engagement in EU affairs. This position led to difficult and sensitive negotiations with the EU and External Relations Committee over exactly what information could be shared in briefings on Council meetings.

This reticence was easily explained and comprehensible from the Scottish Executive's perspective. However, the impression of a lack of transparency and accountability was striking to those external to the Executive, unable to trace the effects of Scottish influence upon UK policy positions. This opened up opportunities for party political attacks on the Executive about the quality and quantity of its involvement as well as accusations that the Labour-led Scottish Executive was not independent of the UK Labour Party which formed the central government. Such attacks made particular play of the fact that devolution and the creation of a Scottish Parliament were supposed to provide greater transparency, accountability and democracy in the way in which Scotland is governed (Paterson, 1998: 239-244).

Such behaviour thus clearly reflected the continued confrontational nature of party politics in the UK, with the main opposition parties seeking to challenge and exploit the SE's record of engagement in EU affairs during the period 1999-2007. This is particularly the case for the SNP who seized on this as a way of demonstrating that Scotland would be in a stronger position in the EU as an independent state. Confrontational tendencies, policy positions and attitudes were all apparent in exchanges between the Executive and the opposition parties on EU affairs.

However, such confrontational party political tendencies were less salient in the operation of the European and External Affairs Committee, the workhorse for the scrutiny of both EU legislation and the SE's EU-related activities. The workings of the Committee lie, for the most part, in sharp contrast to the more showy, media- and public-aware exchanges which took place in the full Scottish Parliament, even when the Committee's convenorship was not held by a Labour MSP.

The Scottish Parliament European and External Affairs Committee

The European and External Affairs Committee, formerly the European Committee, is a statutory, or mandatory, committee, meaning that it was one of the committees required by the Standing Orders of the Scottish Parliament. Its inclusion as a mandatory committee was recommended by the Consultative Steering Group (CSG), a cross-party body established by the Scottish Office after the 1997 referendum in order to consider the manner of operation of the Parliament. The establishment of a European Committee, alongside other committees such as the Business and Equal Opportunities Committees, was considered to be "fundamental to the operation of the Parliament" (CSG, 1998). In addition to such mandatory committees, the Parliament is able to establish subject committees to scrutinise specific areas of public policy. The subject committees of the first parliament corresponded to the original ministerial portfolios of the first Scottish Executive.

Thirteen MSPs were originally nominated to serve on the European and External Affairs Committee, though this was subsequently reduced to nine. The first convenor of the Committee, Hugh Henry MSP, was drawn from Labour's ranks. However, the subsequent convenor, Richard Lochhead MSP, came from the SNP. The Committee was given a broad-ranging and somewhat peculiar remit, given its status as a mandatory committee covering an area of policy broadly reserved to the

Westminster Parliament. Its remit in 1999, under Rule 6.8 of the Standing Orders, was to:

> ...consider and report on:
> – proposals for European Communities legislation;
> – the implementation of European Communities legislation;
> – any European Communities or European Union issue.

It is obvious that this is a very broad remit enabling the Committee to look at a wide range of policy issues, including, under clause (c), issues outside the first, or Community, pillar. Many such issues also, inevitably, fall under the remit of a subject committee. During its first four years, the Committee led inquiries into subjects as diverse as matched funding, football transfers, European governance and Infectious Salmon Anaemia. Within those four years, it received a massive volume of legislative and pre-legislative documentation for scrutiny, recognised as the key function of the Committee.

This heavy workload was anticipated before the Committee was even set up, given the number of documents produced and distributed annually by the EU. The Committee's original members were informed at the outset that it would not be possible to scrutinise such a vast number of documents and that a very selective approach would have to be adopted in deciding which legislative proposals were of particular importance to Scotland (Interview, 2000). This approach underpinned successive subsequent revisions aimed at refining the Committee's working procedures for handling documentation (Interviews, 2003; 2004). It was also anticipated that many issues would be referred to the subject committees for them to pursue further as they deemed necessary.

In general, the Committee meets once a fortnight when the Parliament is sitting. This was expected from the outset and it was even suggested early on that the Committee may have to met on a weekly basis – something that has happened on occasion in order to pursue specific inquiries. A typical Committee meeting agenda would include hearing evidence from witnesses, updates on reports being carried out by individual members of the Committee, recommendations for document scrutiny, recommendations from the document sift and the Convenor's report.

The regularity and intensity of the Committee's work during the Parliament's first term demonstrated quite clearly a keenness to engage proactively with the EU policy process in so far as resources allowed, and that it had no intention of being sidelined. The Committee's determination to both scrutinise European legislative proposals and hold SE Ministers to account for their handling of EU-related affairs led to a number of important revisions and innovations in the operation of the Committee.

Building upon the remit set out in the Standing Orders, the Committee developed a range of methods for handling its business. Firstly, it conducts inquiries into issues of specific interest to Scotland. Secondly, the clerking team, supported by legal advice, conducts a sift of the documentation received from the EU with the intention of highlighting policy proposals with implications for Scotland which, crucially, are still at an early stage in the policy process (Interviews, 2000; 2003). Thirdly, in a significant innovation, the Committee negotiated with the Executive a system of pre-and post-Council reporting, a system so rare that few Member State parliaments have similar mechanisms (Interview, 2004).

In undertaking all-committee inquiries, the Committee has taken evidence from a wide range of witnesses, including SE Ministers and officials, European Commission officials, local government representatives and members of professional associations. The appearance of Commission officials other than the Commission representative in Scotland is particularly interesting. Given their own workload, it is unlikely that they would appear before every committee of a sub-state parliament that invited an appearance. It may be that their willingness to give evidence in Scotland arose in part from the high profile of Scotland as a "historic nation" and the Europe-wide interest in Scottish affairs that the devolution process aroused. The evidence collected from witnesses was then used in the drafting of Committee reports.

In addition to all-committee inquiries, members of the Committee were also nominated as individual reporters for particular issues, producing their own reports for discussion by the Committee. The subjects, and the timescale for these reports, were laid out in the forward work programme of the Committee, a method for scheduling workload that was initiated during its first year of operation. A number of such reports were rapidly completed during the first parliament, submitted for discussion by the Committee as a whole and, where agreed, published as Committee reports.

The most important task of the Committee was the scrutiny of EU legislative proposals. This provided an enormous workload for the Committee and its clerking team. Even though such a workload was anticipated, working procedures were revised just over a year after the establishment of the Committee, in what was described by officials as a shift from the "House of Commons sift model" to a "House of Lords sift model" (Interview, 2003). A document sift was carried out by the Convenor and the Committee clerk, assisted by legal advisors. Documents could then be selected for priority by the Committee as a whole. These documents usually fell in an area of current Committee inquiry, for example, documents relating to fisheries during the Committee's investigation into the proposed reform of the Common Fisheries Policy. Others may be referred to an appropriate subject committee, either for scrutiny or for their information. There were regular and persistent attempts by the Committee to encourage subject committees to engage more intensively with the European dimension of their respective port-folios.

Another category of the sift was the documents for which additional information was requested, usually in the form of a Scottish Cover Note from the Executive explaining the Scottish dimension, or, more rarely, an Explanatory Memorandum from the lead Whitehall department is awaited. A Scottish Cover Note is then sometimes required upon receipt of the Explanatory Memorandum. The majority of documents in the sift, however, fell into the category of "No Further Action", either because the subject was of no relevance to major Scottish interests, or because the proposal was not at a stage where the policy outcome could be influenced, normally because it had already advanced too far through the EU's policy process (Interview, 2000).

The Convenor's report, a regular item on the Committee's agenda, constitutes a round-up of issues such as correspondence received and proposed responses, forthcoming visits from overseas notables and reports on meetings and conferences attended by the Committee. Such a report might contain, for example, notice of letters received from the Scottish Executive or the European Commission and a suggestion as to whether the correspondence should merely be noted or whether a further response is required. With regard to upcoming meetings, members would be asked if anyone was able to attend. Such meetings are usually with sub-state or central government ministers from other EU Member States, but have also included visiting members of foreign royal families and representatives of EU institutions such as the European Parliament. Members who attend such meetings then report back at a subsequent Committee meeting.

The most important innovation for the Committee during the first parliament was the establishment of the system of pre- and post-Council reporting by the Scottish Executive. With the exception of the Danish Folketing, which has the ability to mandate Danish government minis-ters, few parliaments at either Member- or sub-state level have devel-oped similar mechanisms, in such a systematic way, in their attempts to hold executives responsible for their negotiations and decisions in the Council of the European Union.

This system represented a further attempt by the Committee to gather relevant information. Council agendas are received in advance and post-Council ministerial reports are provided. Of central importance was the issue of getting the Executive to agree to provide the information requested. Concerns revolved around how much information could be provided, especially pre-Council, and how it would be handled, because of the need to adhere to the principle of confidentiality as conceived by the UK Government (Interview, 2004). Eventually, agreement was reached whereby in advance of every Council meeting, an agenda, annotated with a short discussion of the Scottish interest of each agenda item would be provided to the Committee.

The above discussion demonstrates the diverse range of activities carried out by the Committee with relation specifically to EU affairs. As a result of changes within the Executive, the Committee subsequently took on an extended remit over European and External Affairs. In addition, the Committee also sought to develop an active role in tracking the implementation or transposition of EU legislation by the Executive. Again, developing such a system required negotiations with the Executive over the nature of the information provided (Interview, 2000). This attempt to tackle the implementation issue demonstrated yet again a determination by the Committee to hold the Executive genuinely accountable for its EU-related activities.

The first years of the Committee's operation provided a steep learning curve for members, some of whom had no previous experience of EU affairs. In order to help with this process, the whole Committee undertook a number of trips to Brussels with the aim of helping members to develop a better understanding of the EU legislative processes and the stages of policy development at which proposals can best be influenced. It also enabled the Committee to develop contacts with the EU institutions and particularly with members of the European Commission. Such visits were considered extremely useful to the Committee (Interviews, 2000; 2003). Consequently, in spring 2001, a visit by all SP committee convenors to Brussels was organised in order to help further their understanding of the workings of the EU and its impact upon their respective policy areas (Scottish Parliament Parliamentary News Release 0015/2001, 21 March 2001).

Such details of the Committee's work indicate that it was pro-active in seeking to engage with EU policy issues. However, the Committee also encountered many of the problems evident in the experience of sub-state parliaments elsewhere. For at least the first year of its operation there was a commonly held belief that the Committee was "finding its feet" as it sought to work out when and where it could best feed into the policy process and how it should select areas on which it should focus its attention. In order to facilitate its engagement, the Committee developed its annual programme on the basis of the European Commission's annual forward work programme and by inviting visits from the UK ambassadors of the Member State holding the upcoming six-monthly Council presidency.

It was recognised by civil servants that the Committee had the potential to influence the decision-making process in highly-specific policy areas by engaging with the Executive (Interview, 2000). Nevertheless, the circulation of the Committee's reports proved to be a sensitive issue in the Committee's relationship with the Executive (Interview, 2000). Some of the Committee's reports, for example on the implementation of the Structural Funds programmes, were sent to the Executive in an attempt to influence the implementation process. It is, however, worth noting that the impact of receiving Committee reports could be reduced if they examined an issue with which the Executive was not deeply concerned at the time.

Other reports were developed in response to Commission consultation initiatives, such as the report on the 6th Environmental Action Plan. This Committee report was sent directly to the Commission, an action that initially caused some consternation, particularly in central government (Interviews, 2000). However, the Parliament is not bound by the MoU and the Concordats and the Committee had responded to a general consultation request, sending the report only in the name of the Committee. Given the status of their report, the move was quietly accepted.

It was recognised, however, that the Committee had to be careful about its role, exercising caution about the issue of being seen to attempt to influence draft legislation at the EU level by circumventing the SE. The emphasis was placed upon openness and transparency, not undermining SE Ministers (unless the Executive's policy position had been overturned by the Parliament). The reports sent to the Commission were viewed as providing feedback as requested, not as attempts to recommend the Commission alter legislative proposals.

In 2003 the Committee produced a legacy paper with the intention of providing advice to its successor committee and thus facilitate the process of learning by experience (Scottish Parliament, 2003). It is clear from the legacy paper that the Committee experienced difficulties managing its workload, even before the size of the Committee was reduced from thirteen to nine. Problems encountered included time constraints, a lack of resources to devote to scrutiny and the preparation of reports, and the issue of determining its position in relation to the subject committees. Many problems derived from the sheer volume of documentation leading to revisions of the documentary sift procedure. The Committee also developed the strategy highlighted above for planning its future workload by tying its priorities to those of the Commission and the upcoming Council presidency.

As with sub-state parliamentary committees elsewhere, difficulties were also created by the time constraints imposed by the scheduling of the EU policy process. Many sifted documents marked "No Further Action" had already reached a stage where it was pointless for the Committee to try and influence the Executive's position as it was too late for the Scottish Executive to try and influence the UK's position or the policy outcome. Alternatively, by the time a document had been sifted and referred to a subject committee, placed on its agenda and discussed, it could also be too late to engage with the Executive. The Committee also encountered problems trying to deal with this workload with the limited resources available to it, including pressure on the clerking team and the lack of researchers' time available to it.

Aside from these problems, which had been anticipated in advance, one highly specific area of tension emerged during the Committee's 2000 inquiry into past and present additionality and matched funding in the Structural Funds programmes. This was the refusal of central government ministers and officials, notably the Chancellor of the Exchequer and the Secretary of State for Scotland, to appear before the Committee. Although the Committee accepted these responses, particularly from the Chancellor, acknowledging that the Scottish Parliament had no power to summon central government representatives, a letter from the Secretary of State arguing that he was only answerable to the Westminster Parliament was leaked, generating media interest in the issue. The Committee was not, on the record, upset, although the situation inevitably created tension between the two levels. The European and External Relations Committee completed its inquiry, though it failed to draw a conclusion on the particular aspect relating to additionality, arguing that the Committee had been unable to acquire sufficient evidence to draw any substantive conclusions about the operation of the additionality principle in Scotland's receipt of Structural Funds (SP Committee News Release CEU027/2000, 8 November 2000). The Finance Committee's parallel inquiry was, however, suspended as a result of the lack of response.

It can be argued that this unanticipated source of tension derived, at least in part, from the issue of the lack of transparency, with the Committee unable to access the information it felt it required. Noticeable in the operation of the Committee, however, was that there was generally much less evidence of the party political tension apparent in the plenary Parliament, even when the convenorship switched from the Labour MSP Hugh Henry to the SNP MSP Richard Lochhead (and later to the former leader of the SNP, John Swinney). In general the members managed to work in a collegiate manner – although the influence of party political tendencies could nevertheless be discerned. This general approach carried through despite subsequent membership changes. Such a co-operative approach derived at least partially from the fact that the Committee examines the potential impact of detailed legislation on Scotland, rather than arguing about issues of clear party political disagreement such as Scotland's status in the EU.

In summary, it can be seen that during the period of the first parliament in devolved Scotland, the Parliament's European and External Affairs Committee pro-actively sought to engage with EU affairs, although it did experience a number of difficulties in establishing its role. However, unlike European committees in other sub-state parliaments, it did not face the additional difficulty of trying to impose itself upon a pre-existing committee structure, which facilitated the establishment of relations with the subject committees. It demonstrated a willingness to be flexible by continually revising and adapting its working procedures to better deal with its enormous workload. As the Committee gained in experience, it demonstrated a growing ability to focus on highly specific policy issues. Although it struggled to make a substantive impact on Executive positions during these early years, its potential to do so was recognised both in the Parliament and in the Executive. Its approach suggested that the Scottish Parliament, not least through the activities of the Committee, was one of the most pro-actively engaged sub-state parliaments anywhere in the EU.

Summary

The principal hypothesis proposed in this study suggests that the growing overlap between EU and domestic politics will be acknowledged by the involvement of the new devolved authorities in domestic EU policy formulation in the UK. The evidence presented here demonstrates the involvement of both Scottish Executive and Parliament in EU affairs. On the part of the Executive, it demonstrates involvement at both ministerial and official levels in the formulation of the UK line and its presentation at the negotiating table in the EU arena across a range of policy areas.

Not only does this demonstrate their involvement, it also belies the argument that "regional" engagement in European affairs is a spin-off of Structural Fund reforms. Although the Structural Funds remained an important area of policy for Scottish involvement in EU affairs, it was clearly not the only area of engagement when the evidence is examined. However, this did not prevent comments from other political parties that the Executive is principally interested in, and motivated by, funding opportunities (Interview, 2000).

With regard to the possible sources of tension between the central government and the devolved institutions in Scotland and Wales, Table 4.1 presents a summary of the findings.

Table 4.1: Potential and Actual Areas of Tension between UK Central Government and the Devolved Scottish Authorities

Multi-level governance – general	Pre-devolution UK	Post-devolution Scotland
Exclusion	Exclusion	Not in first term
Information flow	Information flow/ importance of the civil service	Not in first term. Civil service crucial to maintaining good working relations.
Loss of competences	–	Not in first term
Exclusion of parliament/ sub-state dominance	-	Yes
–	Confidentiality/lack of transparency	Yes – between Scottish Executive and Scottish Parliament, not between executives
–	Party politics	Yes

On the first point, it is clear that there was no systematic exclusion of the devolved administrations from EU policy formulation with the recognition that their exclusion was not feasible. There was no clear evidence during the early years of devolution that the overlap between EU and domestic politics encouraged the Scottish Executive to challenge the UK Government for improved access to EU policy-making. Rather, the main demands related to changing the manner in which the Scottish budget is funded and formulated, an internal UK issue, and they emanated not from the Labour-led Executive, but from other party, academic and media sources (*The Scotsman*, 21 May 2001). The UK Government conceded quite an extensive range of participatory rights for the SE to make use of, including the establishment of a representative office in Brussels, and involvement in Minecor, although these rights have no legal basis and Minecor was subsequently abolished and its functions subsumed into the work of JMC(E).

Thus there were no important challenges direct to the UK central government. However, the SE did become involved with RegLeg, the grouping of "constitutional regions". This group sought more explicit recognition of the role of sub-state authorities in the EU legislative process – a move which could be interpreted as a challenge to all Member State central governments. Through this framework, the Labour-Lib Dem SE gradually began to speak out more on the future development of the EU and the role of sub-state authorities within it.

The first initiative to engage with the broader sub-state agenda came when First Minister Jack McConnell gave evidence at a consultation hearing for the Commission's Governance White Paper (SE0685/2001, 16 March 2001) and submitted a joint Executive/COSLA paper to the Commission. The Executive then engaged with the Flemish initiative which resulted in the formation of RegLeg and the publication of the Flanders Declaration. RegLeg was intended to provide an opportunity for some of the EU's "strong regions" to discuss a joint sub-state approach to the topics to be discussed by the Convention on the Future of Europe and the subsequent 2004 Inter-Governmental Conference.

The Flanders Declaration was published on 28 May 2001 and was entitled "Reinforcing the role of the constitutional regions in Brussels". The declaration was officially submitted to the Belgian Prime Minister, with Belgium holding the presidency of the EU in the second half of 2001. The demands it contained were designed principally as a means of gaining firmer recognition, and the clear application, of the principle of subsidiarity and to achieve a clearer division of competences between the EU, Member State and sub-state levels. It also demanded a greater role for the "regions" in the actual EU legislative process.

According to press reports the Scottish Executive claimed that the declaration was signed with the knowledge, and approval, of then Foreign Minister Robin Cook and there were no immediate public signs of discontent from the UK central government. However, given the party political significance of the issue of representation, the SNP seized on the declaration as a sign of growing divisions between London and Edinburgh (*BBC News*, 30 May 2001).

Two related events did provoke short-term specific friction over the issue of Scottish representation in Europe. The first was the failure of the then First Minister Henry McLeish to notify the Parliament of the declaration he had signed in Scotland's name, leading him to issue an apology to the Convenor of the European and External Affairs Committee (*The Scotsman*, 22 June 2001). This could be taken as an indication of the potential of the parliamentary committees in their scrutiny work of the Executive. Further criticism came from the SNP when the First Minister refused to participate in a parliamentary debate called by the party to examine the Flanders Declaration (*Ibid.*). Meanwhile, SNP MPs in Westminster challenged the new Foreign Secretary, Jack Straw, to back the declaration as signed by Mr McLeish. Again, this provides evidence of the tension introduced by the party political dimension and also of SNP attempts to open up a division between the Scottish Executive and a recently re-shuffled Labour UK Government.

The second event which arose, creating another short-term tension between the SE and the UK Government was a Belgian proposal to examine the balance of powers between the EU, Member States and the constitutional regions (CEU 7/2001, 27 June 2001) which was strongly supported by the region of Flanders. Engagement with the constitutional regions was part of the Belgian Presidency's priorities list for the declaration of the Laeken European Council in December 2001, a declaration that was intended to set the agenda for the debate of the Convention on the Future of Europe. The media reported that central government resistance to these proposals had forced First Minister McLeish to distance the SE from them (*The Scotsman*, 22 June 2001).

This party political allegation of growing central government unease over Scotland's representation in the EU followed on from a growing Executive use of multilateral horizontal coalitions to take a stance on the future development of the EU. As with the German *Länder*, this type of trans-national coalition appeared to be used as a way of speaking out on major "EU-shaping" issues. However, these over-arching issues are reserved and the SE has no policy competence over the future direction of European integration. Thus the SE appeared to be looking for other mechanisms as a way of making its voice heard.

Subsequently, however, a significant Scottish, and Welsh, attempt to engage with the debate on the future of the EU was made through the UK Government, with the Joint Submission of the UK Government *and* the devolved administrations to the Convention (European Convention, 2003). Such a joint submission, which had been largely formulated by the devolved administrations and discussed through the forum of JMC(E), was extremely rare and indeed, a German *Land* official suggested that the *Länder* were almost jealous of the opportunity for the Scottish and Welsh administrations to present such a submission (Interview, 2003). The paper endorsed some key regional demands, even opening up the radical possibility that the "early warning system", designed to engage Member State parliaments in monitoring the application of the principle of subsidiarity, could be extended to the SP and NAW.

Subsequent developments in the Convention and the IGC failed to anchor an enhanced role for sub-state authorities in EU policy-making. Neither of these two arenas focused in great depth upon the question of sub-state engagement with the EU policy process and, even if the Constitutional Treaty had been ratified and come into force, no significant changes to the opportunity structure for sub-state authorities would have been made. What is perhaps most interesting from the UK perspective is that whilst initial attempts by the SE in particular to engage with the debate through horizontal mechanisms appeared to cause some friction between Scottish and UK levels, there appears to have been a subsequent attempt by the UK Government to provide a channel of access where a previously agreed submission was presented.

With regard to the flow of information, the fact that the existing policy process was extended to incorporate the SE demonstrated that the flow of information between the central government and the Executive was not cut off. In this regard, the role of the civil service can be considered crucial to the management of intra-UK inter-governmental relations during the first four, and indeed eight, years of devolution, during which time there were very few instances of *public* dispute between devolved and central government levels.

The third issue raised here is the transfer of policy competences from the Member States to the EU level. There was no suggestion of this emerging as an area of tension between the central and Scottish tiers in the UK during the period of research. This stems partly from the fact that the EU already held an extensive range of competences by the time of devolution, a situation which had to be accepted by the devolved administrations. The contributions of the constitutional regions to the debate on the future of European governance aimed to address issues relating to the distribution of competences. However, subsequent developments in this debate failed to affect the relationship between the Scottish and UK levels with regard to this matter, although this does not preclude future tensions in this respect.

With regard to the potential exclusion of the Parliament from policy-making and scrutiny, the Parliament, through the European and External Affairs Committee, actively sought engagement in EU-related affairs. The Committee produced reports on European policy issues and called members of the Scottish Executive and their officials before it to answer questions on Scotland's role in the UK's policy formulation process, as well as the introduction of pre- and post-Council scrutiny of the Executive. A very specific area of friction was created between the Scottish Parliament and central government over the refusal of central government ministers and officials to appear before the Committee or release sufficient information for them to be able to pursue their inquiries, leading to the closure of the inquiry into additionality and matched funding.

The resistance of the UK Government to the submission of information to the Scottish Parliament relates to the fifth broad area of tension highlighted here – the issues of confidentiality and transparency. The Executive was not openly excluded from EU policy formulation, but was challenged by the Parliament over the transparency of its involvement. It thus appears that the tensions over involvement in EU policy-making that emerged emanated from the Parliament, which targeted not just the UK Government but also the SE, rather than between the executives. Many of the tensions between the Parliament and the executives had, as a background, the UK's party political tradition of adversarialism. Labour domination of the two executives during the first eight years meant that the only way for opposition parties to challenge this dominance and seek political advantage was through the Parliament and by rousing public opinion. This was particularly noticeable in the issue raised by the SNP over the perceived lack of high-profile Scottish representation in European negotiations.

So far, this study has considered the question of Scottish participation in EU policy affairs, and has shown that despite the fact that considerable areas of potential tension exist, the participation of the SE appeared to run smoothly and relationships between central government and the Executive were generally good during the time period under consideration. The following chapter will examine the experiences of the National Assembly for Wales during the same time period and consider whether relationships between central government, the Welsh Assembly Government and the Assembly have developed in a similar manner.

CHAPTER 5

A View from Cardiff

Introduction

This chapter focuses on the Welsh experience of engagement in the UK's EU policy formulation process under devolution. The original status of the National Assembly for Wales as a corporate body meant there were considerable structural differences between the Scottish and Welsh devolved institutions. The chapter begins by considering the involvement of the Welsh Assembly Government, originally designated as the Assembly Cabinet but referred to here as WAG, and officials in the policy formulation process, before considering the role and contributions of both the plenary Assembly and its European and External Affairs Committee. Under the Government of Wales Act 1998, there was no legal separation between Cabinet and Assembly. The Assembly, and its committees, were not initially designed to scrutinise the activities of the Cabinet. Rather the legislative and executive functions were combined in a single body, an arrangement that created friction between the different roles (Osmond, 2000: 37-39) and an effective division rapidly emerged between the two out of both political and operational motivations. Therefore the roles and experience of WAG and of the plenary Assembly will be considered separately.

The Executive Arm: the Welsh Assembly Government and Its Officials

This section will begin by considering the EU-related activities of Cabinet Ministers, before examining the role of the "home" team (the European and External Affairs Division), the "away" team (the Brussels representative office) and the sectoral policy divisions.

After the May 1999 election, Alun Michael, leader of the Welsh Labour Party, which won most seats in the Assembly but without obtaining an overall majority, decided to form a minority administration following the failure of initial exploratory coalition negotiations with the Welsh Liberal Democrats. The Welsh Labour Party was three seats short of an overall majority in the Assembly, holding 28 out of the available

60 seats. However, this decision proved something of a liability as the opposition parties in the Assembly demonstrated a capacity for co-operation in a number of policy areas in order to defeat the Labour executive (Hazell, 2000: 72-77), leading to the eventual formation of a Labour-Liberal Democrat coalition in autumn 2000, which lasted until the 2003 election. In the second devolved election, Labour once again failed to gain an overall majority of seats. However, the nomination of the Presiding Officer from Plaid left Labour with an effective majority of one, enabling the party to attempt to govern alone, which it did until the 2007 Assembly elections.

The Politics of Europe and the Welsh Assembly Government

The scope of competences of the Assembly also created some confusion in policy areas with an EU dimension. The asymmetry of devolution meant that the National Assembly for Wales had no primary legislative competences (see Chapter 3 for details), leading to a number of debates about what the Assembly was legally able to do. A good example of this would be the long-running debate over whether or not the Assembly had the right to make Wales a "GM-free zone". As regulation of GM crops is decided at the EU level, a European dimension was automatically introduced into the debate. In addition, its status as a corporate body led to an extended discussion over the extent to which WAG, when a minority administration, must adopt the line of the Assembly if out-voted by the opposition parties in a plenary debate on a policy issue (*Western Mail*, 3 November 1999). This led opposition parties to accuse the then First Minister, Alun Michael, of ignoring the prevailing views of the Assembly (*Ibid.*; *Western Mail*, 13 December 1999).

As was initially the case in Scotland, no one Cabinet portfolio contained "Europe". The Structural Funds were placed in the Economic Development portfolio, as a consequence of the importance of Objective 1 status for West Wales and the Valleys for 2000-2006. The decision had been taken during the National Assembly Advisory Group (NAAG) discussions that each Cabinet Minister should be aware of, and responsible for, the EU dimension of their respective policy area (Interview, 2000), although this ran counter to the advice of the European Strategy Group which had argued in favour of one Cabinet Minister being allocated responsibility for "Europe" (National Assembly for Wales, 1998: 5).

The first important consequence of this decision was that a large share of the responsibility for co-ordinating the Assembly's approach to the EU lay with the First Minister. The second important consequence of this decision was that the subject committees of the Assembly took on official responsibility for the EU aspects of the policy areas that they cover, leaving the European Affairs Committee with a remit to look at overarching European issues. This Committee was originally chaired by the First Minister of the Assembly but the chair passed to an Assembly Member (AM) in November 2002 when the committee structure was altered as the *de facto* separation between the Assembly and WAG became more entrenched.

From the Welsh perspective, two key portfolios with regard to EU Affairs are those of Economic Development and Rural Affairs. Both of these areas caused major disputes between WAG and the opposition parties during the early years of devolution as the opposition parties used particular policy issues with an EU dimension to launch attacks on the First and Agriculture Ministers. The arguments that arose surrounding them were political, rather than technical, and will be considered in greater detail subsequently. Of interest here is the fact that the two key areas on Wales' EU agenda, the Structural Funds and Agriculture, provoked controversial debate and no-confidence motions against two WAG Ministers during the first twelve months of devolution, demonstrating both the resonance of EU affairs in Welsh political debate and also, as occurred in Scotland, the party political dimension that showed through in policy debates involving the EU.

The Mechanics of Ministerial Involvement

Relations between WAG and the UK government are based on the same overarching Concordats that govern relations between the SE and UK central government. Although the National Assembly was originally designed to operate as a corporate body, the Concordats were established between the Welsh Assembly Government and central government to reassure central government over the operation of the confidentiality principle and to prevent WAG's exclusion from the information flow (Interview, 2000). In particular, UK government concerns related to the possibility of information being accessed by non-governing political parties, in the belief that the UK government's negotiating position in the EU arena could be weakened if information relating to these positions was released into the public domain before EU negotiations had taken place. As well as the uncertainty of UK officials, Assembly officials were also uncertain at the outset as to the extent of information to be made available to members of other political parties. In practice, the principle of confidentiality was maintained during the first four years of the Assembly, although, as pointed out by officials in Whitehall, the potential remained for the information flow to be cut off if the UK Government felt that the confidentiality principle had been breached (Interviews, 2000).

In spite of these concerns on the part of central government, there was no obvious exclusion of Welsh Ministers from the EU policy process, although an initial examination appears to show that their levels of engagement were not as high as those of SE Ministers. As with the Scottish Executive, WAG members attended and spoke at Councils of Ministers as part of the UK delegation, beginning with Christine Gwyther's appearance alongside Nick Brown (then UK Minister) and Ross Finnie (then SE Minister) at an Agriculture Council on 20 March 2000 (*BBC News*, 20 March 2000). Other early examples of this form of participation include Carwyn Jones' attendance at an Agriculture Council on 20 November 2000 (National Assembly press release W001188-Ag, 20 November 2000) and Jane Hutt speaking for the UK at a Health Council discussing nutrition on 14 December 2000 (National Assembly press release W001290-Hlt, 14 December 2000).

In addition to attendance at formal Councils, informal meetings between WAG Ministers and European Commissioners were held, particularly with those Commissioners holding the Agriculture and Regional Policy portfolios, once again demonstrating the importance of these two areas in Welsh politics. There was a belief, amongst officials and observers, that WAG, initially at least, had a narrower agenda with regard to EU affairs than their Scottish counterparts (Interviews, 2000; 2003). To an extent, this concentration upon Structural Funds and Agriculture reflected their position as priorities of the Welsh Office pre-devolution.

Reflecting in 2003, central government officials considered that the Welsh EU agenda had been reactive rather than pro-active, responding to policy developments rather than seeking out issues for engagement. However, there was also recognition that, as intended by devolution, the Welsh were able to set their own policy priorities and that these were considered to be focused in different policy areas to Whitehall's priorities. This latter point does reflect the fact that devolution allowed the Welsh to pursue their own interests and concerns. However, this capacity, under devolution, for WAG to pursue its own specific policy interests was deemed to have a potentially negative impact upon the intensity of WAG engagement with the EU policy formulation, where WAG's priorities differed from those on the EU and UK agendas. It was also suggested that the feeling of the Welsh agenda being more limited than that of the Scottish Executive remained (Interviews, 2003).

As with the SE, there was a lack of clarity surrounding the link between the devolved administrations and the UK Cabinet. WAG is part of the UK's governmental system, but not part of the UK government, and is therefore excluded from the UK Cabinet system. This was circumvented by the pragmatic approach already identified in Chapter 4 – by the attendance of WAG Ministers at Minecor and the JMC(E), through the work of officials and through meetings between UK Cabinet and devolved Ministers (Interview, 2001). Devolved Ministers could be invited to *ad hoc* ministerial groups that are not formally part of the Cabinet committee system when issues are under discussion for which the devolved administrations have responsibilities. There is no reason for their attendance when the functions under discussion are not devolved. Representing Welsh interests in central government on reserved matters is a role of the Secretary of State for Wales. Further evidence of this pragmatic approach was the organisation of occasional *ad hoc* meetings between UK Cabinet and devolved Ministers following Cabinet sub-committee meetings to allow discussion of relevant issues to take place between the two levels of government where these related to devolved functions. A two-way dialogue was therefore able to be sustained, making both levels aware of the other's plans and interests in certain policy areas.

Such evidence thus demonstrates that WAG Ministers were involved in the UK's EU policy formulation process, though with an agenda that was perceived as being narrower than that of the SE. It would also appear that the level of engagement was less than that of their Scottish counterparts, a trend which requires further consideration when examining the role of WAG officials in domestic EU policy-making.

The European and External Affairs Division

The Welsh Office established a European Affairs Division during the 1970s following the entry of the UK into the EEC. The main responsibility of the Division was the implementation of EC/EU regional policy and in particular the Structural Funds. Its other main role was to act as a conduit for information passing between Whitehall departments and policy divisions in the Welsh Office on European issues, in other words, a "post box" role (Interview, 2000).

Post-devolution, responsibility for the management of the Structural Funds programmes 2000-2006 was transferred from the European and External Affairs Division (EEAD) to the Welsh European Funding Office, an executive organisation accountable to the National Assembly. However, EEAD retained responsibility for establishing the Welsh position on Structural Funds policy for the post-2006 period. The transfer of this responsibility necessitated a strategic re-thinking of the role of the Division and it then moved gradually towards focusing on broader strategic issues relating to the EU, for example the implications of the 2004 enlargement for Wales and enhancing the profile of Wales in the EU arena (Interviews, 2000; 2003).

In addition, the EEAD continued its role as a co-ordinator of EU-related activities, although as with its SE counterpart, it was not involved in day-to-day policy formulation. Its early objective was to reduce the extent to which it was called upon to act as a conduit for information and provider of contacts between the different levels of governance and to get WAG policy divisions to take responsibility for dealing with their counterparts in Whitehall and Brussels. In place of the rather large and loose network for contacts initially in place, the EEAD sought to establish key contacts in all WAG divisions with whom it could co-ordinate EU-related issues (Interview, 2000).

The EEAD also promoted a policy of secondment, a move recommended and strongly supported by the Assembly's European and External Affairs Committee. Although it is not true that there was a lack of EU-based experience in Wales, there had been no deliberate policy of promoting secondment to EU institutions to match the one introduced by the Scottish Office during the 1990s. However, the EEAD and the Committee moved to ensure the establishment of a deliberate secondment policy in the first two years of devolution, whilst recognising that the benefits of this policy would not filter through to the policy divisions until two or three years after secondments began (Interviews, 2000).

No ministerial portfolio was directly responsible for EU Affairs. Alun Michael, whilst First Minister, explicitly took responsibility for co-ordinating EU issues and chaired the Assembly's European Affairs committee. He was supported by the Minister for Economic Development who held responsibility for the Structural Funds programme. This situation further intensified under First Minister Rhodri Morgan between February and October 2000, when he temporarily retained his position as Economic Development Minister alongside his new role as First Minister.

One original function of the EEAD, which had no corollary in Scotland, was that of providing support to the European Affairs Committee. Although this added to the workload of the Division, who were involved in preparing briefing papers commissioned through the Committee clerking team, it enabled WAG, through its officials, to exert control over the agenda of the Committee. It also created an unusual situation for the officials involved, in that civil servants traditionally work only for the governing party (or parties). In the case of the National Assembly, however, officials produced papers to which opposition parties had access, requiring the establishment of new guidelines for the handling of information in the drawing up of committee briefing papers (Interview, 2000). This situation directly contributed to the heavy emphasis placed upon the need to respect the principle of confidentiality. However, as the unofficial division between the work of WAG and the Assembly concretised, and WAG Ministers ceded their roles as Committee chairs, this role was removed from the workload of WAG officials, creating a more familiar situation for dealing with Assembly committees and the opposition parties.

The main contacts for EEAD in the UK central government are the Cabinet Office and UKRep. Officials have the right to attend the regular Friday morning meetings, named after the current Ambassador to the EU and the head of the Cabinet Office European Secretariat, though they do not attend all. Nevertheless, an official from WAG always attended for discussion of issues most relevant to Wales (Interview, 2000). As with the Scottish experience, relations with central government departments were generally evaluated in positive terms, particularly links with the FCO, which were described as "very good", and with UKRep, relations which were underpinned during the first four years by what was openly acknowledged as a large element of trust (Interviews, 2000; 2003).

One dispute that did arise between WAG and a government department was with the then DETR over the proposed nomination, through the Assembly, of Welsh members of the UK delegation to the Congress of Local and Regional Authorities (CLRAE), the regional body of the Council of Europe. However, as was generally the case with this type of dispute, it did not reach the public arena. Instead it was resolved in private discussions between the two levels of government.

In general, EEAD carried out similar functions to its SE counterpart once its Committee-related work had been removed. Initially it did not have responsibility for horizontal relations with other regions, as these were handled by the International Relations Unit until 2001, when the two divisions merged. However, even following the merger, it was widely acknowledged that there were a much smaller number of personnel within WAG directly discussing EU issues than was the case in Scotland.

Despite similarities in the "at home" roles, in Brussels the Assembly and WAG initially established operations along very different lines to the model adopted by the SE.

National Assembly for Wales Office in Brussels

The National Assembly Office in Brussels was initially established on a much smaller scale than the Scottish Executive EU Office. It consisted of two members of staff – one main representative and one providing back-up support. Unlike the Scottish Executive Office, which opened on 1 July 1999, the Assembly Office did not open until September 2000, even though representation in Brussels was considered very important and the main representative in Brussels held a key position in maintaining relations between the Welsh and EU levels of governance (Interviews, 2000). Reflecting the trend towards *de facto* division between WAG and the plenary Assembly, the representative office effectively worked for WAG (Interview, 2000). However, the main representative was also originally co-opted onto the Assembly's European Affairs Committee.

The National Assembly, as a corporate body, also joined the Wales European Centre (WEC), a lobbying organisation that, until its closure in 2004, a closure precipitated by the withdrawal of the Assembly and the Welsh Local Government Association, represented both public and private sector members in Brussels. The two offices were co-located but Assembly membership of WEC brought the two closer than was the case with the SE Office and Scotland Europa, even though those two offices were also co-located.

As a consequence of its initial staffing levels, the Assembly Office originally operated in a very different manner from the SE Executive Office. There were no desk officers covering specific policy areas, rather the main representative sought to establish links between relevant European Commission and WAG officials in policy areas of importance to the Assembly. Its main links with officials outside EEAD related to this area of its activity. The objectives of the office were originally threefold – to maximise the advantage to Wales in terms of identifying funding opportunities, to seek to influence policy decisions made at the European level which impact upon Wales and to raise Wales' profile in the EU (Interview, 2000).

By spring 2003, the Welsh Assembly Government's approach to the role and structure of its Brussels office had changed. A decision was taken to recruit six policy officers, one to handle the business of each key policy division. Recruitment was open to external candidates as well as staff being provided through the policy of secondment. This move was considered to represent a major strengthening of the Brussels office with the provision of dedicated policy desk officers, rather than one principal representative trying to handle all EU business (Interview, 2003). This suggested a strategic rethink of the handling of EU affairs, given the dedication of resources that such an extension of the office required. This strengthening followed WAG's May 2002 decision to hand in its twelve-month notice to the Wales European Centre, a decision that precipitated some controversy, as it was initially taken without consultation of the plenary Assembly. WAG thus moved from its "twin-track" approach to representation to one larger and better-resourced Office in Brussels (Moore, 2006).

In terms of benefiting from funding opportunities available at the EU level, Welsh Office officials had always been highly active. However, the new EU Office began from a much lower starting point with regard to seeking to influence policy decisions which impact upon Wales, as much less work had been done in this area in the past (Interview, 2000). This demonstrated the historical importance of European funding to Wales, but also shows that funding opportunities are not the only motivation for the increasing levels of activity of sub-state authorities in the EU.

Like the Scottish Executive EU Office, the Assembly Office found UKRep helpful, and WAG officials were generally very positive about UKRep's level of engagement with the devolved administrations. In the Welsh case, there was a tradition of good relations with UKRep in the field of Structural Funds – a Welsh Office official had been an UKRep desk officer for the Structural Funds for a period during the 1990s. The original sole Assembly representative was an accredited diplomat who worked closely with UKRep and had full use of the facilities at the UKRep premises, as well as the opportunity to attend UKRep meetings of relevance to Welsh concerns (Interview, 2000).

The representative office also had a good relationship with counterparts in the SE Office. Originally it was felt that the Scots had a broader agenda as a consequence of the wider range of powers devolved to the Scottish Parliament and had therefore adopted a different model, i.e. nominating desk officers, to enable them to pursue their objectives (Interviews, 2000). The SE officials in Brussels were also helpful on a practical level when the EEAD was in the process of establishing the office in Brussels, to the extent of providing advice on potentially suitable premises they had already looked at. However, as Welsh priorities and the Welsh Assembly Government's approach to the role of the Brussels Office changed, the Welsh representative office began to more closely resemble the model of its Scottish counterpart.

A problem for the Office, and for the "home" team in EEAD was the fact that there was no Assembly representative in Brussels right at the outset of devolution. Much discussion took place in the Assembly about what type of representation was required and, once this had been decided, about the model of office to be established. A particular difficulty was convincing the then First Minister of the benefits of a representative office connected to UKRep in addition to the proposed membership of WEC (Interview, 2000). By the time such issues had been resolved, and the groundwork for the establishment of the office was underway, nearly a year had passed since the official transfer of powers to the devolved institutions.

To a certain extent, this meant the representative office was able to benefit from following in the footsteps of the Scots. However, it also meant that the Scots had a higher profile in Brussels from the outset. What was initially different in the Welsh case was that the whole Assembly was represented in Brussels as a result of its membership of the WEC. However, the *de facto* separation between the Assembly and WAG and WAG's withdrawal from the WEC meant that the office developed into what was clearly an executive office, reporting back to the Welsh Assembly Government.

The other principal difficulty that originally confronted the Assembly Office was the fact that in its original form it could only play a liaison role, being unable to cover policy areas in the same was as the SE desk officers. This made the nature of its relationship with UKRep even more important, given the consequent reliance on desk officers there for specific policy information. The Assembly Office and officials in Cardiff therefore benefited from UKRep's perceived positive attitude towards devolution and the acknowledgement of UKRep as a resource for all parts of the UK. Again, subsequent changes to the structure of the Brussels Office strengthened the capacity of the Office to engage more thoroughly with policy issues.

Policy Divisions

Chapters 2 and 4 have demonstrated the importance of sectoral policy departments in the UK's domestic EU policy formulation process. Consideration of the Scottish experience also demonstrated that these relationships post-devolution tended to rely on bilateral inter-personal links between civil servants, with very little recourse to the formal consultation mechanisms laid out in the Concordats. The nature and extent of connections varied across the Scottish sectoral departments, sometimes reflecting the level of involvement of the territorial office in that policy area prior to devolution, or reflecting the nature and attitude of inter-personal relationships.

Levels of contact between the devolved administrations also vary widely, depending upon the issue under discussion and its salience in different areas of the UK. For example, there is little contact between the Assembly's Agricultural Division and SEERAD on fisheries because the fishing industry is less significant in Wales (Interview, 2000). However, the Welsh are much more likely to be involved on other agricultural issues, for example hill farming, which are of major importance in the territory (Interview, 2003).

The situation which existed in Wales during the first four years of devolution demonstrated, to a large extent, a continuation of the system for territorial involvement which existed prior to devolution taking place. It has been suggested that the policy divisions of the Welsh Office, now the divisions of the Welsh Assembly Government, had, in the past, demonstrated a tendency not to focus upon the EU dimension of the policy areas they cover, but had been content to follow Whitehall's lead on most EU policy issues. However, there seems to have been a growing realisation that it was up to the policy divisions to influence Whitehall's policy positions through negotiation with their Whitehall counterparts (Interview, 2000). The realisation of the importance of the "Brussels angle" could be seen in the changes made to the EU Office and the introduction of the secondment policy.

Relations between WAG officials and Whitehall departments were aided by the deliberate decision that was taken not to split up the UK civil service. The possibility does exist for this situation to cause friction between the two levels, because WAG officials may be accountable to different political masters than Whitehall civil servants. However, in the first four years of devolution it proved beneficial for devolved officials because they remain tied to the same code of conduct as Whitehall officials. This helped to reassure Whitehall officials that principles such as confidentiality would be respected by their Welsh counterparts (Interviews, 2000; 2003).

As mentioned previously, a shift of emphasis away from EEAD co-ordinating relations with Whitehall and Brussels towards policy divisions taking responsibility for the EU dimension of policy areas was encouraged, with EEAD seeking to create a tight network of contacts across the policy divisions. However, after twelve months of devolution, this had proved a slower process than originally expected. Nevertheless, it was noticeable that the old system of reliance upon EEAD to act as a "post box" and Whitehall for policy leads began to change during this twelve month period, as those divisions with less good links to their Whitehall counterparts increasingly realised the need to develop EU expertise (Interview, 2000), a development that continued subsequently.

With regard to the type of contacts that existed between the two levels, there were, as could be expected, many similarities with the Scottish experience. There was a reliance upon informal channels for input into policy formulation, thus once again the level of engagement could be heavily reliant upon the quality of inter-personal relationships, as recognised in interviews with officials. Some divisions, such as agriculture, had good links with their counterparts which dated back to the situation which existed prior to devolution taking place.

It was also recognised that there is a need for a two-way effort to be made in order for relations between the two levels to be managed smoothly (Interview, 2001). One official noted that there was an acknowledgement from "London" of the need for effective working relationships given the EU agenda, particularly in the area of agriculture (Interview, 2003). In this field, monthly meetings between ministers took place, usually one week before the Council of the EU meeting. These were preceded by a meeting of senior officials. The importance of working relationships was again noted in that Welsh officials had confidence in their relationship with MAFF/DEFRA, and UKRep, and their confidence in return that Welsh dealings with the European Commission were conducted within the UK framework.

As noted previously, there was a feeling that some Whitehall departments had a greater awareness of the new circumstances created by devolution than others. However, no JMC, for EU affairs or otherwise, was instigated to deal with a major public dispute between the two levels. Devolution means that WAG and its officials are now politically separate and could therefore go public in the case of a disagreement. Although tensions in the relationship that emerged in public did not relate specifically to EU issues, frictions were evident concerning domestic policy lines. The then Deputy Minister for Local Government, Peter Law AM, referring to discussions over the Local Government Bill in 2000, commented that:

> There are some difficulties with DETR. They sometimes seem to feel that devolution is below their radar screens. (*Western Mail*, 12 May 2000)

This was, however, a rare example of friction between the different levels of government boiling over into the public arena. Another obvious example, also involving DETR, was DETR's approval of GM trials in Flintshire, in the apparent belief that the land in question was in England, and its subsequent refusal to back down despite the Assembly's commitment to a "GM-free" Wales. Whilst anecdotal evidence of other frictions is available, for the most part these were not played out in public, unlike in other federal and regionalised EU Member States.

In spite of the presence of such frictions, there was an awareness that it was not solely down to Whitehall officials to demonstrate their awareness of the new circumstances of devolution. If WAG wished to engage with the UK's EU policy formulation processes, its officials could not be passive if they wanted to influence the UK's EU policy lines. They also needed to make an effort to engage with Whitehall and not just continually be seen to shift the blame towards central government if Wales' needs were perceived as not being taken into account (Interviews, 2000; 2001).

The workload of Welsh officials increased dramatically as a consequence of devolution. As well as being increasingly involved in policy formulation, officials have to prepare ministerial statements and answers for Assembly questions, although unlike Scottish officials, they were not engaged in the drafting of primary legislation. The number of Welsh officials also remained quite small, far fewer than in Scotland. The size of the body of officials, combined with workload, contributed to a perception that pre-dated devolution, namely that Welsh officials were often happy to follow the UK line in most areas, with the principal exceptions, according to a number of interviews, being Agriculture and the Structural Funds programmes. At the outset, Welsh policy divisions appeared more reliant upon their central government counterparts than their Scottish counterparts were. However, this could be interpreted as a reflection of the asymmetry of devolution, which left the Assembly more dependent upon the UK Government's legislative programme, and not just a reflection of a less pro-active engagement in the EU policy-making process.

One of the most challenging aspects of the relationship with central government at the outset was the Assembly's status as a corporate body. This created a new situation for both politicians and officials, and required a new relationship between civil servants and members of non-governing parties, given the status of the Assembly and officials' early role in servicing Assembly committees. Civil servants are traditionally only used to sharing information with the governing party (or parties), which meant new guidelines needed to be agreed with central government as to how relationships with non-governing parties should be managed (Interview, 2000). However, with the development of the *de facto* division between the Assembly and WAG and changes to the committee structure, this role confusion was subsequently minimised. The 2006 Government of Wales Act subsequently gave this separation of roles legal standing.

Perhaps unsurprisingly, relationships between central government and Assembly officials functioned best at the higher levels of office, where a better understanding of each others' roles existed. Relationships between the devolved and central government levels could be affected by a lack of awareness of each others' roles at lower grades within policy divisions, both within Whitehall and in Cardiff (Interview, 2001). It was also remarked that central government officials' attitudes were shaped by the attitude of Ministers towards devolution. As noted in Chapter 4, some UK Ministers were inevitably more sympathetic towards the concept of devolution than others, and ministerial opinions were considered capable of affecting departmental attitudes towards the devolved authorities in either a positive or a negative manner (Interview, 2000).

Another issue with implications for the management of relationships between the central government and the Assembly level was the lack of specifically developed EU policy expertise amongst Welsh officials. During the 1990s the Scottish Office developed a specific policy of organising secondments to UKRep and the EU institutions in order to create a body of officials with experience of the EU policy process. Although there were, in the early years of devolution, officials working for the Assembly with EU expertise, there had been no systematic policy of secondment under the Welsh Office.

Once the secondment policy was put in place, there was reported enthusiasm amongst Welsh officials to pursue this career option. However, the process of matching officials with secondment opportunities was only put in place after the first year of devolution had passed. It therefore took several years before the results of the move could be felt across WAG policy divisions and a larger body of officials with EU experience and contacts began to emerge.

As suggested above, in the first term of devolution there were few public disagreements between the central government and WAG, although this was not the case between the plenary Assembly and central government, as will be demonstrated later. Again the Concordats were viewed as a "fall-back mechanism" or as general guidelines which were useful to refer back to should problems in communication arise (Interview, 2000). WAG Ministers and officials adhered strictly to the principle of confidentiality, facilitating the management of relations between the two levels, and giving Whitehall civil servants the opportunity to build up their trust in the reliability of their Welsh colleagues, enabling the flow of information to be maintained. However, officials also acknowledged a certain onus upon the devolved administration(s) to safeguard information.

However, and as with Scotland, there remained several potential areas of friction contained within the system. Firstly, this issue of confidentiality remained a key concern in the relationship between WAG and central government. Although its necessity was evident to WAG Ministers and their central government counterparts, it can be, and was, interpreted as a lack of transparency by those external to the relationship. Any breach of the principle of confidentiality could cause problems in the flow of information from central government to WAG. Thus this issue is capable of creating two different sets of tensions, one between the levels of government, and one within the plenary Assembly.

The issue of representation in UK delegations to Brussels has been less salient in Wales than in Scotland where it has been exploited by the Scottish National Party, although it was apparently raised by the Welsh First Minister during the JMC meeting on 1 March 2001. Should the issue emerge as a tension, it is more likely to be between the Assembly as a whole and central government, rather than between WAG and central government for as long as the two levels of government remain Labour-dominated. In case of governmental incongruence, the issue of "participation by invitation" can be expected to become increasingly salient.

Another potential area of friction identified arises from the asymmetrical system of devolution established in the UK. The Spanish experience with asymmetrical decentralisation has demonstrated that those "regions" with weaker levels of competence are likely to demand extra powers, a situation that was reflected in Wales. Demands emanated from Plaid Cymru and the Welsh Liberal Democrats to grant the National Assembly the same competences as the Scottish Parliament.

This apparent lack of stability in the devolution process was reflected in the Assembly Government's establishment of the Richard Commission to examine the question of further devolution to Wales. The Commission was established by Rhodri Morgan towards the end of devolution's first term, and reported in spring 2004. The establishment of the Commission to investigate this question suggests that dynamics for further change were developing, dynamics that were reflected in the passing of a new Government of Wales Act in 2006. This second Act actually contains the possibility of holding a referendum on primary legislative powers for Wales, suggesting that devolution to Wales has yet to reach its final form. The existence of this prospect is likely to occasion continued demands for further devolution to take place, until such a referendum is actually held.

Although there were few public rows between WAG and central government, one area where there was disagreement was over the exact limits of the Assembly's power. One example of this was over the planting of GM seed in Wales after the Assembly had passed a motion banning the growing of GM crops in Wales only to discover that such a trial was already going ahead in Flintshire, as highlighted above. The ensuing debate over whether the Assembly was legally able to ban the growing of GM crops demonstrated the lack of clarity that existed over both the extent of the Assembly's competences and the extent to which motions agreed by the Assembly must be observed by both WAG and the UK Government. This contributed to demands for a clearer separation of competences between the Welsh and UK levels such as that which exists under devolution to Scotland.

One issue that emerged clearly in interviews with relation to Wales, which was not mentioned as frequently in Scotland, was the additional workload created by devolution. There was some concern that the increased workload of officials may lead to more staff being taken on who were unfamiliar with dealing with Whitehall and that this thereby risked a potential increase in the number of misunderstandings or ignorance of the need to abide by the same principles as Whitehall civil servants. In particular there was concern that a lack of awareness of the right procedures to go through to achieve the desired results could have a negative impact upon the levels of trust which had emerged as crucial in the relationships between devolved departments and their Whitehall counterparts (Interview, 2001).

To some observers, WAG Ministers and officials sometimes appeared to be less involved in the formulation of the UK's EU policy process than their Scottish counterparts (Interview, 2000). Writing in 2001, Sir John Gray, a former UK Permanent Representative to the EU, observed that some believed that there was actually less contact between Welsh and Whitehall officials on EU issues than had been the case prior to devolution. This lower level of engagement, he argued, seemed to stem from three factors in particular: the attitude of the Welsh Office towards EU policy-making prior to devolution, the asymmetry of devolution and an apparent lack of resources given the increased workload (Gray, 2001: 38).

Nevertheless, there was evidence of engagement in the EU policy formulation process and a recognition of the need to be able to demonstrate that officials were aware of, and engaged with, EU issues. This was particularly the case with agricultural issues, where connections between the Welsh policy division and their central government counterparts were already considered strong. It was also the case for Structural Funds issues. Welsh engagement on this particular issue was high because of the Objective 1 status of large parts of Wales. This issue also proved to be one of the most controversial areas in the relationship between the central government and Assembly levels, notably the question of matched funding. Policy matters with an EU dimension, including matched funding, were widely debated by the plenary Assembly after it first convened in 1999, and provided further evidence of tensions within the devolved system.

The National Assembly for Wales Plenary

The National Assembly for Wales contained 60 Assembly Members (AMs) at its inception. Its status as a corporate body, combined with its lack of primary legislative power, had implications for the operation of the Assembly and its handling of EU-related business. During the Assembly's early years, the debate on EU issues was dominated by discussion of Structural Funds issues, both the effective use and distribution of the funding gained, particularly under the Objective 1 Programme for West Wales and the Valleys, and ensuring that sufficient matched funding was gained from the UK Treasury for the programme. The second most important policy area with an EU dimension was agriculture, further confirmation of the key importance of these two policy areas in Wales.

This was reflected in written and oral questions asked in the plenary during the first term. Questions focused on Objective 1 funding, and more specifically on the question of matched funding. Many questions asked concerning agriculture and rural affairs also had an EU dimension. Far fewer questions were asked about issues such as attendance in the Council of Ministers (Council of the European Union), relations with UKRep and relations with the European Commission. Further examination of the Official Record of the National Assembly reveals that a similar pattern emerges when considering oral questions asked and oral questions submitted but not reached during plenary. Unlike in Scotland, the question of high-profile representation in the European Union was a less salient issue in the National Assembly, clearly being superseded by the issue of Objective 1 and matched funding.

In terms of plenary debate, issues with an EU dimension appeared more frequently on the agenda in the National Assembly than in the Scottish Parliament during the first term of devolution. One of the earliest short debates held in the Assembly was entitled "A Strong Welsh Voice in Europe", debated on 8 June 1999. Other similar short debates and minority party debates followed. Again, though, most of these debates related to Structural Funds issues rather than dealing with the question of the role and position of Wales within the EU and how WAG seeks to influence the UK's EU policy positions. This also applied to ministerial statements made to the Assembly and to motions moved by WAG Ministers.

The first minority administration proved precarious, soon discovering that opposition parties were willing to put aside their differences to take the Labour administration to task. The fact that the minority administration could be out-voted by the opposition parties acting in concert created difficulties regarding the extent to which WAG was required to heed motions passed by the plenary Assembly. This led to the accusation, highlighted above, that WAG was "ignoring" majority Assembly views (*Western Mail*, 3 November 1999; *Western Mail*, 13 December 1999) and continuing with its own line even though this had been voted down by the opposition.

EU issues presented the opposition parties in the Assembly with some of their best opportunities for attacking the first Labour administration. Both the then First Minister Alun Michael and his Agriculture Minister, Christine Gwyther, who had been an unpopular choice with the opposition parties, were subject to no-confidence motions ostensibly based on EU issues, although in both cases there were more general causes of dissatisfaction amongst opposition politicians.

Christine Gwyther was subject to no-confidence motions on 19 October 1999 and 17 May 2000. The first of these motions related specifically to WAG's ability to negotiate with the European Commission on Wales' behalf, whilst the second was a result of the uncertainty surrounding the Assembly's attempted ban on the planting of GM seed in Wales. With regard to the first motion, the National Assembly had voted in favour of continuing a calf-processing aid scheme which was rejected by the European Commission as a distortion of competition. However, the opposition parties argued that they had been misled by Ms Gwyther about the potential opposition from the Commission to such a scheme. Nick Bourne, Conservative AM, also berated the Agriculture Minister for only spending half an hour discussing the issue with then Agriculture Commissioner Franz Fischler during a one hour meeting:

> Half an hour to represent Welsh interests on a central matter that had the support of the whole Assembly. That was insufficient. We need somebody to provide a strong, robust voice for Wales. (National Assembly for Wales Record of Proceedings, 19 October 1999)

Unfavourable comparisons were also drawn with the actions of Ross Finnie in Scotland who, it was argued, had made no attempt to conceal potential difficulties in the introduction of a ewe-cull scheme (*Ibid.*).

However, there was also a deeper underlying dissatisfaction with First Minister Michael's choice of Gwyther, a vegetarian, to hold the agriculture portfolio during an exceptionally difficult period for both the Welsh and the UK meat industry following the BSE crisis of the mid-1990s. Once again, this underlines the importance of agricultural policy in Wales, but the EU dimension of the policy area is also clearly highlighted by the nature of the issue which brought affairs to a head in this instance. The overlap with the EU policy process resulting from the regulation of the farming industry by the Common Agricultural Policy was clearly demonstrated in both this no-confidence motion and other Assembly debates on the issue.

First Minister Michael's resignation was triggered by a no-confidence motion that was also ostensibly based on an EU policy issue, although reasons for the motion also related to the UK's internal decision-making, rather than explicitly to relations with the European Union. This was the long-running debate over WAG's alleged failure to secure sufficient matched funding from the UK Treasury for the Objective 1 Programme in West Wales and the Valleys.

The opposition parties, particularly Plaid Cymru, argued that Wales would lose out because matched funding for Objective 1 projects would have to be found by re-allocations within the existing Welsh budget, implying that spending cuts would be necessary in areas such as health and education in order to finance spending on Objective 1. It was argued that this would happen rather than matched funding being provided by the UK Treasury as required by the principle of additionality. The Treasury's continued refusal to provide any guarantees of extra funding until after its Comprehensive Spending Review had been completed in July 2000 left Mr Michael in an awkward position, as he could only give assurances that the money would be forthcoming without any apparent concrete proof.

However, the attack on Alun Michael also clearly ranged beyond the issue of Structural Funds and contained elements provoked by resentment of his leadership style, his perceived imposition on Welsh Labour by the UK Labour Party and his alleged inability to stand up for and protect Wales' interests in discussions with the central government. The arguments that raged around Objective 1 funding were political rather than technical, but nevertheless it was an EU-related issue that had provided the opportunity for the opposition parties to attack the governing devolved administration.

These motions of no-confidence also demonstrated the party political dimension apparent within the Assembly. Despite the talk of a "new" politics of inclusivity (Chaney & Fevre, 2001) prior to the establishment of the Assembly, plenary debates proved that the traditions of confrontational politics would take a long time to disappear, if in fact they ever do. As is the case in the Scottish Parliament, the most important cleavage is between the Labour Party and the nationalist grouping. However, Plaid Cymru have, in general, adopted a different approach to that of the SNP which reflects a more evolutionary approach to their objective of autonomy for Wales.

Apart from the debates over agricultural policy and the Structural Funds, other, more general, points of concern emerged from the opposition parties during the first term of devolution. These included concern over the Assembly's status as a corporate body, and particularly this recurrent issue of the extent to which minority administrations had to accept and represent the position of the plenary Assembly if out-voted. After the formation of the Labour-Liberal Democrat coalition in October 2000 this became less significant in the operation of the Assembly, although friction began to re-emerge after the 2003 election result, when the Labour administration initially governed with a majority of one. Following the withdrawal of former Labour AM, Peter Law, from the party in spring 2005, Welsh Labour once again formed a minority administration which, despite a number of challenges and defeats in the Assembly endured until the 2007 Assembly elections.

Another point of concern from the perspective of the opposition parties in the Assembly was the question of confidentiality versus transparency. Michael German AM, leader of the Welsh Liberal Democrats, speaking in the debate following the presentation of the Concordats to the Assembly, remarked:

> The way in which the relationship is to be kept secret and confidential runs counter to the spirit of openness that we are trying to create in this Assembly. (National Assembly for Wales Record of Proceedings, 7 October 1999)

The observance of the principle of confidentiality, as contained in the Concordats, has led to accusations of a lack of transparency and accountability from the opposition parties. They argued that it is impossible to trace the input that Welsh officials and Ministers had into the UK's policy-making processes, including the EU policy process, and that consequently there was no way of holding them accountable for any policy positions presented.

Concerns were also raised by a number of operational difficulties which beset the Assembly's first year in particular, notably several public rows between high ranking civil servants and the Office of the Presiding Officer. The Presiding Officer sought to establish a *de facto* division between the operation of the Assembly and the Cabinet (Welsh Assembly Government) with the consequence that the Assembly was not run as a corporate body. However, the overlap between WAG and Assembly remained an area of sensitivity for policy-making in Wales for the first eight years of devolution, not just for the formulation of EU policy positions, until the legal separation of the two was enacted by the 2006 Government of Wales Act.

The last issue to be mentioned here, whilst not specifically related to the issue of EU policy formulation, also had implications for relations between the National Assembly and central government levels. This was the concern over how much (or little) influence WAG was able to exert, principally via the Wales Office, over the UK Government's legislative agenda for the Westminster Parliament. Again, disquiet was demonstrated over an alleged inability to influence this agenda and have Wales-specific legislation placed upon the Westminster agenda (National Assembly for Wales Official Record, 19 December 2000). This was a further demonstration of the concern over the extent to which WAG is able to influence UK Government policy intentions and positions, whether domestically or at the EU level.

The European and External Affairs Committee

The European and External Affairs Committee of the National Assembly was established with a very different role to that of its Scottish counterpart. Its establishment was recommended by NAAG, although its lack of a scrutiny role led to its purpose being question by the later Standing Orders Commission (Interview, 2000). However, it gained political support from the then Secretary of State for Wales, subsequently First Minister, Alun Michael, in the knowledge that it was politically unwise to be seen to give out a message that the EU was not important or lacked relevance to the operation of the new Assembly.

According to Standing Order 15, the role of the Committee was to:

...keep under review

(i) the Assembly's relations with the institutions of the European Union, and its methods for informing and advising those institutions of the needs of Wales;

(ii) the Assembly's liaison arrangements with UKRep, and with United Kingdom government departments on European issues;

(iii) the Assembly's methods and procedures for the consideration of documents, issues and questions emanating from European institutions, having particular regard to the need for liaison with Members of Parliament responsible for scrutiny of European matters of particular relevance to Wales.

The further terms of the Standing Order make no reference to a scrutiny role, unlike the SP Committee, and the Committee did not, in the first four years, deal with specific policy areas, but is intended to concern itself more generally with overarching EU issues. As with the work of WAG's policy divisions, the subject committees of the Assembly were supposed to handle the EU dimension of their respective policy areas. This approach was recommended by the Advisory Group which argued that every committee should be aware of the impact of the European Union upon their work and that this work should not be duplicated by the European Affairs Committee (Interview, 2000). Standing Order 15 of the National Assembly – Committee on European Affairs specifically states in Section 15.3:

The Committee shall avoid duplicating the work of subject committees but may draw particular issues to the attention of relevant subject committees.

Particularly important with regard to the work of the Committee is the fact that the Structural Funds programme was handled by the Economic Development Committee.

Instead of scrutiny, the European Affairs Committee developed a representational role for itself. As well as Assembly Members, other participants were co-opted onto the first Committee and were able to attend its discussions, although they had no vote. These participants included Welsh MEPs, Welsh members of the Committee of the Regions and Economic and Social Committee, the European Commission's Representative in Wales and the Assembly's chief representative in Brussels. Co-option of members decreased in importance, and eventually halted, as the *de facto* between WAG and the Assembly established itself.

Because it was not involved in legislative scrutiny, the European Affairs Committee did not attempt to fit into the rapid turnaround of the EU's legislative process. It did not meet on a regular basis, partly as a consequence of the problem of finding a time and date suitable for as many of the Assembly Members of the Committee, and at the outset also the co-opted members, as possible (Interview, 2000), but also because its remit allowed it to focus upon longer-term objectives, such as increasing the number of Welsh officials seconded to UKRep and the EU institutions. The Committee's role was considered to be the assessment of the "success" of WAG in dealing with EU and external issues, interpreted as "success" in putting across Wales' "voice".

Officials serving the Committee recognised the practical difficulties inherent in the approach of its Scottish equivalent and acknowledged that the resources were not available to carry out similar tasks in Wales (Interviews, 2000; 2003). The Committee was generally considered to be largely apolitical in the carrying out of its duties, although opposition party members presented complaints about its lack of activity and demanded a more Scottish-style role for the Committee, including the ability to extend invitations to UK civil servants and European Commission officials to hear the Committee's views and:

> to establish formal mechanisms for the Committee to be able to present Wales' views before crucial Councils of Ministers and summit meetings so that the UK delegation is aware of the National Assembly's views. (Plaid Cymru internal paper, 2000)

This issue first emerged in the Committee's March 2000 meeting and was further discussed subsequently. In its first Annual Report, laid before the Assembly in June 2000, no direct recommendations were made to alter the Committee's role. However, the parties were invited to submit views, in response to which Plaid Cymru submitted the position paper quoted above, demanding an enhanced role for the Committee. Such a strengthening of its role did not, however, materialise.

Although the Committee was largely apolitical in its operation, there was resentment from some Committee members over some procedural issues, particularly with the impression being generated that because, unlike its Scottish equivalent, it did not meet frequently, that it did very little (Interview, 2000), neither producing reports nor making policy recommendations. Some of the issues discussed, such as enlargement, are areas on which it is entitled to hold an opinion, but which remain the responsibility of the UK Government.

The lack of a requirement for formal consultation on EU issues also provoked discontent. Although in certain instances the First Minister did write to express the Assembly's collective view on an EU issue to the UK Government, there is no way of judging whether this had any impact upon the central government's approach. Rather the Committee had to focus its attention upon trying to influence the thinking of WAG and bringing it to adopt a position on these over-arching issues.

This situation demonstrated further the conflict between the pragmatism of officials and the expectations of politicians that emerged from the devolution process. The politicians held higher expectations of what the new institutions would be able to do and their potential influence, whereas officials had a greater awareness of the limitations imposed by issues such as available resources and the code of conduct of the UK civil service.

To a certain extent, the Committee benefited at first from the impact of having the First Minister chairing the Committee – if an issue was decided in the Committee, the First Minister is automatically aware of the Committee's opinion. However, this also created problems for the operation of the Committee as it gave WAG/EAD control of the Committee's agenda, an operational feature that was unpopular with the opposition parties. It produced more general concern about the performance of the Committee and the potential negative impact of the First Minister taking on too much work – at least prior to the negotiation of the coalition agreement (*BBC News*, 19 September 2000). It also delayed attempts to set up a trans-UK body of European Committee chairs from both chambers of the Westminster Parliament and the devolved authorities because the Welsh First Minister had a very different working agenda to the other committee chairs (Interview, 2000).

In order for such a closely connected system to function, there was a need for both EEAD and the Committee to be flexible. There was clear potential for friction if either side adopted a very rigid stance on working procedures. However, given the lack of available resources, the Committee may at the time have struggled to function without the support of EEAD officials, unlike the subject committees which are able to "buy in" external expertise (Interviews, 2000). Still, the opportunity that this presented for WAG/EEAD to control which issues appeared on the Committee's agenda and the nature of the papers submitted to the Committee emerged as a point of friction. This situation did not occur in the Scottish Parliament as a result of the constitutional division between Executive and Parliament. In Wales it created the initial difficulties noted previously in establishing the extent of information that could be provided to non-governing parties, as well as providing the opposition parties an opportunity to attack what they saw as a lack of transparency within the decision-making system. As the *de facto* separation between Assembly Government and Assembly became more concrete, the First Minister stepped down from this role as Committee chair in November 2002. This development altered the dynamics of the Committee, although the First Minister continued to attend Committee meetings where he was questioned about his executive's EU and external policies.

The Committee was involved in the negotiations for the Assembly to become a member of the WEC and the establishment of the representation in Brussels, but neither the Committee nor the Assembly plenary were privy to the Welsh Assembly Government's decision to withdraw from the WEC before its announcement. The Committee also played a role in the establishment of a Welsh European Forum which had the aim of providing a discussion forum for interested parties from all sectors to discuss EU issues with implications for Wales. It was also prominent in supporting moves towards a deliberate policy of seconding Welsh officials for work experience in Brussels (Interview, 2000).

Like the members of the SP Committee, members of the Assembly Committee participated in a visit to the EU institutions in Brussels. Several of them already had experience of EU policy-making, but others had no experience at all. Again, this proved a useful experience and the Committee subsequently encouraged the subject committees to undertake similar visits. It was also suggested that each subject committee should nominate one member to follow key EU policy developments in that subject but that proved to be a very slow process which didn't really take hold. Very early on, the Committee also asked every WAG Minister to review their connections to EU policy and present a paper to their respective subject committees for discussion, as a means of raising awareness of the EU dimension of policy areas, particularly on policy issues like education where this had been lacking previously (Interview, 2000).

As with the SP's Committee, there was a sense that the European Affairs Committee of the National Assembly spent the first term searching for its role, leading to the assessment that neither this Committee nor its subject counterparts had particularly "claimed the ground" for dealing with EU legislative proposals. This was clearly demonstrated by party discontent over the role it adopted, the irregularity of its meetings and the apparent lack of concrete output. However, the role and remit of the committee remained fundamentally different to that of the SP European Committee and it did not develop in the same direction.

Summary

Evidence presented in this chapter indicates that the hypothesis that the overlap between EU and devolved competences will lead to the involvement of the devolved administrations in EU policy-making applies in the Welsh case as well as the Scottish one. Nevertheless, the evidence can be difficult to discern with seemingly fewer high-profile attendances at EU meetings than the Scottish Executive. However it is clear that Welsh Ministers attended Councils of Ministers and held informal meetings with European Commissioners, demonstrating their engagement with the EU policy process. They also had the opportunity to contribute to overall UK policy direction with their participation through Minecor (until it was wound up), JMC(E) and the Friday morning meetings which seek to circumvent any difficulties raised by their exclusion from the UK Cabinet system.

Although the involvement of Welsh Ministers and officials can be demonstrated, their agenda was widely considered to be narrower than that of their Scottish counterparts, particularly by officials at the centre, with their main focus perceived to fall upon agriculture and the Structural Funds. However, the fact that agricultural policy is such an important feature of Wales' EU policy interests signifies that purely financial motivations stemming from the Structural Funds programme are not the only cause motivating Welsh engagement with the EU policy process. Taken with the Scottish experience, this demonstrates that further explanation of sub-state mobilisation is required beyond the argument that it was motivated by the 1988 Structural Funds reform and also indicates that the growing policy overlap across numerous policy areas is a significant factor.

The second hypothesis relates to potential and actual sources of friction contained within the devolved system. Evidence from the Scottish experience has already demonstrated that although tensions had not emerged in all of the areas identified, there were tensions emerging from some of these sources (see Table 5.1). The first source of tension, identified primarily from the experience of the German *Länder*, indicates that tension can be created by the exclusion of SSAs from EU policy formulation in areas where they have domestic responsibilities and any subsequent challenges to gain the opportunity to participate. The acknowledgement of the UK Government in the White Papers that such exclusion was not feasible has meant that the issue of exclusion has not emerged as a tension in the UK's post-devolution experience. However, there was some discontent, particularly among opposition parties, about the level of representation of Welsh Ministers in EU meetings and accusations that when they attended such meetings they did not do enough to defend Welsh interests.

There was little evidence of direct challenge from WAG for improved access to EU policy-making during the period of data collection. The issue was apparently raised by First Minister Rhodri Morgan at the first JMC meeting held on European issues on 1 March 2001 and a new course of action to ensure more regular representation at Councils appears to have been agreed, although no record of the meeting was made public. However, there was no sustained challenge or public disagreement surrounding the issue as was the case, for example, in Germany.

Table 5.1: Potential and Actual Areas of Friction Post-Devolution

General	Pre-devolution UK	Post-devolution Scotland	Post-devolution Wales
Exclusion	Exclusion	No	No
Information flow	Information flow/ importance of civil service	Not in first term. Civil service crucial	Not in first term
Loss of competences	-	Not in first term	Not in first term
Exclusion of *Landtage*/executive dominance	Potential for exclusion of SP/NAW	Yes	Yes
-	Confidentiality versus lack of transparency	Yes	Yes
-	Party politics	Yes	Yes
-	-	-	Asymmetry
-	-	-	Structural Funds

As was seen in Scotland, there is a significant party political dimension involved in the relations between the devolved administrations and central government. The Labour Party, widely considered to be a highly centralised political party, was dominant in all the administrations during the first eight years of devolution. This made challenges less likely than if some form of cohabitation, or governmental incongruence, had occurred with different parties in power at different levels in the devolved system. Challenges that emerged in Wales related less directly to the question of access and more often to specific questions such as additionality and matched funding. These challenges also tended to emanate from the plenary Assembly, rather than WAG, again providing evidence of a party political dimension in the tensions emerging at this stage. Party political demands for a greater role have occurred, but not a sustained challenge from WAG to central government.

With regard to exclusion from the flow of information from the UK central government, this did not occur in Wales, despite Whitehall's initial uncertainty over the Assembly's status as a corporate body. However, this remained a potential point of friction and was clearly an area of sensitivity which could be affected by the introduction of governmental incongruence. The formation of the Labour-Liberal Democrat coalition did not appear to have any grave implications for the relatively free information flow.

The fourth point, also identified from sub-state experiences elsewhere, relates to the transfer of sub-state authorities' domestic competences to the EU without consultation. There has been no occurrence of this during the period under investigation. However, it could, in future, create friction if it was to occur without consultation, particularly if there was a party political dimension involved. The implications of such a transfer may, however, affect Wales differently from Scotland as a consequence of the asymmetrical allocation of competences created by the devolution process.

One issue that has clearly created friction was the perceived exclusion of the plenary Assembly, and its European and External Affairs Committee, from the EU policy formulation process and the related dominance of WAG in this area. This is also connected with the fifth area of friction identified, namely the questions of transparency and accountability. Evidence of dissatisfaction with the role of the Committee has been presented, along with evidence of calls for it to take a more pro-active and forceful role in EU-related issues and the representation of Welsh interests. Thus far, the Committee has been less pro-active than its Scottish equivalent. Although the plenary Assembly has been actively engaged in debating EU issues, or Welsh issues with an EU dimension such as the calf processing scheme, it appeared to have little impact, as there was no formal requirement for the plenary Assembly or the Committee to be consulted on EU issues.

The question of confidentiality versus transparency has also proved to be a vexed one for the plenary Assembly. Without the adherence of the Cabinet and its officials to the Whitehall principle of confidentiality, WAG risked effectively being removed from both the flow of information and the EU policy-making process. However, the principle of confidentiality leads opposition parties to argue that they cannot follow the influence or contributions of WAG and its officials to that same policy process.

The background context to the frictions that emerged, as well as the potential sources of friction, was party politics. The evidence from events in the Assembly suggested that the confrontational style of politics continued, despite the intention that a new consensual style of politics would be created post-devolution. This provoked difficulties in the operation of the Assembly until the formation of the Labour-Lib Dem coalition in 2000 ended the awkward position of the minority administration. However, such difficulties resumed when Labour once more formed a minority administration from May 2005 until April 2007.

In addition to the points of friction identified previously, two other sources of tension stood out with regard to the Welsh experience. The first of these was the instability of the asymmetrical system created by devolution, with demands for a greater range of competences, resulting in the establishment of the Richard Commission to inquire into the revision of Wales' devolution arrangements.

The second friction which arose spectacularly in Wales leading to the resignation of the first First Minister, Alun Michael, was the controversy over matched funding and additionality. This issue had several dimensions: central government's (the Treasury's) adherence to its own timetable in spite of the political difficulties of Welsh Labour, the lack of transparency in negotiations between the Assembly Cabinet and Treasury, the Labour central government's "trust us" approach towards the issue and a perceived lack of trust in the then First Minister's leadership skills.

As was the case in Scotland, however, the tensions that emerged appeared in the relationships between the plenary and WAG/central government, rather than between the Welsh and UK administrations. Again this reflects the party political dimension, but it also reflects the executive dominance of the EU policy formulation process. A combination of these two factors provided less incentive for WAG to challenge central government, whereas the lesser role of the Assembly provided the opposition parties with the motivation to challenge both administrations. Thus the pattern of tensions in Wales broadly resembled Scottish experiences, with the addition of one Assembly-specific factor (asymmetry) and one issue-specific factor (the matched funding/additionality controversy).

The next supplementary hypothesis of this study is also related to the question of asymmetry. It argues that asymmetry is likely to result in Welsh attempts to attain the same level of devolved competences as Scotland. There were indeed increasing calls, emanating from outside WAG, for the Assembly to be given a greater range of competences equivalent to those of the Scottish Parliament, as reflected in the establishment of the Richard Commission. The Government of Wales Act 2006 failed to quell this debate. Indeed, by holding out the prospect of a referendum on primary legislative power, it effectively ensured its continuation.

The final hypothesis considered here is the impact of asymmetry and the level of resources available to the different devolved administrations upon the level and nature of their engagement in EU affairs. Different levels of commitment and resources were evident in a number of different aspects of the involvement of the devolved administrations in EU policy-making. For example, the very different models originally adopted in the establishment of representative offices in Brussels demonstrated different levels of resources made available to deal with these issues, decisions which subsequently had an effect upon the way in which the respective representative offices operated. The decision to remodel WAG's office in Brussels and its expansion thus demonstrates a significant commitment of resources to engagement with the EU, reflecting the growing recognition of the EU's importance in policy areas devolved to Wales and also the symbolic nature of being seen to be involved in EU affairs (Jeffery & Palmer, 2003).

Overall, it appears that the level of Welsh engagement was not as high as that of Scottish involvement, nor did it range across so many policy areas in-depth. Although it is not explicitly clear that this is a direct consequence of the asymmetry of devolution and the different level of resources available to the Scottish Executive and the Welsh Assembly Government, these factors may contribute to the explanation. Other factors which may be suggested include the pre-devolution experience of the territorial offices, their preparations for devolution and their level of EU engagement, which enabled the Scots to move forward on these issues more rapidly post-devolution. Questions of identity and self-confidence in that identity, which could be linked to the fourth resource of "legitimacy" identified by Jeffery (2000) may also have a role to play but lie beyond the scope of this study. Nevertheless, the possibility of this influence offers an avenue for continued research into the contribution played by specific types of resource to the effectiveness of sub-state engagement with both domestic and EU-level policy processes.

CHAPTER 6

A Central Government Perspective

Introduction

This chapter will examine the reactions of central government officials to the changes introduced in the process of formulating EU policy positions as a consequence of devolution. The experiences of UK central government officials based in both London and Brussels will be considered to further enhance understanding of the impact of devolution on the UK's EU policy formulation process. Evidence of any resistance to the involvement of the devolved administrations in the policy process will be sought, as will any indications that new tensions have emerged in the relationship, or that existing, pre-devolution, tensions were exacerbated after 1999.

As noted previously, the Acts left EU affairs as a reserved competence of the UK central government. This created a contradictory situation as responsibilities which were now devolved within the UK had also largely been transferred to the EU during the European integration process and the devolved administrations were thus responsible for their implementation. Therefore, the development of coherent EU policy positions necessitated some form of vertical co-ordination between the different levels.

The sections of this chapter will concentrate upon the key players in this process as already identified: lead policy departments, the Cabinet Office and the Cabinet committee system, the FCO and UKRep. Changes to the roles of these institutions and the impact that devolution had on the way they formulated EU policy will be considered, as will apparent differences between the intensity of engagement of the two devolved administrations. The changed role of the territorial offices in the policy process will then be considered, together with any differences in their activities that emerged as a consequence of the asymmetry of devolution.

The Role of Policy Departments

A General Perspective

As demonstrated in Chapter 2, UK government policy departments play a central role in the formulation of EU policy positions, being responsible for most technical policy negotiations. This situation was perpetuated post-devolution. It is made clear within the Concordat on EU affairs that the final responsibility for producing the UK's negotiating line remains with the lead UK department, with the UK Minister taking the ultimate decision on issues such as the composition of the negotiating team sent to Brussels. With regard to the inclusion of devolved Ministers in Council negotiating teams, precedents for their involvement were clearly established during the early years of devolution. However, it was also clear that they attended with the agreement of the UK lead department and adhering to a previously agreed UK line (Interviews, 2000; 2003).

Both the White Papers and the Concordats demonstrate that central governments are expected to involve their devolved counterparts in the formulation of policy positions where there is an overlap between the EU and devolved competences. As demonstrated previously, the participation of the devolved administrations in the formulation of EU negotiating positions frequently took place on a bilateral basis between policy departments. The usual procedure was for Whitehall to prepare papers for comment by the devolved administrations (Interview, 2000). The management of relations with the new authorities was helped by the fact that staffing changed little during the first two years of devolution, allowing for continuity in inter-personal contacts, even though institutional affiliations had changed.

As highlighted previously, it was widely considered amongst officials that some Whitehall functional departments were slower to adjust to the new circumstances created by devolution than others, although awareness subsequently increased (Interviews, 2000; 2003). Departments that experienced a high level of co-operation with their territorial office counterparts prior to devolution, such as MAFF/DEFRA often appeared to be more aware of the changed circumstances of officials in the devolved administrations and more likely to include the devolved administrations in the preparation of EU policy positions (Interviews, 2000; 2003). However, it was clear that the first year of devolution in particular presented a steep learning curve for officials at both levels of government and that after that period the mechanics of managing relations were still being adjusted in some policy areas.

Suggestions of a lack of awareness among some central government officials indicated that there was a need for all Whitehall departments to acquire an understanding of devolution. As with all large organisations, there were, inevitably, different perceptions of devolution which varied between officials, with some more favourable towards the idea than others. There had initially been a certain amount of suspicion and resistance towards such a fundamental change, although generally it was considered that central government officials had been favourable towards the idea of devolution (Interview, 2000).

As noted previously, some of the problems that arose in relations between central government and the devolved administrations were considered to result less from deliberate obstruction on the part of officials, but more often from this lack of awareness or "ignorance" of the realities of devolution (Interviews, 2000; 2003). This tendency towards a lack of awareness varied across departments and the data collected suggested that this could be related to two principal factors. The first of these was the personality of the individual, especially the personality of the Minister, and their attitude towards devolution (Interview, 2000). If a Minister was favourable towards the idea of devolution, the department was generally considered to adopt a more favourable attitude towards co-operation with devolved officials. The other factor was the departmental culture with smaller more cohesive departments being more co-operative and "switched on" to devolution than larger departments which covered a number of distinct policy areas (Interview, 2000). Several policy departments established central units for dealing with the task of raising awareness across the department.

Officials at both levels considered the maintenance of the civil service ethos important. The decision not to territorialize the civil service enabled information flows and channels of communication to remain more open than may have been the case had the civil service been divided. It was suggested that central government officials were likely to have been less willing to co-operate and share information with the devolved administrations than proved to be the case under devolution, if these circumstances had been different (Interview, 2000). There were, however, some accusations reported in the media of insufficient information being passed from the central level to the devolved level, although these did not relate specifically to EU concerns (*icWales*, 4 April 2001).

A strong emphasis was placed upon the use of informal mechanisms in the management of relations between the two levels, which appeared to suit central government officials and Ministers, and which was not challenged by the devolved administrations. There was a view that it was the co-ordination machinery which operates within Whitehall that is central to making the system for involving the devolved administrations in the formulation of EU policy positions work (Interviews, 2000; 2003). The informality of these arrangements stresses yet again the reliance upon inter-personal relationships between key players already discerned from the perspective of the devolved administrations. As a consequence of the importance of relationships between individuals in making the system work smoothly, rather than formal mechanisms, it is thus unsurprising that the system worked better in some policy fields than others.

The reliance upon personal relations also means that trust became increasingly important in the management of relationships between the two levels post-devolution. Good working relationships were characterised by trust and reliability, further underpinned by the sharing of information and it was considered important that this culture should be continued in order for the smooth management of relations to be maintained (Interviews, 2000). The opinions of central government officials, taken in conjunction with those of devolved officials, clearly demonstrate the centrality of communication to the effective handling of policy co-ordination post-devolution.

The importance of trust and reliability was clearly demonstrated in the case of the National Assembly for Wales and the concern noted in Chapter 5 over its original status as a corporate body. Confidentiality was one of the key sensitive areas for central government officials, and reassurances were sought from the Welsh in particular to assuage concerns that most things copied to the Assembly would end up in the public arena (Interview, 2000). These concerns diminished over time, as Assembly officials and WAG Ministers continually demonstrated respect for the principle of confidentiality (Interview, 2003), thereby maintaining the necessary trust between the different sets of officials.

There were also concerns that new officials and policy advisors, in particular those unfamiliar with government procedures, may go public with information at an earlier stage in discussions than officials with more experience of Whitehall procedures (Interview, 2001). Such behaviour could create defensiveness on the part of central government officials, thereby harming the atmosphere of trust necessary for conducting relations between the different levels of government. However, there were no clear-cut public examples of problems of this nature in either the Scottish or Welsh case during the first four years of devolution.

Many of the problems identified by central government officials during the first term of devolution related primarily to procedural issues and were generally resolved by flexibility and compromise on the part of both sides. It is clear that much of the essential work in producing a single UK policy line was carried out behind the scenes (Interview,

2001), and that engagement here was crucial in ensuring that Scottish and Welsh concerns were incorporated in the UK's line. To official minds, influencing this line is more important than ministerial representation in Councils where a pre-negotiated UK line must be presented. Another issue that created problems was the tightness of timescales, both EU and domestic, within which the interests and concerns of the devolved administrations must be put forward to UK counterparts (Interview, 2000).

In terms of appearance, there was little apparent change in the way in which the UK's EU policy formulation processes operated at the official level. This was borne out by the comments of officials who saw little actual change in the practicalities of co-ordinating the process. This suggests that little had changed from the involvement of the territorial offices pre-devolution. Two things, however, seem clear about the participation of the devolved administrations in the EU policy formulation process. The first is that levels of engagement differed between the devolved administrations and across different policy sectors. The second is that although the devolved administrations clearly have access to the EU policy-making process, there is no firm evidence of the extent to which they are able to influence the policy positions adopted by the UK Government. Their influence could be discerned in specific policy issues of particular salience such as fishing quotas for Scotland and cockle bed closures in Wales, but in general terms it is difficult to identify issues where devolved administrations made an impact upon policy positions taken forward to Brussels negotiations. Here the issue of confidentiality makes it difficult for both the plenaries and external observers to discern the impact of the presentation of devolved concerns and interests.

However, the influence of the devolved administrations could also be clearly discerned on a non-sectoral issue when the joint central government-devolved paper was submitted to the Convention on the Future of Europe's plenary session on regional and local authorities (European Convention, 2003). This submission, discussed more fully in the summary of Chapter 4, was considered by other EU "regions" to be remarkably extensive in its content and notable in the mere fact of it taking place. However, it could also be argued that this represents another example of "no surprises", with the devolved administrations engagement in EU "constitutive" politics being channelled through the central government, rather than taking place through bodies like RegLeg.

Having concentrated here upon general trends and attitudes which could be discerned in central government post-devolution, the next section will consider different ways in which specific central government departments reacted to the devolution process, seeking to discern differences in the ways in which arrangements have been adapted. These different reactions by UK departments are potentially a factor in the emergence of different levels of engagement by the devolved administrations in the UK's EU policy formulation process.

Some Departmental Specifics

With most negotiations between central government and the devolved administrations carried out on a bilateral basis between policy departments, any arrangements that the central government ministries made to take account of devolution are of considerable importance. As already indicated, different policy departments are considered to have adjusted to the new situation to varying degrees. Awareness levels also appear to have differed depending on factors already identified, including individual and ministerial attitudes towards devolution, departmental cultures and the size and coherence of the department.

Several policy departments, including MAFF/DEFRA, set up a central unit specifically intended to raise awareness about the department's devolution procedures (Interviews, 2000). This awareness-raising exercise was an important factor in maintaining good relations, with devolved officials holding the opinion that MAFF/DEFRA colleagues generally had a good understanding of the new environment within which the devolved administrations were operating (Interviews, 2000; 2003), implying that not all Whitehall departments were so accommodating.

The role of this central unit, the Constitution and European Affairs Unit, was to raise awareness, advise on devolution issues and promulgate information forwarded from the Cabinet Office. Information regarding devolution from the Cabinet Office, often in the form of a Devolution Guidance Note, or DGN, was passed to all Whitehall policy departments who then decided how it was to be circulated internally. Cabinet Office DGNs were intended to "help departments with the practicalities of working with the devolved administrations". The MAFF unit circulated DGNs to heads of division and placed them on the internal computer network to try and ensure their availability to all members of the department. Some DGNs were circulated in their original form, as distributed by the Cabinet Office. If necessary, additional MAFF-specific "devolution information notes" were also appended, specifying how the department would tackle particular issues (Interview, 2000). This could also happen independently if something was identified as a procedural problem within the department.

MAFF was a central government department that had strong links with the territorial offices pre-devolution, so higher levels of trust had already been established between Whitehall and territorial civil servants.

It was felt that such inter-personal relations helped to smooth the transition resulting from the devolution process. Officials maintained frequent contact with their devolved counterparts and although the political situation had clearly changed, it was felt that actual practices had altered little (Interviews, 2000; 2003). The approach from all sets of officials was to try and work on a reasonable and practicable basis. Communication channels were maintained reasonably well, although, as admitted at the Whitehall level, there were a few breakdowns in communication from the central government side (Interview, 2000). The clearest example of this came on a non-EU related issue, the planting of GM contaminated crops in Scotland. Although MAFF had been aware of the problem since 17 April 2000, the Scottish Executive was not informed until 15 May (*The Scotsman*, 26 May 2000). This was described at the time as a "total lack of communication" (*Ibid.*), with Ross Finnie commenting:

> I'm even more annoyed that there was a total lack of communication between MAFF and ourselves between that date. We are writing to them to make it clear that this is unacceptable. (*Ibid.*)

However, he did mitigate this somewhat by expressing his disappointment at this breakdown because communication between the two had previously been so good (*BBC News*, 26 May 2000). The Scottish Minister succeeded in gaining an apology from the central government department and inquiries were ordered to find out how the issue had been "mishandled" (*The Herald*, 2 June 2000). This demonstrated that even with one of the better working relationships between the devolved and central government levels, frictions and problems could arise.

Nevertheless, both sides judged the relationship in positive terms. From the central government perspective, devolved officials were generally considered good at keeping central government informed of matters like contact with the European Commission or with other sub-state authorities, thereby helping to maintain the basis of trust upon which good relations were founded.

Decisions on devolved ministers' attendance at Councils of Ministers are taken by the lead UK Minister on a case by case basis. Although MAFF/DEFRA adopted a flexible approach to deciding the make-up of delegations to Councils, the practical and logistical constraints upon the size of delegations were recognised (Interview, 2000). This was acknowledged as a particular problem for MAFF/DEFRA as agricultural policy was one area where all of the devolved territories have distinctive interests and concerns and often all devolved representatives wished to be involved, whilst for operational reasons relating to the logistical management of Council meetings only one can be accommodated alongside the UK Minister. During the first term, it was clear that the devolved administrations accepted the approach adopted to representation in Council.

This situation applied across the MAFF/DEFRA policy divisions. For example, for fisheries policy, officials believed external observers would discern little change in the management of relations pre-and post-devolution with the relationship with Scottish officials being described as "very close" (Interview, 2003). The most important change was the way in which the Scottish Executive Minister's role in the Councils of Ministers was presented for public consumption, with one official based in Brussels commenting that it was emphasised to a greater extent than had been the case pre-devolution (Interview, 2000), even though there had also existed a perceived need under earlier Conservative governments to demonstrate the involvement of the Scottish Office in such meetings. At a review meeting held in Edinburgh in the summer of 2000, the conclusion was drawn that overall the system had worked as well as could be expected, with positive evaluations at both levels.

As a consequence of the fact that MAFF/DEFRA led in the EU context as the representatives of the UK Government, inter-departmental meetings were chaired by central government officials. The central government department holds responsibility for putting the UK's position together, but, with regard to fisheries, obviously would want to work closely with SEERAD. If problems did arise, devolved officials could point to the Concordats to ensure their involvement. However, in 2003, officials at the centre suggested that no reference to the Concordats had been made in the last two years.

The situation in the early years of devolution in the fisheries divisions was further helped by the good personal relations that existed between the then UK and Scottish Ministers responsible, Elliot Morley and Ross Finnie. This, combined with existing good relations between officials, helped ensure a smooth running of the system in the early stages of devolution. Nevertheless, there was inevitably disagreement on individual policy issues which were generally resolved through compromise and negotiation (Interviews, 2000; 2003). Central government officials did not concede that any new frictions had emerged as a consequence of devolution. It was remarked, however, that the increased workload of devolved officials actually could restrict their time for commenting on, criticising, or influencing submissions being prepared for UK Ministers, compared with their pre-devolution contributions to this preparation process (Interview, 2000).

Other central government departments did not make the same kind of concerted effort as MAFF/DEFRA to prepare for devolution. However, they did begin to adjust, particularly in those departments such as the Home Office (Justice) and Environment, which, as noted by Whitehall officials, began to feel Scottish and Welsh interests more directly than had been the case pre-devolution (Interview, 2000), with a greater number of Scottish and Welsh Ministers covering a wide range of portfolios in greater depth than had been possible under the territorial offices. For example, DfEE/DfES was described as "pretty assiduous" at keeping the devolved administrations informed of developments and kept in regular contact, asking the devolved administrations for comments on briefing papers it had prepared, although it was the Scottish Executive that most frequently responded, given differences between the Scottish and English/Welsh education systems (Interview, 2000). Indeed, it was Scottish officials who, over the years, had heightened DfEE/DfES' sensitivity to territorial, particularly Scottish, concerns, and it was suggested that the current position with the information flow had taken some time to reach.

DETR/DTLR also further developed its own procedures in response to devolution with desk officers often consulting their counterparts on proposed policy lines and using the formal process of a ministerial write-round. However, their adaptation was evaluated more critically than that of some of the other departments like MAFF/DEFRA and there were several disputes over the involvement of the devolved administrations in policy areas covered by DETR/DTLR (Interview, 2001). There was, for example, disagreement between WAG and the then DETR over the Assembly's desire to nominate a delegate to CLRAE. On non EU-related issues, there was also the controversy of the planting of GM crops in Wales against the express wishes of the Assembly. There is little clarification of why this was the case, although the sheer size of the department at the time and the attendant difficulty of raising awareness of devolution across all of its policy divisions may have been contributory factors.

As well as implications for the formulation of EU policy positions, devolution also affected the way in which EU directives and regulations were implemented. Although the responsibility for implementation is devolved, it is not the devolved administrations, but the UK Government that would appear in front of the European Court of Justice. From that perspective, it was in the interests of central government to ensure co-ordination takes place in the domestic EU policy-making process and that the implications of policy for the devolved administrations were taken into account (Interview, 2000). It was recognised that for implementation to run smoothly, those responsible for implementing the policy must be involved in the negotiating process, an argument that had previously put forward by the German *Länder* to justify their demand for a role in the EU policy process.

In spite of the fact that implementation is a devolved responsibility, when the European Commission was asked how it would prefer to receive notification, it requested UK-wide notification, not individual territorial notification (Interview, 2000). Much of the legislation allows for differential implementation, an element that has been identified as potentially creating future problems by central government officials, although the impact of this possibility did not fully filter through in the first term of devolution.

The Cabinet, Cabinet Committees and the Cabinet Office

As identified in Chapter 2, the Cabinet is traditionally considered to be the locus of decision-making power in the UK. Before devolution took place, Scottish and Welsh interests were represented by the Secretaries of State of the territorial departments. This practice continued post-devolution, although most of their policy responsibilities had been transferred to the devolved administrations in 1999. Because the Cabinet is a central government body, ministers from the devolved administrations are not represented there, nor on the Cabinet committees which deal with specific policy areas.

However, a lot of the work of Cabinet committees is done in the process of writing round the UK Ministers concerned, rather than through actual meetings. The standard format post-devolution, where an issue touched on the responsibilities of the devolved administrations, was for the lead Minister to conclude his letter to the other UK Ministers concerned by saying that s/he was writing in similar terms to the devolved administrations (Interview, 2001). In addition, official involvement in the formulation of UK policy positions also helped to circumvent the exclusion of devolved ministers from actual Cabinet and Cabinet committee meetings.

The Cabinet Office continued to play the central role in the overall co-ordination of EU policy, being described as the "central node" of a large co-ordination network, and it took a very active role in determining what procedures should be applied for involving the devolved administrations post-devolution (Interviews, 2000; 2003), as can be seen with the Devolution Guidance Notes circulated around Whitehall departments. As part of its response to the Labour Government's plans for devolution, the Cabinet Office initially established a Constitution Secretariat (later reformed into a "Devolution and the Regions" Unit) responsible for co-ordinating the UK Government's overall scheme for constitutional reform (Interview, 2000). The work of this Secretariat, to which Scottish Office, later Executive, officials were seconded, combined with the efforts of the European Secretariat, led to the Cabinet Office's response to devolution being evaluated in positive terms by civil servants in the devolved administrations (Interviews, 2000; 2003). The European Secretariat continued to perform much of its practical co-ordinating role at the official level, via the same informal system of networks and *ad hoc* meetings that was employed prior to devolution.

The range of dispute mechanisms, including the JMC, arranged by the Cabinet Office to deal with conflicts of interest post-devolution were not invoked for the purpose of conflict management during the first term of devolution. The first JMC on European Affairs was held on 1 March 2001 and concentrated upon more general issues and a review of the operation of the Concordat's arrangements. Two principal reasons were given as to why this machinery was not invoked. Firstly, most conflicts of interest were dealt with through negotiation and compromise by the relevant Ministers and officials, with the implication that officials would view the decision to call upon conflict resolution mechanisms as a failure on their part to reach a suitable compromise agreement (Interview, 2000). Secondly, there was a concern that the JMC machinery would prove too cumbersome for the pace at which events occur at the EU level and therefore a more informal *ad hoc* approach to resolving disputes was preferable (Interview, 2000).

However, following the replacement of Robin Cook by Jack Straw as Foreign Secretary, and the establishment of the Convention on the Future of Europe, JMC(E) began to meet on a more regular basis, with discussions largely focusing upon developments in the Convention. It was in this forum that the joint submission paper to the Convention mentioned previously was discussed. Since this time, JMC(E) has met much more regularly, eventually replacing Minecor (Carter *et al.*, 2005), to leave this as the key non-Cabinet multilateral forum for discussing issues relating to the management of intra-UK relations on EU policy issues, as well as specific issues themselves.

The role of the Cabinet Office in EU policy-making changed little after devolution. However, the Office did take deliberate steps to raise awareness of the implications of devolution for EU policy-making both within the Cabinet Office and throughout the policy departments of Whitehall. Devolved policy divisions had contact with the European Secretariat and with the Devolution and the Regions Unit as the need arose. As could be anticipated, they had little or no contact with the other main Cabinet Office secretariats such as Defence. The CO European Secretariat was in regular contact with the SE's External Relations division and the Welsh EEAD on over-arching EU issues of interest but in 2003 it was acknowledged that the Scots had been best placed to develop a strategic approach to dealing with EU issues, noting the much smaller size of the Welsh administration (Interviews, 2003).

The FCO and UKRep

The Foreign and Commonwealth Office has a set of reserved powers, so that its role continues to be to represent the UK as a whole, including the devolved territories. Therefore, the FCO, and UKRep, made an active decision on the way in which this function was to be discharged post-devolution. This led to the strategic decision, taken at a very early stage, to include the devolved administrations in relevant aspects of EU policy-making. It thus adopted a positive approach to devolution, to making the co-ordination system work post-devolution and to working with the devolved administrations. Therefore, despite initial concern from territorial officials that the FCO would prove resistant to devolution, its reaction to the process was described as "very good" and it was said that FCO officials "couldn't have been more helpful" (Interviews, 2000; 2003).

Like MAFF, the FCO also created a central unit, the Devolved Administrations Division (DAD), responsible for raising awareness of the new circumstances created by devolution both within the FCO at home and in its overseas posts and also to create links between the relevant officials in the FCO and the devolved administrations. The unit was established in February 1999 and was shut down as a separate unit in September 2000, although it responsibilities were then transferred to the desk responsible for looking after parliamentary relations (Interview, 2000). The main role of the unit appears to have been an awareness-raising one, and also to act as an initial point of contact for officials from the devolved administrations with questions about any impact of international affairs on their work and for Foreign Office officials about the implications of devolution for their work. There does not appear to have been any intention for the unit to become a permanent fixture. Rather it was designed to act as a facilitator during a transitional period as the FCO adjusted to new reality of devolution. The unit was considered at least in part responsible for the FCO's apparent ability to engage positively with the devolved administrations (Interview, 2000).

This positive attitude towards devolution was reflected in the invitation to the devolved administrations to be involved in the Minecor group. Minecor was, until it was wound up in 2004, a cross-cutting ministerial group for EU co-ordination which provided an opportunity for devolved Ministers to discuss European issues with their UK Government counterparts. The two key objectives of Minecor were to concentrate on enhancing the UK's links with other member states and regions of the EU and to raise the profile of the benefits of EU membership in the UK itself. Its activities were subsequently absorbed into the workload of JMC(E) (Carter *et al.*, 2005).

In terms of EU policy co-ordination, however, out of all the FCO's divisions, the key role is played by the Brussels-based UKRep. It is UKRep that is principally responsible for negotiations, for drafting documents and which has the necessary contacts for influencing decision-making at the EU level. It was therefore crucial for the effective involvement of the devolved administrations in the UK's EU policy formulation process that officials belonging to UKRep were aware of the differences created by devolution.

UKRep officials clearly understood that devolution was a change that affected the UK's EU policy-making process, and hence the delivery of a co-ordinated policy line in Brussels (Interviews, 2000). The devolved administrations realised the importance of maintaining close relationships with UKRep which is responsible for actually steering work through in Brussels. From the perspective of the devolved administrations, UKRep officials were initially considered to have been helpful and to have demonstrated a positive engagement with devolution, indeed more positive than some of the Whitehall departments (Interviews, 2000). In fact, UKRep officials attended the Agriculture/Rural Affairs review meeting that took place in Edinburgh at the end of devolution's first year. This demonstrated the perceived importance that was attached to engaging with the devolved administrations and making them feel that their concerns and interests were well-represented by UKRep. If the devolved administrations felt well-represented by UKRep, they would have less incentive to try and represent their own concerns in Brussels which could, potentially, cause UKRep serious problems of co-ordination.

From the perspective of UKRep officials, it was considered to be in their interests to work with the devolved administrations and also to ensure that Whitehall departments co-operate closely with their devolved counterparts (Interview, 2000). Although UKRep desk officers were willing to take implications for the devolved administrations into account, they did not have the time or resources to actively seek out new dimensions created by devolution (Interview, 2000). In other words, although UKRep was happy to incorporate devolved concerns, these had to be brought to the attention of the extremely busy desk officers. This meant that it was essential for the devolved administrations to engage pro-actively with the EU policy formulation process.

The establishment of the representative offices of the devolved administrations in Brussels led to the creation of what was referred to as the UKRep "family" in Brussels. Again, UKRep was deemed to have been helpful towards those offices and established good relations with both the Scottish and Welsh Offices, which felt that they were close to UKRep (Interviews, 2000). Good information flow from UKRep to these offices placed the devolved administrations in the UK in a better position to engage constructively with the EU policy process.

During the first four years, there was little friction between the representative offices and UKRep. As with the policy departments in the UK, their relationship was based firmly on mutual trust. UKRep made it clear that it was willing to share information on the basis of confidentiality and a respect for their need to do business without leaks of material and policy positions. Like the devolved administrations in the UK, the representative offices respected this position and acted accordingly to facilitate their engagement with the policy process. However, as discussed in Chapter 4, the "Aron Paper", leaked to the media in 2007, suggested that there were more tensions in the relationship than were readily apparent to outside observers.

UKRep desk officers play three principal roles – intelligence officer for gathering and distributing information, tactical advisor on negotiating strategies and often chief negotiator, and lobbying. Although they lacked the time and resources to seek out specific devolution dimensions in their policy areas, they had a definite self-interest in identifying any potential problems at an early stage (Interview, 2000). In certain areas, such as fisheries policy, where central government and Scottish officials and Ministers have always collaborated closely, little changed post-devolution. Inevitably, devolution had a greater impact in other policy areas and the relationship between central government and the devolved administrations was felt to be more separate and formal post-devolution. However, in many cases, it was often just a question of placing additional copy recipients on material for circulation to make sure that the devolved administrations were involved (Interview, 2000).

Taking the example of fisheries policy, interventions by Scottish Ministers in Fisheries Councils were felt to have increased post-devolution. Rather than being a consequence of procedural change, however, this was a deliberate decision by the UK and devolved Ministers concerned, partly for reasons of political presentation (Interview, 2000). The devolved Minister was openly seen to participate in meetings, thus placing the devolved executive in a better position to rebut opposition claims of a lack of representation in the EU arena. In this area, devolved involvement was facilitated by the good personal relations that existed between the UK and Scottish Ministers in post at the time.

For the most part, any conflicts of interest in fisheries were sorted out between London and Edinburgh and were resolved before policy positions were forwarded to Brussels. During the first four years of devolution, officials found that any policy differences were susceptible to being resolved "without any great dramatics" (Interview, 2000). If

UKRep officials received conflicting advice from central government and devolved officials, they felt they had a role to bring the different sides together to work towards a single UK line. UKRep's paramount concern was the need to ensure that the UK was able to present a single united policy line in EU negotiations.

It can be seen from the situation described in these sections that surprisingly little changed on a practical level in terms of European coordination from the pre-devolution procedures described in Chapter 2, with much of the work continuing to be carried out by informal contacts between officials. However, there was a need for awareness-raising exercises within the central government about the changed circumstances created by devolution and the need to involve devolved Ministers and officials in the EU policy formulation process, a process that was more effective in some departments than others. Nevertheless, two departments within central government had their role dramatically altered as a consequence of devolution, namely the territorial offices.

The Scotland and Wales Offices

The changed role of the territorial offices and the Secretaries of State was an area of uncertainty in the devolution process and continued to be an issue of debate with suggestions ranging from the complete abolition of the offices through their integration into a single department or their continuation in a reduced form (*The Herald*, 8 May 2000; *Western Mail*, June 2000). In 2001, their roles were incorporated into the new Department of Constitutional Affairs and the roles of Secretary of State were held part-time alongside functional ministerial portfolios. However, for the first two years of devolution they were retained as independent offices, although reduced in size and resources, acting as the representatives of the devolved territories (*not* the devolved administrations) in central government and the representatives of central government in the devolved territories. The majority of their former officials transferred to the Scottish Executive and the National Assembly *en bloc* in 1999. From a central government perspective, the Secretaries of State continued to play an important role as "facilitators and fixers" (Interview, 2001) in relations between central government and the devolved administrations. However, it was made clear that the two offices were not to be considered as conduits between central government and the new devolved institutions (Cabinet Office Devolution Guidance Notes 3 and 4) at the expense of bilateral departmental contacts and communications.

An inevitable consequence of the asymmetry of devolution was the fact that the Scotland Office saw a much greater reduction generally in the extent of its role in policy formulation than was the case for the

Wales Office (Cabinet Office DGN 4). There was little contact between Scottish Executive departments and the Scotland Office on specific policy issues, although the Scotland Office continued for a period to have some curious transitional roles where, for example, the Secretary of State's signature might be required on a document for implementation (Interview, 2000). However, these were gradually phased out and thereafter there appeared to be minimal involvement of the Scotland Office, particularly at the official level (Cabinet Office DGN 3) in the day-to-day management of intra-UK relations dealing with EU policy co-ordination. The Secretary of State had a continued role to play as Scotland's representative in the Cabinet.

The Secretary of State for Scotland was, however, involved in one of the most salient points of tension to emerge during the first term of devolution which was the then Secretary of State's refusal, along with the then UK Chancellor of the Exchequer, Gordon Brown, to give evidence to the Scottish Parliament's European Committee during their inquiry into additionality, matched funding and the Structural Funds. It is quite clear that the Scottish Parliament cannot summon UK Government ministers and the Secretary of State made his position clear in a letter to the SE Minister for Parliament following unfavourable press reporting of the incident (Scotland Office news release SS0148, 22 June 2000). They may, however, choose to appear should they consider it appropriate, as Peter Hain, then the FCO's Europe Minister, agreed to do in response to the European Committee's inquiry into the "Future of Europe" (Scottish Parliament Committee News Release CEU009/2001, 1 November 2001).

There were two principal reasons for the emergence of this tension. First was the actual refusal by the Secretary of State to appear for questioning by the Committee, saying that the SE Finance Minister was capable of answering the questions of the Committee, and also that the Secretary of State himself was due to give evidence on the issue to the Westminster Parliament's Scottish Affairs Select Committee. This was represented as a snub to the Scottish Parliament by the opposition parties on the Committee. Secondly, the substance of the letter from the Scotland Office to the Committee was also leaked into the public arena (although it would have been placed on the internet eventually anyway).

This created further tension on both sides for different reasons – for the parliamentary committee because of the nature of the reply sent, which they considered to be insensitively worded, and for the central government department because the letter was leaked ahead of its publication (prompting a letter to the SE Minister for Parliament from the Secretary of State for Scotland). This had the effect of souring relations between the Parliament and the Scotland Office, although as a dispute between the Parliament and UK Government, it appeared to have minimal consequences for the involvement of the Executive in the EU policy formulation process.

When the report of the Committee was eventually published in the autumn of 2000, the convenor of the Committee in the accompanying press release (CEUR 027/2000, 8 November 2000) called for "more openness and transparency from Government departments" and noted that:

> Although requests were made to UK Government Ministers to attend our inquiry meetings, they declined. The committee feels that the subsequent written information they provided was not sufficient to verify the net impact of EU funding on economic development spending in Scotland. This was a matter of regret to the committee.

This conclusion from the Committee allowed the opposition parties a further opportunity to go on the attack over the question of the gathering of evidence from central government departments (*The Times*, 9 November 2000).

In contrast to the greatly reduced role of the Secretary of State for Scotland and the Scotland Office, the role of the Secretary of State for Wales and the Wales Office continued to be more prominent as a consequence of the fact that all primary legislation regarding Wales continued to be passed by the UK Parliament. The Secretary of State's role had three principal dimensions – to represent Wales in the Cabinet (and the central government in Wales), to get resources allocated to Wales, and to take through the Westminster Parliament any specifically Welsh bills and any Wales-specific clauses in other primary legislation. The Secretary of State for Wales is also the lead minister for European negotiations on minority languages, although this is not an important role in terms of extensive involvement in EU policy formulation. As well as being involved in negotiating the annual bloc voted to Wales from the UK's budget, the Secretary of State also played a central role in negotiations with the UK Treasury over securing additional funding for Wales in the July 2000 Spending Review in recognition of the Objective 1 status accorded to large parts of Wales (Interview, 2001).

A large part of the Wales Office's role consisted of liaising, and facilitating relations, between the central government and the Assembly Government. However, the vast bulk of both domestic and EU policy business is conducted bilaterally between departments. The Office could act as mediator or prompt WAG to become involved if it recognised the impact of a legislative proposal on Wales. Part of the role of the Office was to look for a differential impact of policy proposals on Wales and then represent these in Cabinet committees to ensure that UK Ministers were aware of implications for Wales. The Office also monitored the reaction of the Assembly Government to contacts on policy positions or proposals from lead UK Ministers (Interview, 2001).

As indicated above, primary legislation affecting Wales continued to be passed by the Westminster Parliament. However, the situation for European legislation is more complex – some EU directives have to be implemented by primary legislation, whilst other directives could be implemented directly by the Assembly through secondary legislation in areas where the Assembly held the relevant functions. Directives in areas where the Assembly had no functions would be implemented through primary legislation for England and Wales. For any EU legislation requiring primary legislation, an agreement had to be reached between the UK department and the Assembly as to how prescriptive or detailed the primary legislation would be that was approved by Westminster before the Assembly could pass its secondary legislation. This was, however, a general issue, indeed tension, between the two levels, where the Assembly had policy responsibilities, although it did not emerge specifically with regard to EU legislation during the first term.

On a broader point, although the role of the Wales Office and the Secretary of State is to represent Wales in the UK central government, the Secretary of State did not act as a mouthpiece for the views of WAG. Rather the Secretary of State's role was to form his own view, which may be similar to that of WAG, but which takes into account, from a central government perspective, how realistic the proposals are overall (Interview, 2001).

The roles of the territorial offices inevitably altered dramatically as a consequence of devolution. As a result of the asymmetrical nature of devolution, the Wales Office retained a greater role in the policy formulation process than the Scotland Office, although both continued to have a role in representing Scottish and Welsh interests in central government. The reduction in their resources in the wake of devolution did, however, limit the extent to which they could adopt an active role and instead, they tended to watch over proceedings and intervene as facilitators and mediators, rather than seeking to actively engage in the policy-making process.

The Political Dimension

Much of the evidence in the preceding chapters on Scotland and Wales indicates that tensions are most likely to arise between the devolved and central tiers of government on issues which are politicised or contain the potential for politicisation, such as the question of matched funding and Objective 1 in Wales. It is also clear that much of this tension emerges not from the devolved executives, but from within the UK's confrontational party political system, with the opposition parties in the Parliament and the Assembly attempting to gain party political advantage over the parties in coalition and/or the Labour central government.

The political dimension of devolved participation in EU policy formulation was recognised to some extent by the Labour UK Government Ministers, for example, the importance of devolved (mainly Labour) Ministers being able to point to their participation in Councils of Ministers in Brussels. There was a focus amongst opposition (nationalist) parties, particularly in Scotland, to seize on the high-profile questions of representation in order to press their claims for "independence in Europe". This focus on the outward manifestation of involvement meant that central government departments tried to recognise and accommodate these changed expectations in order to minimise political challenges to the devolved executives (Interview, 2000). Under governmental incongruence, the pressure for central government ministers to ensure the visible engagement of devolved ministers out of party political motivations will be absent.

Some central government departments discussed issues such as Council of Ministers attendance with the devolved administrations in order to identify potential situations where devolved ministers could attend and speak at Councils. However, the outcome of these discussions was to maintain the principle of the delegation's make-up being decided on a case by case basis, so there are no hard and fast rules determining under what conditions devolved ministers form part of the delegation (Interview, 2000). In some policy areas, like fisheries, the situation changed little, with a Scottish Office Minister always forming part of the UK's delegation pre-devolution, and a Scottish Executive Minister participating at Councils post-devolution. What changed was not the situation during negotiations in Brussels, but the way it was represented by the Executive in Scotland as clear evidence of their participation and also of the benefits of working through the UK government, a large Member State, in the EU.

Another element of the political dimension that was identified as being of importance by officials was the attitudes of Ministers towards devolution and co-operation with the devolved administrations, as suggested in the section on lead UK departments. Attitudes towards devolution rest upon individual opinions which inevitably meant that some Ministers were more sympathetic towards devolution than others (Interview, 2000). This represented a political reality and was something that the devolved administrations needed to be aware of, and to work around, in order to ensure that their concerns and interests are taken into account at the central government level.

One final element that was identified as smoothing relations between the devolved administrations and central government during the first four, indeed it could be argued eight, years of devolution, remaining of central importance in the years 2003-7, was the dominance of one party at all levels of government, albeit, at times, in coalition in the devolved executives. This meant that there was no political advantage to be gained from creating problems between the two levels of government for most Ministers as it would only damage the standing of their own party. It also meant that most devolved Ministers could make party-based appeals to their UK counterparts regarding policy issues as an alternative way of getting their concerns taken into account and offered internal party channels as an alternative mechanism for dealing with differences of opinion (Interview, 2000). The difficulties of maintaining the smooth running of devolved involvement in the EU policy formulation process with different political parties forming administrations at the different levels is identified as a major theme in this chapter and will be discussed further in the postscript.

Potential Challenges

When asked about potential challenges to the smooth running of the devolved system of intra-UK intergovernmental relations, officials at both devolved and central government levels replied that the question of governmental incongruence, with different parties forming governments at different levels of the system, would provide the sternest test for its operation (Interviews, 2000; 2003). Under this situation, the Concordats would become more important for both sides, for one to demonstrate their right to involvement, for the other to insist upon the principle of confidentiality. In addition, ministers would not be in a position to make political appeals to their central government counterparts through intra-party channels, as they had been able to do during the first two terms of devolution.

Each set of officials is obliged to represent the views of its minister (Interview, 2000), which under governmental incongruence would make compromise more difficult to reach, as the nature of the party political system in the UK would be likely to make the positions of each side less flexible. A party might also identify a potential political advantage in breaking off negotiations and placing the blame for their failure on the other government. This might particularly be the case with a devolved administration led by a nationalist party which would gain advantage from depicting the UK central government as resistant to Scottish or Welsh concerns.

However, it has also been suggested that intergovernmental incongruence would not automatically provoke this type of tension, particularly with regard to Wales. From this perspective, it was argued that it is not self-evidently in the interests of central government to cut communication with the Assembly level as this would automatically encourage different policies that the central government may wish to avoid. Equally there would be no immediate benefit a government majority in Wales to provoke an early dispute with the central government whilst it remained reliant upon the central government to draft the primary legislation that provides the framework within which the Assembly can enact its secondary legislation (Interview, 2000). Even under the 2006 Government of Wales Act, the Assembly remained more closely tied to events in Westminster than is the case for the Scottish Parliament.

The second element that was identified as a potential future challenge is the maintenance of the information flow between the different levels of government. Again, this is a situation that could be exacerbated by governmental incongruence. In order for the flow of information to continue, the culture of trust which exists between the devolved and central government levels would need to be maintained. If, for whatever reason, this trust were to break down, the potential exists for the flow of information to be restricted very rapidly if officials were so instructed (Interviews, 2000; 2003). Any problem which affected the levels of trust could create a major challenge for the EU policy co-ordination process that would have implications for both levels. The devolved administrations would no longer have access to papers on central government positions, although EU documentation that is already in the public domain would remain readily available. Central government would receive less information about the activities of the devolved authorities, thereby weakening their "no surprises" strategy.

Other potential challenges were also identified, although the two described above represented the primary concerns for most officials at both levels. Another area that was identified as potentially creating friction in the future was that of staffing and recruitment. As argued previously, the fact that a large staffing transfer did not take place around the time of devolution made the system operate more smoothly in its initial stages as most officials were dealing with the same people as was the case before devolution. However, some central government officials were of the opinion that recruitment to the new devolved administrations may alter the nature of relations with Whitehall departments. In the early years of devolution, officials of the devolved level had worked for either the territorial offices or other central government policy departments and therefore had an understanding of Whitehall's operating procedures. Newly recruited staff would lack such experience and lack awareness of the way in which Whitehall operates, and might therefore not fit into the policy formulation processes as well as other colleagues with that experience.

Another issue that was raised as a potential area of concern, rather than a probable challenge, was the representative officesin Brussels (Interview, 2000). Their close engagement with UKRep was considered crucial to the representation of UK interests in Brussels. UKRep sees its role as representing the whole of the UK with a co-ordinated single policy line and considered it imperative that a situation should be avoided where the devolved administrations' offices in Brussels were representing different opinions from the single UK line. Again this situation could change under governmental incongruence, and it was recognised that the representative offices of the devolved administrations contained the potential to undermine the UK's policy co-ordination system, although such a situation did not arise during the first four years. The leaking of the Aron Paper, however, confirmed this as a potential area of dispute between the devolved and central government levels.

A final area of concern that was identified by both Scottish and central government officials was the question of the representation of English concerns and interests. The current situation is that the Whitehall (UK) department is also responsible for representing English concerns and interests which has created some functional problems for UK ministers and officials who have to represent both UK and English interests, although these may not necessarily be identical, particularly in areas like fisheries policy. There was a concern demonstrated that it could be possible to "lose" the English dimension if the UK minister is accompanied by a devolved minister, that is to say there is a small possibility that in listening to the opinion of the devolved administrations some of the English dimension may be lost. Alternatively, without devolved involvement, the English angle could come to dominate (Interviews, 2000; 2003).

Summary

In practical terms, from a central government perspective there were few obvious major changes in the way in which EU policy positions were formulated as a result of devolution. Although the relations with devolved officials became more separate and formalised post-devolution, much of the work continued to be carried out by informal contacts between officials. There were no widespread public disputes as was the case between the Federal Republic and the *Länder* executives in Germany as a result of their push for involvement in the EU policy formulation process, or between the Spanish central government and the Autonomous Communities. Nevertheless, disputes did occur over specific policy issues such as matched funding. There were also signs of policy divergence emerging, particularly in Scotland, which could contain the seeds of potential friction between the central government and devolved levels.

The central hypotheses of this study relate to the experiences of the devolved authorities. However, they also raise issues with regard to the experiences and behaviour of the central government during the early stages of devolution. The first hypothesis, contending that the concept of European Domestic Policy would apply in the UK post-devolution, appears to be borne out by both the experiences of the devolved administrations and those of central government.

The UK central government acknowledged from the outset that it would not be practicable to exclude the devolved administrations from the formulation of the UK's EU policy positions. It was suggested during an interview in Whitehall that EU policy is an extension of domestic policy and this must also apply to the way in which EU policy is formulated, therefore the devolved administrations must be involved in those areas where they have domestic responsibilities (Interview, 2001). This appears to confirm that increasingly less of a distinction is made between EU and domestic policy arenas as a consequence of the overlap between the functions and responsibilities of the different levels of governance.

There is no clear evidence of sustained public resistance on the part of central government to the involvement of the devolved administrations in EU policy formulation, although, as has been apparent throughout this chapter and the preceding ones, devolution created uncertainty as to how procedures would operate. There is some evidence that attitudes towards devolution vary across departments, with some being more positively engaged with the devolved administrations than others.

These different levels of engagement appear to result from a number of factors. The first of these is the attitudes of the central government departments towards devolution and involving the devolved administrations in EU policy-making. Secondly, post-devolution levels of engagement often appeared to reflect the level of engagement of the territorial offices in that policy area pre-devolution. Another factor is whether the devolved policy divisions are actively seeking to engage in a given policy area and, indeed, whether or not they have the resources to do so. Officials at the centre acknowledged that Scottish officials were better placed to engage with EU policy formulation, but by 2003 were impressed at the extent to which the SE had developed its EU strategy during just four years. Where the devolved administrations did seek to engage, there was little clear evidence of obvious continued resistance from central government departments, although it was noted that some problems had been created by an apparent lack of awareness of the changes resulting from devolution on the part of central government officials, particularly those in the larger departments which cover a number of policy areas.

Although there were no large-scale disputes over the right to participate, as was the case in the Federal Republic, there have been both policy and procedural problems during the first four years. Differences of opinion over policy issues were resolved through negotiation and compromise. Some of the procedural problems were not overcome in the first years of devolution, and two in particular caused some concern. The first of these regards Scotland and concerned the differences between the Scottish and Westminster legislative timetables when a directive or regulation needs to be implemented across the UK, but cannot be implemented simultaneously because of the difficulty of co-ordinating two different legislative timetables (Interview, 2000).

The second issue regards Wales and the length of time that the Welsh policy formulation and legislative procedure can take. This was considered to impede Welsh policy divisions from inputting into the UK's policy formulation process in a timely manner and created concern in central government policy departments, both about timely input and timely implementation. For the most part, procedural issues have been dealt with in a pragmatic manner, with reference to the Concordats if necessary (Interviews, 2000; 2003).

With regard to the tensions identified previously, there is less evidence of the impact of such areas of friction at the central government level. However, the key areas of concern from a central government perspective concerning the smooth management of intra-UK relations are the inter-connected issues of the information flow and the question of confidentiality. One of the most important concerns for central government officials was that the principle of confidentiality would be respected and information passed to the devolved executives would not find its way into the public arena. During the first four years, this concern was not realised, however the potential remained for this to be an area of major tension between the UK and devolved levels.

As suggested previously, although there is no difficulty in establishing that officials from the devolved administrations are participating in the formulation of the UK's EU policy positions, it is difficult to determine the quality of that access, that is the influence that they are actually able to exert upon the policy positions being adopted. The fact there was little change in practical terms in co-ordinating the policy formulation process suggests that there was little change from the pre-devolution system, where the territorial offices were only able to have an impact upon rather limited and specific policy issues, largely of a technical nature. The difficulty in discerning the extent to which the devolved administrations are able to exercise influence in the policy process was also reflected in the comments of non-governing political parties regarding the lack of transparency in the system.

In summary, the central government machinery demonstrated flexibility in adapting to the new situation created by devolution and did not prove as resistant to change as some observers had anticipated in the run-up to devolution, or create as many frictions as comparative experiences suggested. In fact the adaptation appeared to take place more smoothly than even some officials anticipated. The pattern of responses to devolution varied, with some departments considered to have responded better to the task of incorporating the devolved administrations into their policy formulation process. However, few major areas of tension were apparent in relations from the central government perspective, a situation undoubtedly helped by the Labour Party's dominance of UK politics during the first eight years of devolution. Nevertheless, the party political dimension does create problems external of the official management of relations which civil servants are, or need to be, aware of.

CHAPTER 7

Conclusions

This study commenced with the aim of enhancing understanding of sub-state mobilisation in the domestic EU policy formulation processes of Member States and re-examining the concept of multi-level governance. It has simultaneously provided an exploration of the early experiences of the UK's devolved administrations in the domestic EU policy formulation processes of that Member State. In order to explore this engagement, it drew upon existing interpretations of sub-state mobilisation and the experiences of sub-state authorities elsewhere in the EU to help place the UK's devolved administrations in the context of sub-state mobilisation across the EU.

After reviewing the strengths and deficiencies of existing interpretations with regard to their explanatory potential for understanding sub-state mobilisation, an analytical framework was drawn up with which to examine the UK's post-devolution experiences. Elements of the multi-level governance concept were adopted as part of this analytical framework, but complements were sought to try and increase the explanatory potential of this approach. In particular, the concept of European Domestic Policy, as developed by the German *Länder*, was identified as a potential means of complementing the concept of multi-level governance.

The principal hypothesis tested in this study thus argued that:

The concept of European Domestic Policy, as developed by the German Länder governments in response to the continuing process of European integration, will apply in the post-devolution United Kingdom. This will see the increasing overlap of European and sub-state policies reflected in the involvement of the newly established Scottish and Welsh authorities in EU policy formulation, both within the UK and in the EU arena.

The second chapter of this study then demonstrated that the debate over the extent of the inclusion of the devolved authorities in the UK's domestic EU policy formulation process was indeed underpinned by a UK central government acceptance that it was not feasible (or even desirable) to exclude the devolved administrations from that process in areas where they held domestic responsibilities. This effectively demonstrated an acceptance, on the part of the UK central government, that an overlap existed between the EU and domestic spheres of competence. Two important considerations arise from this acceptance. Firstly, a similar acceptance was not so easily forthcoming in other federal and regionalised Member States of the EU (Germany, Spain). This indicates that the UK, devolving power at a later date, may have learnt from the experiences of other states. Secondly, and most importantly for the hypothesis being tested, it implies a theoretical acceptance of the concept of European Domestic Policy, an acceptance which was subsequently recognised by some civil servants in actual practice.

Motivations for such acceptance derived from a combination of the political and the practical. Nevertheless, the overall acceptance did not preclude resistance and/or reluctance to engage with the devolved administrations at both ministerial and official level. Some of this apparent nervousness translated into a heavy emphasis upon respect for the principle of confidentiality, evident in both the Concordats and in interviews with central government officials.

However, the broader acceptance of the participation of the devolved administrations in EU affairs can be demonstrated by the evidence of ministerial and official level engagement by the devolved administrations presented in the preceding chapters. Although the levels of engagement demonstrate some inconsistency – the Scottish Executive appears more heavily involved than its Welsh counterpart and there is also sectoral variation – there is clear evidence that the devolved executives, during the first term of devolution, did engage with the formulation of EU policy positions, engagement which continued throughout the second term. Sectoral variation can, at least in part, be argued to derive from the non-binding nature of the Concordats, which means that the level of engagement by the divisions of the devolved administrations can be dependent upon the attitude adopted by their central government departmental counterparts.

The evidence that devolved engagement has extended across a range of policy areas clearly contests the argument that sub-state mobilisation is a consequence of the 1988 reform of the Structural Funds programme. If this were the case, then the devolved administrations would not have sought (and would not have been permitted by the centre) to engage with, and ultimately attempt to influence, policy in areas as diverse as fisheries, education, agriculture and the environment. This suggests that further explanation is in fact required to enhance our understanding of sub-state mobilisation in EU policy formulation. In this respect, the complement used in this study, the concept of European Domestic Policy, appears to add a further dimension by arguing that the overlap between EU and sub-state responsibilities will lead SSAs to seek to engage with EU policy issues across the full range of policy competences where they hold devolved functions.

As noted above, in other cases, notably those of Germany and Spain, the quest for regional participation in EU affairs met with resistance on the part of the federal and central governments respectively. In the UK, the central government accepted at an early stage that it was not practical to exclude the devolved administrations. Instead, the UK government chose to structure the ways in which this engagement could take place in order to facilitate devolved involvement whilst also minimising any potential negative impact upon the presentation of the all-important unified policy position in Brussels. In Germany, for example, a cycle of challenge and resistance had emerged between *Bund* and *Länder* over the question of sub-state engagement with the EU. This cycle led to the construction of a supplementary hypothesis tested in the case of the UK, namely:

> The overlap between European and devolved domestic competences is likely to create (or exacerbate) sources of tension in the relationship between the devolved executives and the UK central government over the degree and nature of the involvement of the devolved authorities in European policy formulation.

Sources of tensions are summarised in Table 8.1. The first point to note is that in the UK no obvious cycle of challenge and resistance to parallel the German experience emerged between the domestic levels of government. Central government's tacit acceptance of European Domestic Policy appeared to preclude challenges from the devolved administrations for participation in the EU policy formulation process. Nevertheless, this did not mean that the relationships were without their frictions created by the actuality of an overlap between EU and domestic responsibilities, as Table 8.1 demonstrates.

What has been noticeable in the UK in comparison with other federal and devolved EU Member States is the fact that tensions between the different levels have largely been contained in private. It could be argued that one of the reasons for this is the lack of a UK equivalent of a "Constitutional Court" to which disputes between the levels can be referred. Frequent referrals have marked relationships between central and sub-state levels elsewhere, most notably in Spain. However, during the first eight years of devolution, no referrals were made to the formal dispute resolution mechanism, the Judicial Committee of the Privy Council. This implies therefore, that the political dominance of the Labour Party during this period has also played a role in containing tensions between the different levels of government.

In other EU Member States, tensions principally emerged in relations between federal/central and sub-state levels of government. Although similar areas of friction were clearly acknowledged to exist in potential in the devolved UK, the challenges and frictions within the UK have tended to emanate in the first instance from the devolved legislatures, rather than the devolved executives. Such challenges targeted not only their respective executives, but also the UK Government.

There is less evidence of an impact of these tensions at the central government level with regard to domestic EU policy formulation (Chapter 6). However, there was one clear area of major concern for central government civil servants, namely respect for the principle of confidentiality. At the devolved level, areas of concern included the information flow, the question of confidentiality versus the need for transparency and the exclusion of the Parliament/Assembly from substantive engagement with the EU policy formulation process and also the difficulties for the EU Committees in exercising effective scrutiny over the involvement of their respective executives' engagement with EU policy formulation.

Table 8.1: Potential and Actual Areas of Friction Identified in the Post-Devolution UK

General	Pre-devolution UK	Post-devolution Scotland	Post-devolution Wales
Exclusion	Exclusion	No	No
Information flow	Information flow/ importance of civil service	Not in first term. Civil service crucial	Not in first term
Loss of competences	–	Not in first term	Not in first term
Exclusion of *Landtage*/executive dominance	Potential for exclusion of SP/NAW	Yes	Yes
–	Confidentiality versus lack of transparency	Yes	Yes
–	Party politics	Yes	Yes
–	–	–	Asymmetry
–	–	–	Structural Funds

What also emerges from the identification of frictions in the post-devolution UK is that a number of the areas of tension that have arisen relate to characteristics that are specific to the UK's political system and traditions. These characteristics, most noticeably the confrontational nature of party politics, have often served to exacerbate other areas of tension as political advantage was sought. A salient example was the ongoing debate over access to the Council of the European Union that periodically broke out between Labour and the SNP in Scotland. Nevertheless, it can be argued that some of the areas of tension identified can be related to wider EU trends that occur in political systems such as the Federal Republic of Germany which differ from that of the UK. An example of this kind of friction would be the issue of the *de facto* exclusion of sub-state legislatures from the EU policy formulation process.

It also needs to be borne in the mind that a lack of concrete evidence of tensions in the specific areas identified clearly does not mean that the potential for friction is absent. Rather it simply means that specific frictions did not arise during the first four years of devolution and may yet occur as circumstances change, particularly with changing governments and coalitions. The range of existing and potential frictions indicates that the ever-increasing overlap between EU and sub-state domestic policy responsibilities contributes to intra-state tensions between central and sub-state levels of government.

Moving away from the identification of specific sources of friction, another source of potential instability could also be identified in the case of UK devolution, namely its asymmetry. This asymmetry led to the formulation of a further supplementary hypothesis:

> The UK devolution process does not create a stable equilibrium. Its asymmetry is likely to result in Welsh attempts to attain the same level of devolved competences as Scotland.

It is clear that during the first four years of devolution there appeared to be a level of dissatisfaction with the level of competences allocated to the National Assembly, demonstrated in opinion polls suggesting a growing majority in favour of a parliamentary model of devolution (Wyn Jones & Scully, 2004). There were also disputes over the extent of its powers and the overlap with the responsibilities of central government and the work of the Westminster Parliament. With devolution already having been described as "a process rather than an event" by a former Secretary of State for Wales, there was a suggestion that the path for further devolution to Wales was open.

Outside the Welsh Assembly Government, there were a growing number of calls for the Assembly to be awarded a range of competences comparable with that of the Scottish Parliament. This highlighted once more the party political dimension of both British politics and the devolution debate, with many of these calls emanating from Plaid Cymru, the Welsh nationalists. A further element contributing to this discussion was the apparent lack of public support for the Assembly in its initial form, with people either not knowing what powers the Assembly held or believing that it did not have sufficient power to make a difference in Wales (Curtice, 2000: 272, 238).

During the earliest years of the Assembly, no calls were heard from within the Welsh Assembly Government to extend the competences of WAG and NAW, with the argument made that until the current settlement had been fully tested and found wanting, there was no case to be made to support the call for further powers. Indeed, during the first two years, calls for further devolution were met with some resistance and reluctance, not just on the part of the UK central government, but also by the Labour-dominated administration in Wales. This situation changed with the review of the Richard Commission, set up by First Minister Rhodri Morgan. The Commission's initial remit was to examine "the powers and electoral arrangements of the National Assembly in order to ensure that it is able to operate in the best interests of the people of Wales" (Richard Commission, 2004).

In its report, published in March 2004 and thus outside the timescale of the empirical research conducted for this study, the Richard Commission argued for a clearer separation of responsibilities between Westminster and Cardiff Bay, a change in the electoral system from Additional Member to Single Transferable Vote, a legal separation of executive and plenary (replacing the *de facto* separation), and an increase in the number of AMs to 80. A legislative response to continuing demands for further devolution to Wales resulted in the Government of Wales Act 2006 which enhanced the powers of the Assembly whilst still falling clearly short of the Scottish model of devolution. This outcome suggested that demands, at least from outside the Welsh Labour Party, were likely to continue and that a certain instability in the asymmetrical devolution arrangements would continue to exist. The prospect of a referendum on primary legislative powers, as contained in the 2006 Government of Wales Act, ensures that demands will continue to be made, at least until the referendum is held.

As well as creating instability, it can also be argued that the asymmetrical nature of devolution also impacted upon the way in which, and the extent to which, the devolved administrations were able to engage with the domestic EU policy formulation process:

> In addition, the asymmetry and the different level of resources available to the devolved authorities will affect both the level and nature of their engagement in EU affairs.

This initial study of the early years of the devolution process gathered some evidence to support the argument that different levels of engagement could be discerned in a number of aspects of the devolved administrations' involvement in EU policy formulation. During the first four years, the level of engagement of the Welsh Assembly Government appeared neither as deep, nor as wide-ranging as that of the Scottish

Executive. One point is worth noting here. It must be borne in mind that the Welsh Office was deemed to be less engaged with EU affairs than its Scottish counterpart and thus it can be argued that the starting points of the two devolved administrations were not equal. As a consequence, it could be argued that during initial stages, engagement by the Welsh administration could not be expected to be as high as that of its Scottish counterpart.

Despite this caveat, asymmetry and the level of available resources may well contribute to the explanation of this difference. A number of officials commented upon the different resources, available to the respective devolved executives, particularly in terms of personnel. The level of resources was also identified as influencing some of the strategic decisions taken. This could clearly be seen, for example, in the choices on the initial form of representative offices established in Brussels, which were originally structured in very different ways.

Jeffery, writing in 2000, identified four key sets of variables impacting upon levels of sub-state engagement with EU affairs: constitutional/legal position; inter-governmental relations; "entrepreneurship" (including finance; administrative investment and political leadership) and "legitimacy". Taking each of these turn, a few preliminary comments can be made about their relevance in the cases of the devolved UK administrations.

Firstly, with regard to the constitutional/legal position, it must be noted that devolution is not entrenched in a written constitution as the UK does not have a single written constitutional document. Of importance here, as already noted, is the asymmetrical nature of devolution in the UK. Technically, however, with regard to the opportunity structure established by the Memorandum of Understanding and the Concordats, no distinction is made between the different administrations. This can be related to the second set of variables – "inter-governmental relations". Both Scottish and Welsh administrations operate within the Concordat framework and have demonstrated a preference for bilateral inter-personal ties which appears to derive from the pre-devolution experience of co-ordinating the territorial and functional offices. For these two sets of variables, then, asymmetry aside, there is little to distinguish between the two administrations.

The third and fourth sets of variables are more difficult to define. With regard to "entrepreneurship", as noted above, the Scottish Executive had a greater range of administrative resources at its disposal. Nevertheless, strategic decisions were still required in order to maximise engagement. Noticeable here is that the third of the Scottish First Ministers in office during the period in consideration took a keen interest in EU issues, and indeed external affairs more broadly conceived. A good example would be his submission of evidence during the Commission's consultation on its Governance White Paper in 2001.

Both of the devolved territories claim "historic nation" status and both hold a strong sense of distinct identity. Yet "legitimacy", difficult to define as Jeffery readily admitted, could be argued to be stronger in Scotland than in Wales on the basis of the strength of support for the devolved institutions established, as a comparison of the respective referendum results in 1997 demonstrates. An initial summary of this evidence, taken together with the comments made by officials, suggests that the asymmetry and the third set of variables of administrative and entrepreneurial resources, contributed to the different levels of engagement discerned during the first four years. This avenue of research offers potential for further enhancing our understanding of the effectiveness, or otherwise, of sub-state mobilisation in the EU policy processes.

Multi-Level Governance and Sub-State Mobilisation in the European Union

From the discussion above it is clear that the engagement of the UK's devolved sub-state authorities shares some of the motivations and characteristics of structures of multi-level governance in other Member States of the EU, whilst also retaining some characteristics that are UK-specific. The study demonstrated that the devolved administrations sought to engage with a number of policy areas where competences are shared between the EU and sub-state levels, indicating that their motivation related to the ability to participate in decisions taken at EU level that they would otherwise take themselves domestically. This reinforces the need to enhance our understanding of sub-state mobilisation in the EU by continuing to develop and complement the original conception of multi-level governance (Marks, 1992; 1993) to take this "bottom-up" impulse (Jeffery, 2000) into account.

This finding also demonstrates a need to investigate the forms of multi-level governance emerging in those policy areas where there is evidence of sub-state attempts to engage with the EU policy process. This takes the study of multi-level governance in the EU beyond its early predominant focus upon regional policy which is apparent in much of the existing literature of sub-state mobilisation. It is argued here that the concept of European Domestic Policy can be instrumentalised in order to increase further our understanding of how multi-level governance operates in practice in the EU.

This study of devolution in the UK during its first four years also identified and analysed the principal causes of friction between sub-state and central levels of government in the management of the domestic EU policy formulation process. Areas of friction had previously been identified in the experiences of other federal or devolved EU Member States (Jeffery, 1996; Jones, 2000). This study has demonstrated that some of these frictions appear to exist in patterns of multi-level governance across the Member States, whilst others derive from characteristics that are specific to the political systems of individual Member States.

Placing UK devolution in the broader context of multi-level governance in the EU has thus demonstrated both broad similarities and acute differences in the implications of European integration for different systems of territorial governance across the EU. By attempting to further develop understanding of the motivations that have led to the degree of sub-state mobilisation evident in the EU today, this study has raised questions about whether explanations based upon the drawing-down of European funding retain their validity as the "constitutional regions" of the EU seek to influence the shape of the debate on policy-making processes at the EU level and sub-state mobilisation spreads and intensifies in different EU Member States.

Governmental Incongruence
and the 2007 Elections

> In my view, just as Flanders leads for Belgium
> at the Fisheries Council, so should Scotland
> lead for the UK.
>
> First Minister Alex Salmond
> (Scottish Executive, 11 July 2007).

Speaking at Scotland House in Brussels to mark the 90th anniversary of the Battle of Passchendaele, the SNP First Minister Alex Salmond unambiguously asserted Scotland's claim to lead for the UK on fisheries policy. The May 2007 elections to the devolved institutions finally created the circumstances which had previously been identified as the greatest challenge to managing intra-UK intergovernmental relations post-devolution: governmental incongruence.

In Scotland the SNP formed a minority administration having gained one more seat in the Scottish Parliament elections than the Labour Party. In Wales, Plaid Cymru, the Welsh nationalists, entered into a coalition agreement with the Welsh Labour Party. Although the Labour Party remained the largest party in the National Assembly for Wales, with 26 seats, they were four seats short of an effective majority. After coalition talks to renew the 2000-2003 coalition between Labour and the Liberal Democrats failed, and the so-called "rainbow" coalition of Plaid, the Conservatives and the Liberal Democrats also collapsed, Labour and Plaid, the two largest parties in the Assembly, agreed the "One Wales" coalition programme in July 2007. However, Labour held the most posts in the new Welsh Assembly Government, a situation likely to continue facilitating relations between WAG and the UK central government. Inevitably, therefore, most attention focused upon the nature of the relationship between the SNP Scottish Executive and the Labour UK Government.

The evidence presented in the chapters of this book demonstrates that under Labour-dominated executives, intergovernmental relations were largely managed on a bilateral and informal basis, with a reliance upon goodwill, interpersonal relations, trust and confidentiality. Under governmental incongruence, the motivations of the governing parties can be expected to alter. Given the SNP's commitment to an independent Scotland, they have a clear interest in highlighting perceived constraints placed upon the pursuit of Scottish interests by the UK central government. Increased politicisation of the relationship between the Scottish Executive and the UK Government is therefore the likely outcome, with more disputes between the two levels being made public.

Jack McConnell, former Scottish First Minister, argued in June 2007 that Whitehall would need to be aware of an enhanced need for clear communication, particularly on sensitive issues (*The Herald*, 20 June 2007). Other observers, including UCL's Constitution Unit, argued that the UK Government would need to strengthen the formal mechanisms for managing intra-UK relations and dispute resolution, as the likelihood of clashes over both policies and politics increased (*The Herald*, 8 May 2007).

Such clashes, of course, could be over domestic as well as international issues. However, the salient issue of representation in EU Council meetings was demonstrated as a likely flashpoint right at the outset, not least in Salmond's speech at Scotland House in July 2007. Richard Lochhead, Secretary for Rural Affairs and the Environment, was the first SNP Minister to attend a Council, on fisheries policy, in June 2007, later stating: "While this was a relatively low key Council meeting, I ensured that key Scottish concerns were reflected in the UK position." (*The Herald*, 12 June 2007). However, former Rural Affairs Ministers Rhona Brankin (Labour) and Ross Finnie (Liberal Democrat) dismissed attempts to gain control over European fishing negotiations from the UK Government as "wrong" and "misguided" (*BBC News*, 11 July 2007; *The Scotsman*, 23 June 2007).

In early October 2007, all four Fisheries Ministers met in Peterhead, Aberdeenshire, for pre-Council discussions, with the Fisheries Council in October viewed as a key part of the preparations for deciding fishing quotas at the December Fisheries Council. Jonathan Shaw, the UK Fisheries Minister, insisted that the UK would lead on fisheries policy in the EU, despite Mr Lochhead saying that the Scottish Executive would continue to press for the lead in the EU negotiations (*Aberdeen Press and Journal*, 6 October 2007). This public disagreement over the issue of leading the UK's delegation in the Fisheries Council negotiations demonstrates that this will, as argued in Chapter 4, prove to be a source of friction in intra-UK relations under intergovernmental incongruence.

Another area where tension could increase relates to the role of the Scottish Executive EU Office in Brussels, given that the SNP-led Executive has greater incentive to deal directly with the EU institutions, rather than going through UK Government channels. Not using such channels undermines the principle of "no surprises" that had appeared to underpin the management of intra-UK relations during the first eight years of devolution. One approach to handling this situation is increased formalisation of the co-ordination mechanisms.

Noticeable from the first eight years of devolution was the importance of the role played by the civil service in maintaining good communications between the different levels of government. Their pragmatic approach to handling relations, and their respect, particularly at the devolved levels, for key principles such as confidentiality ensured relatively smooth relationships, with those frictions and disputes that did emerge remaining in private. No recourse was made to the official dispute resolution mechanism between 1999 and April 2007. However, under governmental incongruence, the civil servants are accountable to political masters with divergent interests and priorities. With disputes more likely at the political level, and more likely to be made public, the low-key informality evident in the first eight years will be severely tested.

Perhaps the most noticeable change under governmental incongruence in the first few months was the extent to which frictions were becoming apparent in public. Early evidence came with a very public dispute between the UK Government and the re-named Scottish Government over compensation to farmers affected by bans on livestock movement put in place following a localised foot-and-mouth outbreak in the south of England. According to media reports, Labour sources claimed a breakdown in trust following the Scottish First Minister making public confidential information passed to the Scottish Executive from Whitehall (*The Times*, 15 October 2007). Such tension in the early months of governmental incongruence clearly illustrates the issues relating to confidentiality, trust and the information flow highlighted in this examination of intra-UK relations post-devolution.

The evidence presented in this book demonstrates that tensions between the two levels were certainly not absent under Labour-dominated administrations, but also shows that such tensions were largely kept out of the public domain. The media reports referred to here, even though not a reliable method of data collection, clearly demonstrate that this is no longer the case and that tensions between the different levels are now emerging in public. The 2007 election outcomes removed the incentive, at least on the part of the Scottish Executive, to keep instances of conflict private. It will be difficult for the UK central government to go back on the precedents already established, given the widely accepted recognition of the overlap between EU and domestic policy competences, but a formalisation and strengthening of co-ordination mechanisms may prove necessary to contain the emergent tensions that have been identified here.

Bibliography

Documentary Sources

Assembly of European Regions: "The Regions claim more competences in Europe" 5 May 2000.

Assembly of European Regions: "Towards a European Constitutional Framework" 30 November 2001.

Belgian Presidency of the EU: Priorities Note 1 July – 31 December 2001 (available at: http://www.eu2001.be).

Bundesrat: *Bundesrat und Europäische Union* Bonn, Sekretariat des Bundesrates, 1997.

Colloquium of the Constitutional Regions: "Strengthening the role of the constitutional regions in the European Union: Minutes" Brussels, 22 February 2001.

Colloquium of the Constitutional Regions: "Political Declaration by the constitutional regions of Bavaria, Catalonia, North-Rhine Westphalia, Salzburg, Scotland, Wallonia and Flanders" 26 April 2001.

Committee of the Regions: "Wie sollen die Zuständigkeiten in Europa verteilt werden?" press release, 3 July 2000.

Committee of the Regions: "Institutional Reform of the European Union: Point of View of the Committee of the Regions", 31 July 2000.

Committee of the Regions: "The Regions with legislative powers in tomorrow's Europe", Press Release COR/01/10628.en, 15 November 2001.

Committee of the Regions: "Comité des Régions: Déclaration de Laeken", Press Release COR/01/12640, 17 December 2001.

Conference of the Regions with Legislative Power: "Towards the reinforced role of the Regions with legislative power within the European Union: Resolution", 15 November 2001.

Consultative Steering Group: *Report of the Consultative Steering Group on the Scottish Parliament – Shaping Scotland's Parliament*" (available at: http://www.scotland.gov.uk/library/documents-w5/rcsg-00.htm).

Cosla: *COSLA and the European Union*, no date.

Cosla: *The COSLA European* Strategy, COSLA internal paper, May 2000.

Council of the European Union: "Subject: 2335th Council Meeting – Environment", Press release 13859/99, 13 December 1999.

Council of the European Union: "Subject: 2278th Council Meeting – Environment", Press release 9420/00, 22 June 2000.

Department of Trade and Industry: *Concordat between the Scottish Executive and the Department of Trade and Industry* London, HMSO, 1999.

European Commission: *Consultations conducted for the preparation of the White Paper on democratic European Governance: Report to the Commission*, SG/8533/01-EN, June 2001.

Foreign & Commonwealth Office: "Speech by Joyce Quin, Europe Minister, to the Northern Ireland Assembly", 26 February 1999 (available at: http://www.fco.gov.uk/news/speechtext.asp?2063).

Foreign & Commonwealth Office: "Daily Bulletin – Wednesday 28 February 2001"(available at: http://www.nds.coi.gov.uk/coi/coipress.nsf).

Foreign & Commonwealth Office: *Annual Departmental Report 2001* (available at: http://www.fco.gov.uk/directory/dynpage.asp?Page=94).

Hansard Report: Official Record of Proceedings of the House of Commons, Volume 302, 8 December 1997.

Hansard Report: Official Record of Proceedings of the House of Commons, Volume 304, 12 January 1998.

HM Treasury: *Funding for the Scottish Parliament, the National Assembly for Wales and Northern Ireland Assembly: A Statement on Funding Policy* London, HM Treasury, 2000.

Ministry of Agriculture, Fisheries and Food: "Main Concordat between the Ministry of Agriculture, Fisheries and Food and the Scottish Executive" London, MAFF, 1999.

National Assembly for Wales: *Standing Orders of the National Assembly for Wales* (available at: http://www.wales.gov.uk/keypubstandingorders/index.htm).

National Assembly for Wales Record of Proceedings: *Assembly Business* – various, as cited in text (available at: http://www.wales.gov.uk/).

National Assembly for Wales: "Alun Michael and Rhodri Morgan hold high level talks in Brussels", Press release W000069-Ind, 26 January 2000.

National Assembly for Wales: "Christine Gwyther presses Franz Fischler on Tir Mynydd", Press release W00790-Ag, 17 July 2000.

National Assembly for Wales: "Carwyn Jones at European Agriculture Ministers' meeting", Press release W001188-Ag, 20 November 2000.

National Assembly for Wales: "Voice of Wales in Europe is getting louder, says Rhodri Morgan", Press release W01207-Eur, 23 November 2000.

National Assembly for Wales: "Jane Hutt leads on nutrition at European Community Health Council in Brussels", Press release W001290-Hlt, 14 December 2000.

National Assembly for Wales European Affairs Committee (2000): "International Relations and the Profile of Wales" EUR-01-00 (p. 2), 9 March 2000.

National Assembly for Wales European Affairs Committee (2000): "Newsletter 6 – June/July 2000" (available at: http://www.wales.gov.uk/subieurope/content/newsletters/).

Plaid Cymru: *Internal Paper: Comments on the role of the European Affairs committee of the National Assembly for Wales*, 2000.

Scottish Executive: *Memorandum of Understanding and Supplementary Agreements between the UK Government, Scottish Ministers and the Cabinet of the National Assembly for Wales*, 1 October 1999.

Scottish Executive: "McConnell announces plans for Scotland Week in Brussels", News Release SE0734/1999, 29 September 1999.

Scottish Executive: "Home Robertson secures good all-round deal for Scottish fishermen at EU negotiations" News Release SE0895/1999, 17 December 1999.

Scottish Executive: "Jim Wallace meets EU Justice Commissioner in Brussels", News Release SE1037/2000, 7 April 2000.

Scottish Executive: "Nicol Stephen represents UK at European Council of Education Ministers", News Release SE1651/2000, 8 June 2000.

Scottish Executive: "Acceptable balance struck for Scottish industry – Rhona Brankin comments on crucial European fisheries talks", News Release SE3220/2000, 15 December 2000.

Scottish Executive: "McConnell calls for greater Scottish influence in the EU", News release SE0685/2001, 16 March 2001.

Scottish Executive: "Liege Conference", News Release SE4937/2001, 28 November 2001.

Scottish Executive: "The Scottish Government's relationship with Europe", Speech by First Minister Alex Salmond on the 90th Anniversary of the Battle of Passchendaele, Scotland House, Brussels, July 11 2007.

Scottish Executive Education Department: *Working level agreement between the Scottish Executive and the Department for Education and Employment on European and other International Activities in Education and Training*, no date.

Scottish Executive Education Department: *Outlook International: Promoting the International Dimension in Scottish Schools* Edinburgh, HMSO, 2000.

Scotland Office: "Reid writes to Tom McCabe", news release SSO1488, 22 June 2000.

Scottish Office: *Scotland's Parliament* London, HMSO, 1997.

Scottish Office: *Scotland Bill* London, HMSO, 1997(b).

Scottish Office: "Lessons to be learned from Munich meetings on devolution", news release, 3 October 1997.

Scottish Office: *Scotland Act 1998* London, HMSO, 1998.

Scottish Office: "Dewar: Scotland can be a new type of European region", news release 0313/98, 20 February 1998.

Scottish Office: "Parliament will place Scotland at the heart of Europe – Henry McLeish", news release 1216/98, 12 June 1998.

Scottish Office Education Department: *Scottish Education and the European Community: Policy, Strategy and Practice* Edinburgh, Scottish Office, no date.

Scottish Parliament: *Standing Orders of the Scottish Parliament* (available at: http://www.scottish.parliament.uk/parl_bus/sto-c.htm).

Scottish Parliament: *The European Committee of the Scottish Parliament* Edinburgh, Scottish Parliament, 1999.

Scottish Parliament Official Records of Proceedings: *Parliamentary Business* – various debates as cited in text (available at http://www.scottish.parliament. uk/official_report).

Scottish Parliament Official Records of Proceedings: *Written Answers* – various as cited in text (available at http://www.scottish.parliament.uk/official_ report).

Scottish Parliament: "Scotland receives 'appropriate share' of European funding, says European Committee report – but calls for more openness and transparency from Government departments", Committee News Release CEU027/2000, 8 November 2000.

Scottish Parliament: "Parliamentary delegation pushes for closer links between Edinburgh and Brussels", News release 0015/2001, 21 March 2001.

Scottish Parliament: "Committee launches inquiry into the future of Europe – call for evidence", Committee news release CEU7/2001, 27 June 2001.

Scottish Parliament: "Peter Hain to be first UK Minister to address a committee", Committee News Release CEU009/2001, 1 November 2001.

Scottish Parliament: "Committee calls for greater openness in Europe and bigger role for Scotland", Committee News Release CEU 012/2001, 11 December 2001.

Scottish Parliament European Committee: *Reports* – various, as cited in text (available at: http://www.scottish.parliament.uk/official_report/cttee/europe. htm).

Scottish Parliament European Committee: *Europe Matters*, various issues.

Scottish Parliament European Committee: *Report on the Governance of the European Union and the Future of Europe: What Role for Scotland?*, SP Paper 466, Committee 9th Report 2001.

Welsh Office: *A Voice for Wales: The Government's Proposals for a Welsh Assembly* London, HMSO, 1997(a).

Welsh Office: *Government of Wales Bill* London, HMSO, 1997(b).

Welsh Office: *Government of Wales Act* London, HMSO, 1998.

Secondary Sources

Aldecoa, F. & Keating, M. (eds.): *Paradiplomacy in Action: The Foreign Relations of Subnational Governments*, London, Frank Cass & Co, 1999.

Anderson, J. J.: "Skeptical reflections on a Europe of Regions: Britain, Germany and the ERDF", *Journal of Public Policy*, Vol. 10, 1990, pp. 417-447.

Armstrong, K. & Bulmer, S.: "United Kingdom" in Rometsch, D. & Wessels, W. (eds.): *The European Union and Member States: Towards institutional fusion?*, Manchester, Manchester University Press, 1996, pp. 253-290.

Bache, I., George, S. & Rhodes, R. A. W.: "The European Union, Cohesion Policy and Sub-National Authorities in the United Kingdom" in Hooghe, L.

(ed.): *Cohesion and European Integration: Building Multi-Level Governance*, Oxford, Clarendon Press, 1996, pp. 294-319.

Baker, D. & Seawright, D. (eds.): *Britain for and against Europe. British Politics and the Question of European Integration*, Oxford, Clarendon Press, 1998.

Balthazar, L. (1999): "The Quebec Experience: Success or Failure?" in Aldecoa, F. & Keating, M. (eds.): *Paradiplomacy in Action: The Foreign Relations of Subnational Governments*, London, Frank Cass & Co, pp. 153-169.

Bayerischer Landtag: *Die Landesparlamente im Spannungsfeld zwischen europäischer Integration und europäischem Regionalismus*, München, Filmsatz GmbH, 1988.

Baylis, J. & Rennger, N. J. (eds.): *Dilemmas in World Politics* Oxford, Clarendon Press, 1992.

Bender, B.: "Whitehall, central government and 1992" *Public Policy and Administration*, Vol. 6, 1991, pp. 13-20.

Benz, A. & Eberlein, B.: *Regions in European Governance: The logic of multilevel interaction*, Florence, EUI Working Paper RSC No. 98/31, EUI, 1998.

Bogdanor, V.: *Devolution in the United Kingdom*, Oxford, Oxford University Press, 1999.

Bomberg, E. & Peterson, J.: "European Union Decision Making: the Role of Sub-national Authorities", *Political Studies*, Vol. XLVI, 1998, pp. 219-235.

Bomberg, E. & Peterson, J.: *Policy transfer and Europeanisation: Passing the Heineken Test?*, Belfast, Queen's Paper on Europeanisation No. 2/2000, 2000.

Borkenhagen, F. H. U. *et al.* (Hrsg.): *Die deutschen Länder in Europa*, Baden-Baden, Nomos-Verlagsgesellschaft, 1992.

Borkenhagen, F. H. U. (Hrsg.): *Europapolitik der deutschen Länder. Bilanz und Perspektiven nach dem Gipfel von Amsterdam*, Opladen, Leske & Budrich, 1998.

Börzel, T. A.: "Does European Integration Really Strengthen the State? The Case of the Federal Republic of Germany", *Regional & Federal Studies*, Vol. 7, No. 3, 1997, pp. 87-113.

Boyle, C.: *The New Scottish Parliament: Scotland's changing relations with Europe*, Edinburgh, European Commission Representation in Scotland, July, 1998.

Bradbury, J. & Mawson, J. (eds.): *British Regionalism and Devolution: The Challenge of State Reform and European Integration*, London, Jessica Kingsley Publishers, 1997.

Bradbury, J.: "The Blair Government's White Papers on British Devolution: A Review of Scotland's Parliament and A Voice for Wales", *Regional and Federal Studies*, Vol. 7, No. 3, 1997, pp. 115-133.

Bristow, G. & Blewitt, N.: *Unravelling the Knot: The Interaction of UK Treasury and European Funding for Wales*, Cardiff, Institute of Welsh Affairs, 1999.

Brown, A.: "Designing the Scottish Parliament", *Parliamentary Affairs*, Vol. 53, 2000, pp 542-556.

Brown, A., McCrone, D. & Paterson, L.: *Politics and Society in Scotland (Second Edition)*, Basingstoke, Macmillan, 1998.

Budge, I. *et al.* (eds.): *The New British Politics*, Harlow, Addison Wesley Longman, 1998.

Buller, J. & Smith, M. J.: "Civil service attitudes towards the European Union" in Baker, D. & Seawright, D. (eds.): *Britain for and against Europe. British Politics and the Question of European Integration*, Oxford, Clarendon Press, 1998, pp. 165-184.

Bullman, U. & Eißel, D.: "Europa der Regionen: Entwicklung und Perspektive", *Aus Politik und Zeitgeschichte*, B20-21, 1993, pp. 3-15.

Bullmann, U.: "The Politics of the Third Level" in Jeffery, C. (ed.): *The Regional Dimension of the EU*, London, Frank Cass & Co, 1997, pp. 3-19.

Bulmer, S.: "The governance of the European Union: a new institutionalist approach", *Journal of Public Policy*, Vol. 13, No. 4, 1993, pp. 351-380.

Bulmer, S.: *New institutionalism, the Single Market and EU Governance*, Arena Working Papers WP 97/25, available at www.arena.uio.no, 1997.

Bulmer, S. & Burch, M.: "Organising for Europe: Whitehall, the British State and European Union", *Public Administration*, Vol. 76, 1998, pp. 601-628.

Bulmer, S. & Burch, M.: "Coming to terms with Europe: Europeanisation, Whitehall and the challenge of devolution", paper for the UACES Conference, Budapest, 6-8 April 2000.

Bulmer, S., Jeffery, C. & Paterson, W. E.: *Germany's European Diplomacy. Shaping the Regional Milieu*, Manchester, Manchester University Press, 2000.

Bulmer, S. *et al.*: *European Policy-Making Under Devolution: Britain's New Multi-Level Governance*, European Policy Research Unit Paper No. 1/01, Manchester, 2001.

Burch, M. & Holliday, I.: *The British Cabinet System*, Hemel Hempstead, Prentice Hall/Harvester Wheatsheaf, 1996.

Burrows, N.: "The Scottish Executive" in Hassan, G. (ed.): *A Guide to the Scottish Parliament: The Shape of Things to Come*, Edinburgh, The Stationery Office, 1999(a), pp. 57-64.

Burrows, N.: "Relations with the European Union" in Hassan, G. (ed.): *A Guide to the Scottish Parliament: The Shape of Things to Come*, Edinburgh, The Stationery Office, 1999(b), pp. 125-132.

Cafruny, A. & Rosenthal, G. (eds.): *The State of the EC Vol. 2, The Maastricht Debates and Beyond*, Boulder, Lynne Riemer, 1993.

Caparoso, J. A. & Keeler, J. T. S.: "The European Union and Regional Integration Theory" in Rhodes, C. & Mazey, S. (eds.). *The State of the European Union Vol. 3. Building a European Polity*, Harlow, Longman, 1995, pp. 29-58.

Carter, C. *et al.*: *Scotland and the European Union*, ESRC Devolution Briefing No. 27, Economic and Social Research Council Devolution and Constitutional Change Programme, 2005.

Central Office of Information: *The British System of Government (Second Edition)*, London, HMSO, 1994.

Clement, W.: *Perspektiven nordrhein-westfälischer Europapolitik*, Bonn, Zentrum für Europäischen Integration, Discussion Paper C48, 1999.

Cram, L.: *Policy-making in the EU: Conceptual lenses and the integration process*, London, Routledge, 1997.

Curtice, J.: "The People's Verdict: Public Attitudes to Devolution and the Union" in Hazell, R. (ed.): *The State and the Nations: The First Year of Devolution in the United Kingdom*, Thorverton, Imprint Academic, 2000, pp. 223-240.

Davies, R.: *Devolution: A Process not an Event*, Cardiff, Institute of Welsh Affairs Gregynog Paper, Vol. 2, No. 2, 1999.

Deeg, R. E.: "Germany's *Länder* and the Federalization of the European Union" in Rhodes, C. & Mazey, S. (eds.): *The State of the European Union, Vol. 3: Building a European Polity*, Harlow, Longman, 1995, pp. 197-216.

Dowding, K.: *The Civil Service*, London, Routledge, 1995.

Downs, W. M.: "Constructing a New Scottish Parliament for the 'Europe of Regions': Can Institutional Engineering assure subsidiarity?", *Journal of Legislative Studies*, Vol. 6, No. 2, 2000, pp. 67-92.

Elcock, H. & Keating, M. (eds.): *Remaking the Union. Devolution and British Politics in the 1990s*, London, Frank Cass & Co, 1998.

Engel, C.: *Regionen in der EG*, Bonn, Europa Union Verlag, 1993.

Europäisches Zentrum für Föderalismus-Forschung: *Jahrbuch des Föderalismus 2000: Föderalismus, Subsidiarität und Regionen in Europa*, Baden-Baden, Nomos Verlagsgesellschaft, 2000.

European Strategy Group: *The National Assembly for Wales and the European Union*, Cardiff, Welsh Office, 1998.

Evans, M. & Davies, J.: "Understanding policy transfer: A Multi-Level, Multi-Disciplinary Perspective", *Public Administration*, Vol. 77, No. 2, 1999, pp. 361-385.

Foley, M.: *The Politics of the British Constitution*, Manchester, Manchester University Press, 1999.

Garnett, J. C.: "States, state-centric perspectives and interdependence theory" in Baylis, J. & Rennger, N. J. (eds.): *Dilemmas in World Politics*, Oxford, Clarendon Press, 1992, pp. 61-84.

George, S.: *An awkward partner: Britain in the European Community (2nd edition)*, Oxford, Oxford University Press, 1994.

George, S.: *The Europeanisation of UK Politics and Policy-making: the Effect of European Integration on the UK*, Belfast, Queen's Paper on Europeanisation No. 8/2001, 2001.

Gerstenlauer, H-G.: ",,Bremser" in der Europapolitik? Probleme zwischen Bund und Länder", *Universitas*, 2. Band, 1986, pp. 1037-1044.

Gray, Sir. J & Osmond, J.: *Wales in Europe: The Opportunity Presented by a Welsh Assembly*, Cardiff, Institute of Welsh Affairs, 1997.

Gray, J.: "Welsh Europeans in Whitehall and Brussels", *Agenda*, Journal of the Institute of Welsh Affairs, Winter 2000/1, 2001, pp. 37-39.

Greenwood, J. (ed.): *Representing Interests in the European Union*, Basingstoke, Macmillan, 1997.

Greß, F. (Hrsg.): *Die Rolle der Bundesländer in einem geeinten Deutschland und geeinten Europa: eine Herausforderung für Landesparlamentarismus und Föderalismus*, Wiesbaden, Hessischer Landtag, 1992.

Hahn, O.: "EG-Engagement der deutschen Länder: Lobbyismus oder Nebenaussenpolitik?" in Hrbek, R. & Thaysen, U. (Hrsg.): *Die deutschen Länder und die europäischen Gemeinschaften*, Baden-Baden, Nomos Verlagsgesellschaft, 1986, pp. 105-110.

Hannaleck, I. & Schumann, W.: "Die Beteilungung der Länder an der EG-Politik des Bundes: Probleme und Alternativen" *Zeitschrift für Parlamentsfragen*, Vol. 14, No. 3, 1983 pp. 362-371.

Hardy, S. *et al.* (eds.): *An Enlarged Europe: Regions in Competition?* London, Regional Studies Association, 1995.

Hassan, G. (ed.): *A Guide to the Scottish Parliament: The Shape of Things to Come*, Edinburgh, The Stationery Office, 1999.

Hassan, G. & Warhurst, C.: *A Moderniser's Guide to Scotland: A Different Future*, Edinburgh, The Centre for Scottish Public Policy and the Big Issue in Scotland, 1999.

Hassan, G. & Warhurst, C.: *The New Scottish Politics: The First Year of the Scottish Parliament and Beyond*, Edinburgh, The Stationery Office, 2000.

Hazell, R.: *An Assembly for Wales*, London, Constitution Unit, 1996.

Hazell, R. (ed.): *Constitutional Futures: A History of the Next Ten Years*, Oxford, Oxford University Press, 1999.

Hazell, R. (ed.): *The State and the Nations: The First Year of Devolution in the United Kingdom*, Thorverton, Imprint Academic, 2000(a).

Hazell, R.: *An Unstable Union: Devolution and the English Question. State of the Union Annual Lecture*, London, Constitution Unit, 2000(b).

Hellwig, R.: "Die Rolle der Bundesländer in der Europa-Politik. Das Beispiel der Ratifizierung der Einheitlichen Europäischen Akte", *Europa Archiv*, Folge 10, 1987, pp. 297-302.

Hocking, B. (1999): "Patrolling the 'Frontier': Globalization, Localization and the 'Actorness of Non-Central Governments" in Aldecoa, F. & Keating, M. (eds.): *Paradiplomacy in Action: The Foreign Relations of Subnational Governments*, London, Frank Cass & Co, 1999, pp. 17-39.

Hoffman, S.: "Reflection on the nation-state in Western Europe today", *Journal of Common Market Studies*, Vol. 21, 1983, pp. 21-37.

Hooghe, L.: "Subnational Mobilisation in the European Union" in Hayward, J. (ed.): *Crisis of Representation in Europe*, London, Frank Cass & Co, 1995, pp. 175-198.

Hooghe, L. (ed.): *Cohesion and European Integration: Building Multi-Level Governance*, Oxford, Clarendon Press, 1996.

Hooghe, L. & Keating, M.: "The politics of European Union regional policy", *Journal of European Politics*, Vol. 1, No. 3, 1994, pp. 367-390.

Hooghe, L. & Marks, G.: "The making of a polity: The struggle over European integration" in Kitschelt, H. *et al.* (eds.): *Continuity and Change in Contemporary Capitalism*, Cambridge, Cambridge University Press, 1999, pp. 70-97.

Hooghe, L. & Marks, G.: *Multi-Level Governance and European Integration*, Oxford, Rowman & Littlefield Publishers, 2001(a).

Hooghe, L. & Marks, G.: "Types of Multi-Level Governance", *European Integration On-line Papers*, Vol. 5, No. 11, (available at: http://eiop.or.at/ eiop/texte/2001-011a.htm), 2001(b).

Hrbek, R.: "Doppelte Politikverflechtung: Deutscher Föderalismus und europäische Integration. Die deutschen Länder im EG-Entscheidungsprozess" in Hrbek, R. & Thaysen, U. (Hrsg.): *Die deutschen Länder und die europäischen Gemeinschaften*, Baden-Baden, Nomos Verlagsgesellschaft, 1986, pp. 17-36.

Hrbek, R. & Thaysen, U.: *Die deutschen Länder und die europäischen Gemeinschaften*, Baden-Baden, Nomos Verlagsgesellschaft, 1986.

Hrbek, R. & Weyand, S. (Hrsg.): *betrifft: das Europa der Regionen*, München, Verlag C H Beck, 1994.

Hrbek, R.: "The effects of EU integration on German federalism" in Jeffery, C. (ed.): *Recasting German Federalism: The Legacies of Unification*, London, Pinter, 1999, pp. 217-233.

Huelshoff, M. G.: "Germany and European Integration: Understanding the Relationship" in Huelshoff, M. G., Markovits, A. S. & Reich, S. (eds.): *From Bundesrepublik to Deutschland. German politics after Unification*, Michigan, University of Michigan Press, 1993 pp. 301-314.

Huelshoff, M. G., Markovits, A. S. & Reich, S. (eds.): *From Bundesrepublik to Deutschland. German politics after Unification*, Michigan, University of Michigan Press, 1993.

Hunter, L.: *Managing Conflicts after Devolution: A Toolkit for Civil Servants*, London, Constitution Unit, 2000.

Große-Hüttmann, M. & Knodt, M.: "Die Europäisierung des deutschen Föderalismus", *Aus Politik und Zeitgeschichte*, B52-53, 2000, pp. 31-38.

Jachtenfuchs, M.: "Democracy and Governance in the European Union", *European Integration On-line Papers*, Vol. 1, No. 2 (available at http://eiop. or.at/eiop/texte/1997-002a.htm) 1997.

Jeffery, C.: "The German *Länder* and the 1996 Intergovernmental Conference", *Regional and Federal Studies*, Vol 5, No. 3, 1995, pp. 356-365.

Jeffery, C.: "Towards a 'Third Level' in Europe? The German *Länder* in the European Union", *Political Studies*, Vol. 44, No. 2, 1996, pp. 253-266.

Jeffery, C. (ed.): *The Regional Dimension of the EU*, London, Frank Cass & Co, 1997.

Jeffery, C.: "Farewell the Third Level? The German *Länder* and the European Policy Process" in Jeffery, C. (ed.): *The Regional Dimension of the EU*, London, Frank Cass & Co, 1997(a) pp. 56-75.

Jeffery, C.: "Conclusions: Sub-national authorities and 'European Domestic Policy' in Jeffery, C. (ed.): *The Regional Dimension of the EU*, London, Frank Cass & Co, 1997(b), pp. 204-218.

Jeffery, C.: "Sub-National Authorities and European Integration: Moving Beyond the Nation-State?" paper presented at The Fifth Biennial International Conference of the European Community Studies Association, May 29-1 June 1997, Seattle, USA, 1997(c).

Jeffery, C.: "The Decentralisation Debate in the United Kingdom: Role-Modell Deutschland", *Scottish Affairs*, 19, 1997(d) pp. 42-55.

Jeffery, C.: "The German *Länder* and Europe: Interests, Strategies and Implementation Capacities in European policy-making: A comparison of Bavaria and Saxony-Anhalt" *Unpublished manuscript*, 1998(a).

Jeffery, C.: "The Operation of Multi-Layer Democracy in Germany: Implications and Insights for Scottish Devolution", *Written Evidence for the Scottish Affairs Committee of the House of Commons*, submitted February 1998, 1998(b),

Jeffery, C.: "Sub-National Mobilization and European Integration: Does it make any Difference?", *Journal of Common Market Studies*, Vol. 38 (1), 2000, pp. 1-23.

Jeffery, C. & Yates, J.: "Unification and Maastricht: The Response of the *Länder* Governments" in Jeffery, C. & Sturm, R. (eds.): *Federalism, Unification and European integration*, London, Frank Cass & Co, 1993, pp. 58-81.

Jeffery, C. & Sturm, R. (eds.): *Federalism, Unification and European integration*, London, Frank Cass & Co, 1993.

Johne, R.: *Die deutschen Landtage im Entscheidungsprozeß der Europäischen Union*, Baden-Baden, Nomos Verlagsgesellschaft, 2000.

Jones, J. B.: "Wales: A Developing Political Economy" in Keating, M. & Loughlin, J. (eds.): *The Political Economy of Regionalism*, London, Frank Cass & Co, 1997, pp 388-405.

Jones, J. B. & Keating, M. (eds.): *The European Union and the Regions*, Oxford, Clarendon Press, 1995.

Jones, J. B. & Balsom, D. (eds.): *The Road to the National Assembly for Wales*, Cardiff, University of Wales Press, 2000.

Jones, R.: *Beyond the Spanish State: Central Government, Domestic Actors and the EU*, Basingstoke, Palgrave, 2000.

Jordan, A.: "The European Union: an evolving system of multi-level governance...or government?", *Policy & Politics*, Vol. 29 (2), 2001, pp. 193-208.

Kalbfleisch-Kottsieper, U.: "Die Europakommission der Länder und die Verhandlungen in Brüssel – auf dem Weg zu einer neuen Staatspraxis?" in Borkenhagen, F. U. *et al.* (Hrsg.): *Die deutschen Länder in Europa*, Baden-Baden, Nomos-Verlagsgesellschaft, 1992, pp. 9-16.

Keating, M.: "Europeanism and Regionalism" in Jones, J. B. & Keating, M. (eds.): *The European Union and the Regions*, Oxford, Clarendon Press, 1995, pp. 1-22.

Keating, M.: *The New Regionalism in Western Europe*, Cheltenham, Edward Elgar, 1998.

Keating, M.: "Regions and International Affairs: Motives, Opportunities and Strategies" in Aldecoa, F. & Keating, M. (eds.): *Paradiplomacy in Action: The Foreign Relations of Subnational Governments*, London, Frank Cass & Co, 1999, pp. 1-16.

Keating, M. & Jones, J. B.: "Scotland and Wales: Peripheral Assertion and European Integration", *Parliamentary Affairs*, Vol. 44, 1991, pp. 311-324.

Keating. M. & Hooghe, L.: "By-passing the nation-state? Regions and the EU policy process" in Richardson, J (ed.): *European Union: Power and Policy-making*, London, Routledge, 1996, pp. 216-229.

Keating, M. & Jones, J. B.: "Nations, Regions and Europe: The UK Experience" in Jones, J. B. & Keating, M. (eds.): *The European Union and the Regions*, Oxford, Clarendon Press, 1995, pp. 89-114.

Keating, M. & Loughlin, J. (eds.): *The Political Economy of Regionalism*, London, Frank Cass & Co, 1997.

Kellas. J. G.: *The Scottish Political System (Fourth Edition)*, Cambridge, Cambridge University Press, 1989.

Kellas, J. G.: "European Integration and the Regions", Parliamentary Affairs, Vol. 44, 1991, pp. 226-240.

Kerremans, B. & Beyers, J.: "Belgian Sub-National Entities in the European Union: Second or Third Level Players?" in Jeffery, C. (ed.): *The Regional Dimension of the EU*, London, Frank Cass & Co, 1997, pp. 41-55.

van Kersbergen, K. & Verbeek, B.: "Politics of Subsidiarity in the European Union", *Journal of Common Market Studies*, Vol. 32 (2), 1994, pp. 215-236.

Knemeyer, F-L.: "Subsidiarität, Föderalismus, Dezentralisation: Initiativen zu einem 'Europa der Regionen'", *Deutsches Verwaltungsblatt*, Jg 109 (5), 1990, pp. 449-454.

Knodt, M.: *Tiefenwirkung Europäischer Politik*, Baden-Baden, Nomos-Verlagsgesellschaft, 1998.

Kohler-Koch, B.: "The Strength of Weakness: The Transformation of Governance in the EU" in Gustavson, S. & Lewin, L. (eds.): *The Future of the Nation-State: Essays on Cultural Pluralism and European Integration*, London, Routledge, 1996, pp. 169-197.

Kohler-Koch, B. *et al.* (Hrsg.): *Interaktive Politik in Europa*, Opladen, Leske & Budrich, 1998.

Kohler-Koch, B. (ed.): *The Transformation of Governance in the European Union*, London, Routledge, 1999(a).

Kohler-Koch, B.: "Europe in Search of Legitimate Governance", *Arena Working Papers* WP99/27 (available at: http://www.arena.uio.no/publications/wp99_27.htm), 1999(b).

Laffin, M.: "Constitutional Design: A framework for analysis", *Parliamentary Affairs*, Vol. 53, 2000, pp. 532-541.

Laffin, M. & Thomas, A.: "Designing the National Assembly for Wales", *Parliamentary Affairs*, Vol. 53, 2000, pp. 557-576.

Le Galès, P. & Lequesne, C. (eds.): *Regions in Europe*, London, Routledge, 1998.

Lee, M.: "The Ethos of the Cabinet Office: A Comment on the Testimony of Officials" in Rhodes, R. A. W. & Dunleavy, P. (eds.): *Prime Minister, Cabinet and Core Executive*, Basingstoke, Macmillan, 1995, pp. 149-157.

Leicester, G.: *Scotland's Parliament*, London, Constitution Unit, 1996.

Lenz, A. & Johne, R.: "Die Landtage vor der Herausforderung Europa", Aus *Politik und Zeitgeschichte*, B 6, 2000, pp 20-29.

Leonardy, U.: *Working Structures of Federalism in Germany: Crossroads German and European Unification*, University of Leicester, Discussion Paper in Federal Studies No FS 92/4, January 1992.

Leonardy, U.: "Federation and *Länder* in German Foreign Relations: Power-Sharing in Treaty-Making and European Affairs" in Jeffery, C. & Sturm, R. (eds.): *Federalism, Unification and European Integration*, London, Frank Cass & Co, 1993, pp. 119-133.

McAteer, M. & Mitchell, D.: "Peripheral Lobbying! The territorial dimension of Euro lobbying by Scottish and Welsh Sub-central Government", *Regional and Federal Studies*, Vol. 6, No. 3, 1996, pp. 1-27.

McFadden, J. & Lazarowicz, M.: *The Scottish Parliament: An Introduction*, Edinburgh, T & T Clark, 1999.

McLeod, A. J.: *Regional Participation in EU Affairs: Lessons for Scotland from Austria, Germany & Spain*, Brussels, Scotland Europa Centre, Paper No. 15, April 1999.

Marks, G.: "Structural Policy in the European Community" in Sbragia, A. M. (ed.): *Euro-politics: Institutions and policy-making in the 'new' European Community*, Washington, The Brookings Institution, 1992, pp. 191-224.

Marks, G.: "Structural Policy and Multilevel Governance in the EC" in Cafruny, A. & Rosenthal, G. (eds.): *The State of the EC Vol. 2, The Maastricht Debates and Beyond*, Boulder, Lynne Riemer, 1993, pp. 391-410.

Marks, G.: "An Actor-Centred Approach to Multi-Level Governance" in Jeffery, C. (ed.): *The Regional Dimension of the EU*, London, Frank Cass & Co, 1997, pp. 20-38.

Marks, G., Hooghe, L. & Blank, K.: *Integration Theory, Subsidiarity and the Internationalisation of Issues: The Implication for Legitimacy*, Florence, EUI Working Paper RSC No. 95/7, EUI, 1995.

Mazey, S. & Mitchell, J.: "Europe of the Regions: Territorial Interests and European Integration: The Scottish Experience" in Mazey, S. & Richardson, J. (eds.): *Lobbying in the European Community*, Oxford, Oxford University Press, 1993, pp. 95-121.

Mazey, S. & Richardson, J. (eds.): *Lobbying in the European Community*, Oxford, Oxford University Press, 1993.

Mény, Y., Muller, P. & Quermonne, J.-L. (eds.): *Adjusting to Europe*, London, Routledge, 1996.

Mitchell, J.: "Scotland, the Union State and the International Environment" in Keating, M. & Loughlin, J. (eds.): *The Political Economy of Regionalism*, London, Frank Cass & Co, 1997, pp. 406-421.

Mitchell, J. & Leicester, G.: *Scotland, Britain and Europe. Devolution and Diplomacy*, Scottish Council Foundation Occasional Paper No. 12, 1999, (available at:

http://www.scottishpolicynet.org.uk/scf/publications/oth16_diplom/frameset.sht ml).

Moravcsik, A.: "Negotiating the Single European Act: National Interests and Conventional Statecraft in the European Community", *International Organization*, Vol. 45, No. 1, 1991, pp. 19-56.

Moravcsik, A.: "Preferences and power in the European Community: A liberal intergovernmental approach", *Journal of Common Market Studies*, Vol. 31, No. 4, 1993, pp. 473-524.

Moravcsik, A.: *The Choice for Europe: social purpose and state power from Messina to Maastricht*, London, UCL Press, 1999.

Morgan, K. & Mungham, G.: *Redesigning Democracy: The Making of the Welsh Assembly*, Bridgend, Seren, 2000.

Murkens, J. E.: *Scotland's Place in Europe*, London, Constitution Unit, 2001.

Ohmae, K.: "The rise of the region state", *Foreign Affairs*, Vol. 72, No. 2, 1993, pp. 78-87.

Olsen J. P.: "Europeanization and Nation-State Dynamics" in Gustavson, S. & Lewin, L. (eds.): *The Future of the Nation-State: Essays on Cultural Pluralism and European Integration*, London, Routledge, 1996, pp. 245-275.

Osmond, J. (ed.): *The National Assembly Agenda: A Handbook for the First Four Years*, Cardiff, Institute of Welsh Affairs, 1998.

Osmond, J.: *Adrift but Afloat: The Civil Service and the National Assembly*, Cardiff, Institute of Welsh Affairs, 1999.

Osmond, J.: *The Irish Experience of Objective One: Some Lessons for Wales*, Cardiff, Institute of Welsh Affairs, 2000(a).

Osmond, J. (ed.): *Devolution in Transition: Monitoring the National Assembly, February to May 2000*, Cardiff, Institute of Welsh Affairs, 2000(b).

Osmond, J. (ed.): *Coalition Politics Comes to Wales: Monitoring the National Assembly, September to December 2000*, Cardiff, Institute of Welsh Affairs, 2000(c).

Osmond, J.: "A Constitutional Convention by Other Means: The First Year of the National Assembly for Wales" in Hazell, R. (ed.): *The State and the Nations: The First Year of Devolution in the United Kingdom*, Thorverton, Imprint Academic, 2000(d), pp. 37-78.

Patchett, K.: "The New Welsh Constitution: The Government of Wales Act 1998" in Jones, J. B. & Balsom, D. (eds.): *The Road to the National Assembly for Wales*, Cardiff, University of Wales Press, 2000, pp. 229-264.

Paterson, L.: *The Autonomy of Modern* Scotland, Edinburgh, Edinburgh University Press, 1994.

Paterson, L. (ed.): *A Diverse Assembly: The Debate on a Scottish Parliament*, Edinburgh, Edinburgh University Press, 1998.

Peters, B. G. & Pierre, J.: "Developments in intergovernmental relations: towards multi-level governance", *Policy & Politics*, Vol. 29 (2), 2001, pp. 131-135.

Pollack, M. A.: "Regional Actors in an Intergovernmental Play: The Making and Implementation of EC Structural Policy" in Rhodes, C. & Mazey, S. (eds.). *The State of the European Union Vol. 3: Building a European Polity*, Harlow, Longman, 1995, pp. 361-390.

Rallings, C. & Thrasher, M.: *Why the North-East said 'No': the 2004 referendum on an elected Regional Assembly*, ESRC Devolution Briefing No. 19, ESRC Devolution and Constitutional Change Programme, 2005.

Rawlings, R.: "Concordats of the Constitution", *Law Quarterly Review*, 116, 2000, pp. 257-286.

Reilly, A.: *The role of subnational government in the EU policy process: The case of the Structural Funds in Germany, Spain and the UK*, unpublished PhD Thesis, University of Birmingham, 2000.

Rhodes, R. A. W. & Dunleavy, P. (eds.): *Prime Minister, Cabinet and Core Executive*, Basingstoke, Macmillan, 1995.

Richardson, J. (ed.): *European Union: Power and Policy-making*, London, Routledge, 1996.

Rometsch, D.: *The Federal Republic of Germany and the European Union: Patterns of Institutional and Administrative Interaction*, University of Birmingham, Institute for German Studies Discussion Paper, No. 95/2, 1995.

Rometsch, D. & Wessels, W. (eds.): *The European Union and Member States: Towards institutional fusion?*, Manchester, Manchester University Press, 1996.

Sandholtz, W. & Zysman, J.: "1992: Recasting the European Bargain", *World Politics*, Vol. 40, 1989, pp. 95-128.

Sbragia, A. M. (ed.): *Euro-politics: Institutions and policy-making in the 'new' European Community*, Washington, The Brookings Institution, 1992.

Scharpf, F. W.: "The joint-decision trap", *Public Administration*, Vol. 66, 1988, pp. 239-278.

Scharpf, F. W.: "Community and autonomy: multi-level policy-making in the EU", *Journal of European Public Policy*, Vol. 1, No. 2, 1994, pp. 219-242.

Scharpf, F. W.: *Notes towards a Theory of Multi-level Governing in Europe*, Köln, Max-Planck-Institut für Gesellschaftsforschung, Discussion Paper 00/5, November 2000.

Scott, A., Peterson, J. & Millar, D.: "Subsidiarity: A 'Europe of the Regions' v the British Constitution", *Journal of Common Market Studies*, Vol. 32 (1), 1994, pp. 47-67.

Sloat, A.: "Scotland and Europe: Links between Edinburgh, London and Brussels", *Scottish Affairs*, No. 31, 2000, pp. 92-110.

Sloat, A.: *Scotland in Europe*, Oxford, Peter Lang, 2002.

Smith, M. J.: *The Core Executive in Britain*, Basingstoke, Macmillan, 1999.

Smith, M. J., Marsh, D. & Richards, D.: "Central Government Departments and the Policy Process" in Rhodes, R. A. W. & Dunleavy, P. (eds.): *Prime Minister, Cabinet and Core Executive*, Basingstoke, Macmillan, 1995, pp. 38-60.

Smyrl, M. E.: "Does European Community Regional Policy Empower the Regions?", *Governance: An International Journal of Policy and Administration*, Vol. 10, No. 3, 1997, pp. 287-309.

Spence, D.: "The role of the National Civil Service in European Lobbying: The British Case" in Mazey, S. & Richardson, J. (eds.): *Lobbying in the European Community*, Oxford, Oxford University Press, 1993, pp. 47-73.

Stewart, M.: "The shifting institutional framework of the English regions: The role of Conservative policy" in Bradbury, J. & Mawson, J. (eds.): *British regionalism and devolution: The challenges of state reform and European integration*, London, Jessica Kingsley, 1997, pp. 135-157.

Stoiber, E.: "Auswirkungen der Entwicklung Europas zur Rechtsgemeinschaft auf die Länder der Bundesrepublik Deutschland", *Europa Archiv*, Folge 19, 1987, pp. 543-552.

Stone Sweet, A. & Sandholtz, W.: "European integration and supranational governance", *Journal of European Public Policy*, Vol. 4, No. 3, 1997, pp. 297-317.

Sturm, R. & Jeffery, C.: "German Unity, European Integration and the Future of the Federal System: Revival or Permanent Loss of Substance?" in Jeffery, C. & Sturm, R. (eds.): *Federalism, Unification and European Integration*, London, Frank Cass & Co, 1993, pp. 164-176.

Taylor, B.: *The Scottish Parliament*, Edinburgh, Polygon, 1999.

Taylor, P.: "The EC and the State: Assumptions, Theories and Propositions", *Review of International Studies*, Vol. 17, 1991, pp. 109-125.

Tindale, S. (ed.): *The State and the Nations*, London, IPPR, 1996.

Tömmel, I.: "Transformation of Governance: The European Commission's Strategy for Creating a 'Europe of the Regions'", *Regional and Federal Studies*, Vol. 8, No. 2, 1998, pp. 52-80.

Trench, A. (ed.): *The State of the Nations 2001: The Second Year of Devolution in the United Kingdom*, Thorverton, Imprint Academic, 2001.

Wallace, H.: "Relations between the European Union and the British administration" in Mény, Y., Muller, P. & Quermonne, J.-L. (eds.): *Adjusting to Europe*, London, Routledge, 1996, pp. 61-72.

Wallace, W.: "The sharing of sovereignty: the European paradox", *Political Studies*, XLVII, 1999, pp. 503-521.

Wessels, W.: "Die deutschen Länder in der EG-Politik: Selbstblockierung oder pluralistische Dynamik" in Hrbek, R. & Thaysen, U. (Hrsg.): *Die deutschen Länder und die europäischen Gemeinschaften*, Baden-Baden, Nomos Verlagsgesellschaft, 1986, pp. 181-195.

Wessels, W. & Rometsch, D.: "German administrative interaction and European Union. The fusion of public policies" in Meny, Y., Muller, P.& Quermonne, J-L. (eds.): *Adjusting to Europe*, London, Routledge, 1996, pp. 73-109.

Winetrobe, B. K.: *Realising the Vision: A Parliament with a Purpose. An audit of the first year of the Scottish Parliament*, London, Constitution Unit, 2001.

Woods, C.: *Europe's Regions: Engines or Millstones?* Brussels, Scotland Europa Paper No. 1, 1995.

Wright, V.: "The national co-ordination of European policy-making. Negotiating the quagmire" in Richardson, J. (ed.): *European Union: Power and Policy-making*, London, Routledge, 1996, pp. 148-169.

Newspaper reports (cited in text)

Aberdeen Press and Journal: "UK Minister snubs call for Scotland to lead fisheries talks", 6 October 2007.

BBC News: "Assemblies campaign stepped up", 8 March 2000.

BBC News: "Gwyther attends EU food safety talks", 20 March 2000.

BBC News: "MP backs Plaid power call", 16 April 2000.

BBC News: "GM trial reveals power gap", 10 May 2000.

BBC News: "Assembly battle for GM-free Wales", 15 May 2000.

BBC News: "SNP 'contempt' blast at Reid", 17 May 2000.

BBC News: "Anger grows in GM seeds row", 26 May 2000.

BBC News: "Assembly review is announced", 12 July 2000.

BBC News: "Assembly in Europe under fire", 19 September 2000.

BBC News: "Ministers under fire over inquiry 'snub'", 8 November 2000.

BBC News: "SNP on Euro warpath", 27 March 2001.

BBC News: "Scotland urges more Euro devolution", 30 May 2001.

BBC News: "Scotland 'should lead fish talks', 11 July 2007).

The Economist: "The choice for Scotland and Wales", 6 September 1997.

Financial Times: "A painful progression down the devolution trail", 4 September 2000.

icWales: "Assembly accuses Whitehall", 4 April 2001.

The Herald: "Reserve our seat at the top table, by Jim Wallace", 31 March 1998.

The Herald: "Scottish Secretary's role for scrapheap", 8 May 2000.

The Herald: "Brown challenged over snub to Holyrood", 24 May 2000.

The Herald: "Minister wins apology over GM rape seed", 2 June 2000.

The Herald: "MSPs hit stone wall", 20 September 2000.

The Herald: "The pledge: free care for old in 2002", 30 January 2001.

The Herald: "SNP to challenge ministers' EU attendance", 14 February 2001.

The Herald: "SNP to challenge Straw on access to EU," 19 June 2001.

The Herald: "Scotland 'finding itself frozen out of Brussels'", 22 January 2007.

The Herald: "Prime Minister must 'devise a way' to handle SNP clashes", 8 May 2007.

The Herald: "Fisheries minister deems Euro debut a 'valuable experience'", 12 June 2007,

The Herald: "McConnell warns Whitehall on need to communicate", 20 June 2007.

The Scotsman: "Scotland's Ministers frozen out over Europe", 6 October 1997.

The Scotsman: "Anger at bill's plan for place in Europe", 19 December 1997.

The Scotsman: "SNP anger as Reid 'snubs' MSPs' Europe Committee", 18 May 2000.

The Scotsman: "MSPs vent anger over GM secrecy", 26 May 2000.

The Scotsman: "Executive's EU summit record attacked", 27 March 2001.

The Scotsman: "Give Scotland control of tax, demand experts", 21 May 2001.

The Scotsman: "Holyrood wins right to greater say on Europe", 22 June 2001.

The Scotsman: "SNP 'misguided' over fishery powers bid", 23 June 2007.

South Wales Echo: "Threat of fines forces GM climbdown", 24 October 2001.

Süddeutsche Zeitung: "Bayern fordert von der EU Kompetenzen zurück", 23 March 2000.

Süddeutsche Zeitung: "Union droht mit Nein zu EU-Vertrag", 6 June 2000.

The Times: "MPs want English assemblies", 5 May 2000.

The Times: "German states threaten to sabotage EU treaty", 27 May 2000.

The Times: "Reid and Brown raise MSPs' hackles", 9 November 2000.

The Times: "Finnie criticised over European meetings' record", 15 February 2001.

The Times: "Salmond 'cannot be trusted with sensitive information' claims furious Scottish Office", 15 October 2007.

Western Mail: "Assembly delivers warning to Labour", 3 November 1999.

Western Mail: "New structure for Assembly urged", 13 December 1999.

Western Mail: "Devolution settlement could spark a constitutional crisis", 19 April 2000.

Western Mail: "Formal letter will protest lack of powers being given to Assembly", 12 May 2000.

Western Mail: "MPs in favour of keeping post of Welsh Secretary", 15 May 2000.

Western Mail: "Assembly urged to put GM crop battle to legal test", 16 May 2000.

Western Mail: "Assembly hardline on GM release cannot be enforced", 25 May 2000.

Western Mail: "Plans for Welsh Office merger revealed to Committee", 8 June 2000.

Western Mail: "Assembly finds joint approach to banning GM crop trials", 30 June 2000.

Western Mail: "Lib Dems seek wider powers", 27 February 2001.

Western Mail: "Plaid demands more powers for Wales", 14 May 2001.

Index

Regionalism & Federalism

The contemporary nation-state is undergoing a series of transformations which question its traditional role as a container of social, political and economic systems. New spaces are emerging with the rise of regional production systems, movements for territorial autonomy and the rediscovery of old and the invention of new identities. States have responded by restructuring their systems of territorial government, often setting up an intermediate or regional level. There is no single model, but a range, from administrative deconcentration to federalization. Some states have regionalized in a uniform manner, while others have adopted asymmetrical solutions. In many cases, regions have gone beyond the nation-state, seeking to become actors in broader continental and transnational systems.

The series covers the gamut of issues involved in this territorial restructuring, including the rise of regional production systems, political regionalism, questions of identity, and constitutional change. It will include the emergence of new systems of territorial regulation and collective action within civil society as well as the state. There is no *a priori* definition of what constitutes a region, since these span a range of spatial scales, from metropolitan regions to large federated states, and from administrative units to cultural regions and stateless nations. Disciplines covered include history, sociology, social and political geography, political science and law. Interdisciplinary approaches are particularly welcome. In addition to empirical and comparative studies, books focus on the theory of regionalism and federalism, including normative questions about democracy and accountability in complex systems of government.

Series Editor
Michael KEATING, *European University Institute and University of Aberdeen*

Editorial Board
Charlie JEFFERY, *University of Edinburgh*
Jacques ZILLER, *European University Institute*
Arthur BENZ, *Fernuniversität Hagen*
Frank DELMARTINO, *University of Leuven*

Series Titles

No.12 – Harlan KOFF (ed.), *Deceiving (Dis)Appearances. Analyzing Current Developments in European and North American Border Regions*, 2007, 232 p., ISBN 978-90-5201-369-5

No.11 – Michael KEATING (ed.), *Scottish Social Democracy. Progressive Ideas for Public Policy*, 2007, 289 p., ISBN 978-90-5201-066-3

N° 10 – Yann FOURNIS, *Les régionalismes en Bretagne. La région et l'État (1950-2000)*, 2006, 252 p., ISBN 978-90-5201-095-3

N° 9 – Jacques PALARD, Alain-G. GAGNON & Bernard GAGNON (dir.), *Diversité et identités au Québec et dans les régions d'Europe*, 2006, 417 p., ISBN 978-90-5201-054-0, en coéd. avec les PUL, ISBN 2-7637-8215-9

No.8 – Henrik HALKIER, *Institutions, Discourse and Regional Development. The Scottish Development Agency and the Politics of Regional Policy*, 2006, 598 p., ISBN 978-90-5201-275-9

No.7 – Jörg MATHIAS, *Federalism in Practice. Regional Economic Development and Welfare Reform in the Berlin Republic*, forthcoming, ISBN 978-90-5201-254-7

No.6 – Daniele CARAMANI & Yves MÉNY (eds.), *Challenges to Consensual Politics. Democracy, Identity, and Populist Protest in the Alpine Region*, 2005, 257 p., ISBN 978-90-5201-250-6

No.5 – Nicola MCEWEN, *Nationalism and the State. Welfare and Identity in Scotland and Quebec*, 2006, 212 p., ISBN 978-90-5201-240-7

No.4 – Carolyn M. DUDEK, *EU Accession and Spanish Regional Development. Winners and Losers*, 2005, 202 p., ISBN 978-90-5201-237-7

N° 3 – Stéphane PAQUIN, *Paradiplomatie et relations internationales. Théorie des stratégies internationales des régions face à la mondialisation*, 2004, 189 p., ISBN 978-90-5201-225-4

No.2 – Wilfried SWENDEN, *Federalism and Second Chambers. Regional Representation in Parliamentary Federations: The Australian Senate and German Bundesrat Compared*, 2004, 423 p., ISBN 978-90-5201-211-7

No.1 – Michael KEATING & James HUGHES (eds.), *The Regional Challenge in Central and Eastern Europe. Territorial Restructuring and European Integration*, 2003, 208 p., ISBN 978-90-5201-187-5